Missing Mom

A True Crime, True Family Stroy

A work of creative nonfiction, by Daniel L. Murphy

ISBN: 1514893401

ISBN 13: 9781514893401

Preface

I FELT COMPELLED to write this book because I wanted to share this unusual story. This story is about my mother, Dorothy Lee Murphy. This is a truthful narration, and all of the names, dates, and events are factual. Throughout this book I have tried, as best I could, to be accurate with all my facts and revelations.

This ordeal was an odd, twisting drama, one that I have lived though and shared equally with my brothers and sister, so this book is specially dedicated to them: Timothy Lee Murphy, Mary Ann (Murphy) Deering, and Michael Mark Murphy.

It is also dedicated to our mother, because truthfully, this is her story.

⊷⊜ ⊜⊶

I would also like to thank my generous extended family for supporting me in this endeavor and for helping me raise the capital to get this book published. Also, I wish to thank my good friend Linda Molto for her advice and support, Mike Turner for his expert editing services, and Jorgen Vonsegebaden for his technical assistance.

⊷⊜ ⊜⊶

Lastly, this book is dedicated to the citizens of Flint and Genesee County, Michigan, in acknowledgment of all their assistance.

Thank you, one and all.

List of Chapters

The Second of July

MICHIGAN IS APTLY described as having nine months of winter and three months of bad sledding; consequently northern Michigan's summers are extra precious and fleeting, a blessed gift bestowed upon those hardy souls who have managed to survive those many miserable months of winter.

But winter was over, now it was summer, and this golden day was truly a gift. Warm morning breezes sweetly scented with honey locust blossoms floated across the turquoise lake, into the wide opened French windows, and back out the cottage's wooden screen door. Summer's zenith, the Fourth of July, was just around the corner, and luckily this year it was falling on a Friday, making it easy to spend a long holiday weekend vacationing.

Here to help me celebrate the holiday were my good friends Joe, Joyce, and their two rambunctious dogs, Dugan and Zeppelin. For as long as I've known Joe and Joyce, they have owned a pair of dogs. Now, the names of those dogs have changed over the years, but the breed remained the same. Each cocker spaniel was male; one was black and the other black and white.

I could hear those boys howling with excitement as their van bounded down the sandy two-track trail leading back to my shady cottage. They loved this special place, too. Here those lucky dogs were off the leash, being able to run through the piney woods tracking wild critter scents, and kept quite busy by digging deep cooling holes in the sugary white sand, and jumping into the lake. They'd love to get wet, dirty, and smelly, as dogs can sometimes do. When tired of barking, running, swimming, and scratching, they'd park in the shade close to the grill and snooze, and probably dream of eating leftover treats.

Years ago Joe, Joyce, and I worked together and saw each other regularly, but now we were living at different ends of the state. Fortunately we were all together now, and our taxing holiday agenda was to include picnics and cookouts, canoeing, fishing, fireworks, a parade, and plenty of just plain lazing around. After all, isn't that what vacations are for?

Joyce and I parked ourselves outside at the old picnic table that my mom had painted a bright aquamarine blue, and we were halfheartedly playing a game of Scrabble just to kill the time. Joyce was taking forever to make a word because she took this game quite seriously. You see, she held a master's degree in English literature, whereas I was merely an artist, an illiterate with a measly bachelor of fine arts degree. And in case you didn't know it, on the very first day of art school we learned that spelling was opshunal, opcional, opshinal…not really that impotent.

But I did not protest too loudly while waiting my turn. Instead I savored the cool dappled shade of the wispy white pines and watched as a family of bluebirds took turns drinking from the goldfish pond. Daydreaming, I was planning the evening's menu. Of course we'd have something grilled, maybe salmon or chicken, and cook some peaches-and-cream sweet corn, too. I'd make a salad with greens freshly harvested from the garden, and bake a tart cherry pie for dessert.

Almost all of our summertime cooking took place outside on the old Weber grill. This ancient, copper-colored enameled cooker now sat on cement blocks, because the legs rusted off it ages ago. It was already used when Dad bought it forty years earlier, and for many years our folks put it to work at the family's cottage; now it was being used at mine. This old grill had come to represent the eternal flame of our family, and while at the cottage, the fire never went out.

The grill was not the only thing getting old; within the next month, I would be turning forty-nine, and my birth-day gift to myself was a cleared calendar for the entire month of August. No work was scheduled, not one appointment was made, because I'd planned on having a relaxing month at the lake, spending time with my family and a few close friends.

While waiting for Joyce to take her Scrabble turn, my cell phone abruptly rang its annoying electronic chimes, start-ling me; I'd forgotten it was there.

It was most unusual to have it turned on, let alone outside with me. There are definitely times when one needs to disconnect and unplug, and this was one of them; I was annoyed at the very intrusion. After noticing it was my sister, Mary, I decided to take this call and then turn the damned thing off.

⊶⊷

"Hello," Mary chirped, as she usually did. "What's up?"

"The cost of living," I said. That was my usual response.

"Hey. Did Mom go up north with you?"

"No. She didn't feel up to a long weekend away because she thinks she is getting another bladder infection and wanted to see her doctor. I'm pretty sure it was today."

"OK," Mary replied, sounding somewhat confused. "Because I just stopped by her place on my way home from work, and I see she's not home."

"Maybe she's at the doctor's office."

"Ya, that's probably where she is. I guess I was just a little confused, because when I walked into her bedroom I saw her suitcase sitting there packed, as if she was going somewhere."

"Maybe she hasn't gotten around to unpacking it yet because she isn't feeling well."

"Ya. OK."

"So, what are your plans for the Fourth?"

"I'm going up to Lake George to visit my old high-school friend Jodi. It should be fun. She just got a brand-new speedboat."

"You'll have fun with Jodi. And don't worry about Dort. She's probably just out playing cards."

"Ya. OK. Well, I thought I should check up on the old lady, don't ya know. I'll leave her a note and let her know I stopped by. You have a good Fourth, and say hello to Joe and Joyce for me."

"Ya, you have a good Fourth, too. 'Bye."

⊶⊷

I immediately turned the phone off. My family and friends would know I was at my cottage and could reach me here. Everyone and everything else could wait until after the holiday. My next appointment was ten o'clock on Friday, the Fourth of July, attending Manistee's big parade. This annual spectacle included everything with four legs, four wheels, an engine, or a tail that could be paraded down River Street, the main drag.

Manistee is a picturesque Victorian-era town sitting upon the sandy shores of Lake Michigan. The handsome historic downtown is built upon the banks of the mighty Manistee River, following its gentle curves until it empties into "The Big Lake."

This is a solidly working-class town consisting of mostly Polish and German descendants, with a healthy sprinkling of Nordic types: Swedes, Danes, and a few Fins. There are also some French Canadians thrown in for color, and a token Irishman, too: Danny Murphy, me.

Well over a hundred years ago these hardy immigrants built this prosperous little lakeside town with the virgin timbers harvested from the area's dense native forests. When the forests were cleared and the trees disappeared, so did the lumbering era.

Many of my great-uncles who once worked in those sawmills still carried the scars from those difficult days. A favorite family joke goes like this: Hold up your right hand. Now fold down your three middle fingers, leaving only your thumb and pinkie standing. What is that, you ask? Why, that's your Great-Uncle Pete ordering five beers.

During the last century, logs harvested from these dense native forests were processed in one of the twenty-two sawmills that surrounded the Manistee River basin. Then this premium lumber was shipped out of the busy harbor to build the nation's rapidly growing cities during the last century's industrial-boom years. Nowadays the lumber trade has been replaced by tourism, light industry, paper making, a maximum-security prison, and a bustling Indian casino and resort complex.

The name Manistee is a Chippewa Indian word, meaning "Spirit of the Woods," and the expansive Manistee National Forest is the largest forest in all of Lower Michigan. This picture-perfect harbor town is just the sort of idyllic place that Garrison Keillor would conjure up, very much a Lake Wobegon sort of town. It is a delightful home, for grown-ups and children alike.

The Third of July

MOST YEARS THE entire family would make it up to "Murphy's Bed-and-Breakfast," as sister Mary dubbed my cottage, for the holiday, but this year they all had other things to do. Older brother Tim, his wife, Patty, and their fourteen-year-old, Patrick, would be going to Delaware because their lovely daughter, Aimee, was becoming engaged. Mary's kids were grown and she was going up north to visit with Jodi, and our brother Mike was going to his buddy Stu's in Kalkaska. And since Mom didn't feel up to a long weekend away, this year the B and B would be housing only one Murphy, me.

⊷⊷ ⊶⊷

Last night, while watching the sunset over the lake, my thoughts turned back to Mary and her inquiry about Mother's whereabouts. I hoped she was all right. Truthfully, Mom was getting up there. She'd just turned eighty a couple of months ago, and I knew that she wasn't feeling very well when I left Flint a couple days ago. She was quite prone to bladder and kidney infections. Maybe that's all it was.

At times we would even tease her about her excessive doctoring, because she took really good care of herself. But it was easy for her, because she had a good "Generous Motors" (local vernacular for General Motors) health insurance plan. Mom is really quite healthy and independent for being eighty, she is structured and disciplined, and expects nothing less from us children; being a widow for nearly twenty-five years, she is a very capable woman.

Dorothy Lorraine Lee Murphy, or Dort, as her children like to affectionately call her, was the first child of ten, born to Mark and Lena Verona Lee from the tiny village of Marion, Michigan. We knew that Mother didn't care for life on the farm and she couldn't wait to shake the manure from her polished shoes.

Mom graduated high school in June 1941. In early December of that same year, Pearl Harbor was bombed, and we entered World War Two. Most of the young men of her graduating class went off to fight in the war, and many of them died doing so. When the men left to join the battle, women were suddenly needed in the factories for the war effort. So Mother moved to the glamorous big city of Flint, where she immediately secured a job in the DuPont plant, working alongside her father.

Picturing a better life for herself, Mom saved up her money and put herself through the Baker Business College in downtown Flint. After graduating she was employed as a secretary at the Gillespie Insurance Agency, where she remained until marrying our dad at the age of twenty-eight, which was quite late for her wartime generation.

Now, in spite of her persistent complaints of aches and pains, she is in excellent health, living independently, remains mentally aware, and appears to have a great many years left in her. She might be a sweet, little; white-haired old woman, but she doesn't know it, she is quite feisty. But truth fully, her bark is much worse than her bite. Just the same, she has a very loud bark and still possesses every one of her teeth.

·•⟫⟩ ⟨⟨•·

As the swollen summer sun disappeared, dousing itself into my tranquil lake, it flashed a few final flourishes of amber, red, orange, and lavender, streaking the darkening sky. The cooling evening air brought on a smoky warming campfire, complete with roasted marshmallow s'mores, glasses of cheap boxed wine, and friendly conversation, finishing a perfect summer's evening.

·•⟫⟩ ⟨⟨•·

Otherworldly-sounding loon calls came echoing in from the misty morning lake, bouncing through the open bedroom window and waking me. The sun had not thought of rising yet as I crept down the creaky wooden stairs to start a pot of coffee brewing. Coffee cup in hand, I quietly slipped outside to let my guests slumber in peace and quiet, poked in the garden, pulled a few weeds, and picked some salad greens while still cool and crisp.

Thanks to plentiful spring rains, a nice crop of tart blueberries was just now ripening in the piney woods, so I picked a couple of cups for our breakfast's pancakes. They'd be perfect when served with thick-cut hickory-smoked bacon, butter, and Gloria Savory's gifted real maple syrup.

By now the sun had risen over the pines, the morning was moving along nicely, and I was getting hungry. So I headed in to rustle up some grub. Joe and Joyce were still upstairs snoozing, but the smell of coffee brewing, pancakes flapping, and bacon frying, brought them to life.

The rest of the lazy morning was spent loafing around in the yard and doing absolutely nothing. Afterward, we dined on grilled hot dogs served on white paper plates—how American. Later that afternoon we went to the market to pick up the season's first peaches, some sweet corn, a couple of quarts of great big black sweet cherries for munching and pie making, and a couple of loaves of homemade bread.

Most unexpectedly, I gave in to the most delicious nap right in the middle of the afternoon. Decadently rising well over an hour later, I brewed another pot of coffee and began preparing the evening meal. Smelling a pot of coffee percolating, Joe and Joyce ambled in for an afternoon dessert break and stayed on to help pit the cherries for the night's pie.

"Hey, Murphy, you want me to take the sweet corn out and shuck it for you?" Joe asked.

"Yeah, that sounds good. Maybe you should do about half a dozen ears."

"Come-in' right up."

"What can I do, Danny?" Joyce inquired.

"How 'bout if you set the table. We'll eat outside on the picnic table."

"All right. Can we use paper plates again?"

"Sure, and we'll burn the evidence when we're through."

Tonight's main course would be easy: hot dogs, again. Joyce's favorite meal was a hot dog. She could eat them breakfast, lunch, and dinner, if allowed.

Tonight they would be served with grilled corn on the cob, sweet potato salad, grilled baked beans with bacon, and a sweet black cherry pie served with vanilla-bean ice cream.

The cottage's old wall phone began to ring, so I ceased my hovering over the stove to answer it.

"Hello. Murphy's Bed-and-Breakfast, how may I direct your call?"

"Dan, its Mary," my sister said flatly.

"Happy third of July to you. What's up? I thought you were going to Jodi's."

"No. I'm at Mom's place."

There was a lengthy, punctuated pause.

"She hasn't been here, Dan."

"What do you mean, she hasn't been there?"

"Her car is gone. Her mail is still sitting on the counter, right where I left it yesterday, untouched and un-opened. Her bed looks the same as yesterday, too, still unmade. But her medications are still sitting on the counter, and if she went somewhere she'd definitely be taking her medicine with her. She hasn't been home, Dan."

"Wow. Are you sure she didn't go somewhere with the seniors? Maybe she's on a trip."

"No," Mary said flatly, "I don't think so. She always tells me when she's going somewhere. And I have already called the Burton Senior Center. She's not there."

I could tell she was trying her best to remain calm, but her voice revealed how stressed she really was.

"Have you heard from her, Dan?"

"No, I haven't. Have you called her traveling friend, Mary Rohen?"

"Yes. I've called her. I've called all around, and she doesn't seem to be anywhere."

"This does sound funny, doesn't it?"

There was another lengthy pause. Mary breathed in deeply before continuing.

"There's more, Dan. Her answering machine has a message on it; it's from Dr. Lloyd's office. She never made it to her appointment yesterday. They left a message to see if she was all right. Just a minute and I'll play it for you."

"Hello, Mrs. Murphy? Dorothy, this is Sarah from Dr. Lloyd's office, and we're just calling to see if you're all right, honey, because you missed your appointment today. So, why don't you just give us a call back and let us know that you're all right, now. Thank you. Buh-bye, now."

This didn't sound good. This didn't sound good at all, because Mom always made it to her appointments, especially with her doctors, and if she was unable to make them she'd definitely call and cancel.

"I'm calling the police," Mary said.

"I'll be down first thing in the morning."

Friday, the Fourth of July

A LARGE ROCK was thrown into my tranquil lake, making ripples that would prove far-reaching.

❖

Mary didn't call back with any further updates about Mom, but I sensed that something was terribly wrong. After a long and practically sleepless night, I rose way before dawn, threw a few things into my travel bag, and prepared to leave for Flint. I'd previously invited some friends over for a Fourth of July get-together, but that plan was discarded. Not wanting to wake Joe and Joyce, who were still upstairs and blissfully lost in slumber, I wrote them a brief note explaining my sudden departure, and split.

Usually it took between three and four hours to drive downstate, depending on weather and traffic, but today driving was a breeze because the roads were practically deserted. With the holiday falling on a Friday, most people had long ago arrived at their holiday destinations.

When daylight finally arrived, I could hear the sounds of people already beginning to celebrate by lighting whizzing bottle rockets, and igniting packs of annoying firecrackers. But I didn't feel much like celebrating because I was becoming worried, and there was plenty of time to fret while driving south. Slowly a feeling of dread crept over me, gripping me. Something was definitely wrong.

My mom could be missing. For the first time I acknowledged it to myself. Mother not making it to a doctor's appointment spoke volumes to me. She would always make it to her appointments, and if she was not able to, she'd call from her sickbed to cancel and reschedule.

A few years earlier she'd experienced these unusual, disabling, vertigo-like symptoms. When these phantom dizzy spells and accompanying huge blood pressure spikes would mysteriously come over her, she would completely lose her equilibrium. This disabling imbalance made it impossible for her to perform any of her daily chores, such as cooking, driving, or even getting out of bed. And let me tell you, she was a terrible patient, because she was cranky and demanding. For several months she was practically bedridden and needed transportation to her appointments, as well as to have all of her cooking, shopping, and household chores completed.

So naturally we were thrilled when Dr. Lloyd diagnosed her as having Meniere's disease, an inner-ear disturbance. Treating this illness he cured her vertigo and also eliminated a few medications she was taking that were causing those sudden and unexplained blood pressure spikes. Since her recovery, she was nearly as good as new, and we were all greatly relieved.

Mom has always been very active, and since her recovery she fully resumed her busy life. She currently belongs to Holy Redeemer's Altar Society and the Senior Adventurers travel group, and she is quite active with the Burton Senior Center. She plays cards regularly, and is quite the card sharp. She fully participated and is well-liked.

Quietly over the past few years Mother also became rather devout, which was surprising, because when we were young she hardly ever attended church with us. Thinking back, she was probably glad to have a private moment to herself. Mom fully converted to Catholicism only after Dad died, and I assumed she probably did then because she wanted to set a good example for Mike, as he was eleven. She now reads the Bible and prays daily, went to Mass quite often, and has even attended several religious retreats.

⋅⊳═◉ ◉═◁⋅

My cell phone was a recent, yet necessary, acquisition. Since most of my work was out of town, it just made it much easier to conduct my life and business while I was away. But the damned thing was both a blessing and a curse, because now friends and pests alike could reached me anywhere, anytime. And also, I could now talk on the phone while driving, just like everyone else.

Since my friend Mike worked first shift and was always up this early, I decided to call him. "Morning, Mike, sorry for calling so early. Are you up?"

"Yeah, I'm up, just lying around, smoking cigarettes, and ruminating. What's up?"

"I'm driving back to Flint, because we can't seem to find my mom. We don't know where she is.""It's the Fourth of July. She probably went somewhere fun."

"She was supposed to come up here, with me…"

"Like I said, pumpkin, she wanted to go somewhere *fun*. Don't you worry. She's probably just gone off with some friends. My mom does that sometimes. She just goes off for a couple days, to the casino, or the cottage. Don't worry, it's probably nothing."

"Mike, it's different with my mom. She is eighty years old, she's been a widow thirty years, and she doesn't just 'go off' and not let any of us know where she is."

"Well, I'm just sayin', *my* mom does that sometimes. That's all I'm saying, pumpkin."

It always pissed me off when he called me "pumpkin." It was so dismissive.

"All right, thanks for listening. Happy Fourth."

•→═◉ ◉═←•

A little after eight I called Mary to let her know that I was on the way. After not getting much sleep last night, I didn't want to call too early and chance interrupting her rest. We made arrangements to meet at Mom's trailer around nine, and figure out what to do next.

After reaching Mom's place, I let myself in and closely scanned it to see if any thing appeared out of place. It looked just as tidy as always, with nothing seeming to be disturbed. I saw her unopened mail lying on the counter, and her medicine sitting next to it. As I walked into her bedroom I immediately saw her half-packed suitcase on its stand. Her tousled unmade bed told me that she was really feeling poorly, because Mom always made her bed, always. It was her number one law.

Mother's mobile home was a vision in teal and raspberry sherbet, with the obligatory old lady's cream-and-dusty-rose Victorian floral sofa. Her double-wide trailer was so fancy that it had custom-made coordinating draperies, to match the flowery couch. Her trailer was always clean, nice, and orderly, but it reeked of old lady, smelling like Bengay ointment, Hall's menthol cough drops, mothballs, and floral potpourri. She would always bristle at my calling her place a "trailer."

"It's a modular home," she would say, correcting me every single time.

◦→▷ ◁◦

When Mary arrived we sat at Mom's table, stunned, and tried to figure out what to do next.

"I filed the missing persons report yesterday, but they told me that someone has to be missing for twenty-four hours before they can initiate a search, and we don't even know when Mom left."

"I know. But what I don't know is what we should do next. Do you think we should call the police back to see if they have any news for us?"

"Ya. Do you want to call them this time?"

"Sure."

I dialed the local police station, the phone rang three times, and then an answering machine clicked on. A recorded message began to play, "Hello, you have reached the Mundy Township Police Department. We are sorry, but we will be closed for the Fourth of July holiday, beginning on the evening of Thursday, July 3, until Monday morning, July 7. If you have an emergency, please dial 911."

I looked at Mary, took a deep breath, and said, "They're closed for the holiday. The entire police station is closed. Their recording said to call 911."

So, for the first time in my life, I dialed 911.

"911 operator. What is the nature of your emergency?"

"Our mother is missing."

For the first time I said it out loud, and saying that suddenly made it real.

"How long has she been missing, sir, and, does she have any mental or physical conditions?"

"I don't quite know where to begin. As near as we can figure, our mother hasn't been home for the last two nights. Yesterday my sister filed a missing person report with the Mundy Township Police. We just called them back for an update, and discovered that they are closed for the entire holiday weekend. This can't wait till Monday. We need to talk to someone today. And no, she does not have any conditions."

"OK. Yes sir, you're right, their office is closed. Would you please drive over to the Speedway Gas Station, on the corner of the US-23 expressway and Grand Blanc Road, where an officer will be dispatched to meet you."

"Yes, we will. Thank you."

Mary and I drove to the gas station as instructed, pulled in, and waited for what seemed to be an eternity for an officer to arrive. Unlike northern Michigan's beautiful weather, downstate it was miserably hot and sticky, and the skies were becoming more menacing with each passing minute. As we waited, dark threatening clouds crackled with lightning, unleashing violent electric bolts dropping drenching downpours, and inundating the already rain-soaked fields.

Even with the truck's air conditioner running on full blast, the windows of the cab still steamed up, because the stifling air was completely saturated. Mary and I sat nervously waiting while scanning the road for a police car and silently trying to figure out where mother could possibly be.

"Last night I called Mike on his cell phone and told him that he'd better come home. He said he'd be here later today, as soon as possible. But we don't have any way of getting a hold of Tim yet because they are somewhere on the road between here and Delaware. They don't have a cell phone either."

"We can figure that out later."

Where could Mother possibly be? Did she have another dizzy spell and drive off the road somewhere? You always heard stories on the news about some old lady who crashed her car and became stranded in a snake-filled ditch for days, and was then miraculously found alive. About a million possible scenarios raced through my mind, and none of them were good.

Mary looked flushed and worried.

Missing Person

A STEALTH BLACK police car, with doors marked Mundy Township Police Department, pulled into the gas station and parked on the far west end. Taking a deep breath, I braced myself as we left the comfort of the air conditioned truck to meet the officer. As we stepped outside, the saturated stifling air felt like walking into a steamy shower, and condensation immediately clouded my glasses.

"Good morning. I am Officer Joel Grahn. How may I be of service to you two?" He seemed to be looking to me for an answer, so I responded.

"Morning, Officer. I'm Dan Murphy, and this is my sister, Mary Deering, and, we can't seem to locate our mother."

Somehow that sounded better than she was missing.

"Can you tell me, when was the last time that any body saw her?"

"I last saw her on Sunday afternoon," Mary said.

"That was the last time I saw her, too," I added.

"OK. Where does your mom live? And, does she suffer from any physical, mental, or medical conditions that we should know about?"

"She lives in the Chateau Torrey Hill mobile home community. Our mother is eighty years old, but she's in good shape. She is very independent and still quite sharp; she lives alone, drives, and is mentally aware. Yesterday I filed a missing person report with your department, and we wanted to know if you have any news for us."

"You both realize, don't you, that it's a long holiday weekend? Did you consider the possibility that maybe your mom has gone off somewhere with friends and forgot to tell you guys about it?"

"No," Mary said firmly. "She wouldn't do that. That's not like her. She has been widowed for many years now, and she always keeps us informed of her comings and goings."

"And you do realize that a person has to be missing for twenty-four hours before a missing person report can be filed, don't you?"

"I already filed a report with your department late yesterday afternoon," Mary interjected.

The officer looked at her as if he was puzzled, but I believed he could sense her genuine concern.

"Her doctor's office, in Flushing, called and left a message on her phone. They were checking on her because she missed her appointment. That was two days ago, on July 2. That is very unlike her."

"She hasn't been heard from in two days now," I added.

"OK," the officer said, looking confused, but wanting to comprehend.

Mary continued. "Two days ago, when I stopped at her home, all of the medications she takes daily were still sitting on the kitchen counter. She would never go away with out taking them along. And her car is missing too. No one has seen or heard from her for two days now."

Sliding into his highly technical vehicle, he switched on the dashboard computer and began to type, apparently attempting to bring up the missing person report that Mary filed yesterday.

After several minutes of typing while still seated inside his patrol car, he turned in his seat to speak to us again. "Apparently the storms that are blowing through here have knocked out our computers, and I can't seem to locate the report you filed yesterday, Mary. I'm really very sorry about that. But if you guys don't mind, you can re-file another report, right here, right now, with me."

After posing questions to us for twenty minutes, he had entered all the necessary information into his computer. "OK. The new missing person report is filed now, so I suggest that you go home now and call up all of your mother's friends. Call all of her relatives and acquaintances, too, and ask if anyone knows her whereabouts. I will file this new report and also put an APB, or all points bulletin, out for her missing blue Buick. I'm very sorry about the confusion, but that's about all I can do for now."

Mary and I returned to Mother's trailer, found her personal phone book, divided up the numbers, and called every single friend and acquaintance listed therein, from A to Z. After calling over two hours, speaking to many white-haired old ladies and a lot of answering machines, no one had reported seeing her. Believe me, it was difficult phoning all of Mom's elderly friends and asking if they had seen her recently while trying not to scare them to death.

Not one of Mother's friends knew where she was. Several of them commented that they thought she was going up north with me for the holiday. If only she had, I thought, we probably would not be looking for her now.

·•·►▬◉ ◉▬◄·•·

While phoning Mother's friends, I glanced around her home, and evidence of her deep spiritual devotion was everywhere. A pile of inspirational books always sat on the side table, beside her favorite sage green La-Z-Boy recliner. Next to the front door a painted resin plaque was decorated with flowing angels, and it read, "Lord, there is nothing that you and I cannot face today, together." That was the first and last thing you saw before coming or going.

By mid-afternoon Mike arrived, accompanied by his good friend and neighbor, Todd Weaver. We explained the events to date to them and then sent them over to Tim's house, in Flushing, to track down a phone number to reach them in Delaware. An hour later they called to report that they'd gotten into the house, found the phone number of Aimee's fiancé's parents, and contacted them. They also explained about Mom's disappearance. Tim said they'd turn around and head home as soon as possible.

While still in Flushing, a downriver suburb of Flint, Mike and Todd decided to search for Mom and her car; because that's where we assumed she was headed. All afternoon they drove every possible route she could have taken to reach her doctor's office; assuming that she may have become dizzy and pulled off the road somewhere. It sounded logical, since we had nothing else to go on.

Mother never drove when we were young. It wasn't until after our dad died that she started, but that was nearly thirty years ago now. Still, she always avoided the busy main roads and would instead take the less-trafficked neighborhood streets. She would drive to the post office clear across town just to avoid making a left-hand turn. But she had no problem competing with traffic, having a serious lead foot.

"You have to keep up with traffic," she'd innocently say as she zoomed along in her shiny new Buick as if she was driving the Indianapolis 500's pace car.

The idea of something bad happening to Mother had not yet been fully entertained, and we were still assuming that she was out there somewhere, disoriented while on the way to her doctor's. She never owned a cell phone, so I vowed the first thing we were going to do when she got home was buy her one.

By now several calls were returned from the messages we'd left earlier, and no one had heard from Mother. Mary and I were feeling useless and anxious, so we departed to also drive and search the possible routes she could have taken to her doctor's.

Driving extremely slowly, we scanned the sides of every road, looked down every alley, and took every side street or two-track that spurred off Flushing Road. We were scanning and searching for a dark blue car and paying particular attention to the roads that followed the Flint River.

Day Four, July 5

SATURDAY JULY 5, 2003, slowly crept into being, and another eternity of a night passed into day. There was not a word from Mother, or any further information from the police department either. This began the fourth day that she had been missing.

I showered and dressed, drank a pot of black coffee, and smoked a pack of cigarettes, stoking myself for the coming day; it would undoubtedly be another long one. Mary, Mike, and I arranged to meet at Mother's place to plan our day's search strategies. Tim and his family would be back in town by tomorrow.

Being unable to just sit and let this passively play out, we felt we needed to be doing something, anything, and every-thing we could think of to help find our missing mother. We started by calling the three area hospitals to see if anyone had been admitted matching Mom's description, who seemed to be somewhat disoriented, or even a "Jane Doe." But she wasn't found at any of them. We procrastinated until late in the day before calling the Genesee County Morgue, and thankfully, she was not reported to be there either.

For the rest of the day we drove any and all possible routes to her doctor's office in Flushing. While driving the same few possible routes, and searching for any signs of her missing car, I wondered where she was. But I wondered even more why we hadn't heard anything from the police.

By now we'd acquired reinforcements, and my longtime friend Linda was the first to volunteer. So I teamed her up with my good friend Mike, and they headed out in Linda's little red ashtray of a car to help search. Brother Mike had a couple more of his buddies joining him, too, and they all departed to scan the countryside for a glimpse of a late-model, dark blue Buick Century, out in a field, off the side of the road, over by the river, down in a ditch, in an empty parking lot, anywhere, everywhere, or nowhere at all.

Mary and I decided that it was probably time to make up a "missing person" flier. So we patched together an eight-by-eleven page, using the most recent photo of Mom that we could find. The photo was all lavender and pink, with her smiling face placed front and center, and MISSING printed in big bold black letters at the top. Our contact information was printed at the bottom; pretty basic.

Finding a copy shop open during the Fourth of July weekend was not easily accomplished. But thank God, and thank Kinko's, we were able to have five hundred copies printed on brightly colored paper, to be more easily noticed. Volunteers delivered them around town to post upon kiosks, message boards, and in common places where people gathered. "Wallpaper Flint with them," was our instruction.

Next we decided to contact the local media outlets and inform them of Mother's disappearance. Press releases were written for all three of the local television networks, Channel 12–ABC, Channel 25–NBC, and Channel 5–CBS. The local radio stations and *The Flint Journal*, our hometown paper, were also notified. Volunteers hand-delivered these press packets to the media outlets, because this was most urgent and we didn't have the time to waste by mailing them. Working feverishly, we did everything we could think of to alert the entire community that our mother was missing. We saw that as our job.

That evening we all reassembled back at Mom's trailer at dusk to compare notes on the day's searches, and after reporting we made plans for tomorrow's expanded search parameters. After our meeting we shared a communal dinner of take-out pizza and a bagged salad while watching the evening news. After, Mary called our attention to a small article that appeared in yesterday's Police Blotter section of *The Flint Journal*.

Thursday, July 3, 2003 POLICE BLOTTER
FLINT: Driver Shoots Man in Shoulder and abdomen
    A man was shot in the shoulder and abdomen on Wednesday Afternoon as he walked on a city street, police said.

The victim, was walking on Grand Traverse near Leland Street about 5 p.m. Wednesday when he was approached by a Man driving a four-door, blue vehicle, police said.

The driver pointed a gun at the victim and fired five to seven shots, striking the victim twice, police said.

The suspect drove off and the victim was taken to a local hospital where he was listed in good condition, police said.

—Edward L. Ronders

This inner-city shooting, as described in the article, happened on the same day that we assumed Mother disappeared, along with her late-model, dark blue Buick. But another drive-by shooting in Flint was nothing new; that sort of thing happened all the time. In fact people got shot almost every day, and Flint has been named the most violent city in the country. I didn't see the significance in this shooting, other than a blue car was used. But Mary sensed some greater importance in the clipping and made a point of showing it to us.

Sunday, July 6

ANOTHER VIRTUALLY SLEEPLESS night finally passed into Sunday morning, July 6, 2003, and five days had passed. Mother was still missing, and there had not been any word from the police. Today Mary, Mike, and I met at Mom's place to formulate the day's search plans. Tim and Patty called, using their new cell phone, to say that they'd be joining us later in the day. They expected to be back in Flint around 10 a.m.

Somewhere around nine, and while we were still at Mom's trailer, I received a phone call. The caller ID stated it was the Mundy Township Police.

"Hey, you guys, it's the police," I said. We all stopped dead in our tracks. I answered the call.

⋯⟫⟪⋯

"Mr. Murphy, good morning, sir. This is Chief Dave Guigear from the Mundy Township Police Department; and I am calling to request that you, and your family, come into the police station for a ten o'clock morning meeting, if that will give you enough time to notify everyone."

"Yes. I think we can make that happen. We'll be there."

Since filing the second missing person report, we hadn't heard a single word from them for three whole days. We were anxious and nervous. Contacting Tim on his new cell, we arranged for them to meet us at the police station instead of Mother's place.

At ten o'clock sharp, Mike, Mary, and I arrived at the new, brown brick station, but it was still locked up tight for the holiday. A note, handwritten in black felt pen, was taped to the back door. "The Mundy Township Police Station is closed for the holiday. We will reopen on Monday, July 7, 2003. If you have an emergency, please dial 911. Have a safe and happy holiday."

Buzzing the doorbell, we anxiously waited until a fit and trim older man, somewhere around my age, appeared to open the locked door. Smiling, he said, "Hello, I'm Chief Guigear. Please come on in."

"Hello, I'm Daniel Murphy. This is my brother Michael and our sister, Mary Deering."

"Good morning, everyone, we're meeting in the coffee-break room. Come on back with me. It's way in the back." Obviously he was a policeman in street clothes, but he also looked as if he'd just returned from church. He silently escorted through the darkened station to the employee lounge, and the only room with windows and daylight.

"Thank you for coming in on a Sunday morning, and on such short notice," he politely said. "Can I offer any of you a coffee, a bottle of water, or maybe a soda?" We all declined.

"Our older brother, Tim, and his family will be joining us here at any minute. They're driving back from Delaware," I explained.

"All right. We'll wait until they get here before we begin," Chief Guigear said, taking a seat.

Except for the constant buzzing of the vending machines, the room was excruciatingly quiet. Everyone in the room fidgeted while staring out the picture window at the empty parking lot, as if it was a big-screen television. Then, as if in silent slow motion, we saw Tim's powder blue Buick sedan pull into the parking lot. They slowly unfurled themselves after their long drive and tottered to the back door. A few minutes later, they joined us at the big oval table.

Introductions were made and beverages once again offered. Patrick, like any teenager would, requested a soda. Rather abruptly, two men who were clearly police officers in street clothes entered the room and silently sat at the far end of the table. Chief Guigear introduced them and then began.

"Good morning, everyone. We have asked you all here today... because we have some news to share with you... in your mother's case."

For the first time this was being referred to as "a case." I felt myself stiffening, and bracing for the news about to come.

"I am afraid, that the news we have... is not very good. And, we are very sorry that it's taken so long for us to get back to you ...about this. We have located your mother's vehicle."

He took a long pause before resuming.

"It was located in the city of Flint, behind a nightclub, on Lapeer Road. And it was burned, pretty badly...nearly beyond recognition, actually."

A deeper silence fell over the room. Mike let out his air all at once and slumped onto the table with his head lying between his hands. Chief Guigear paused. After an extended silence, he continued.

"Your mother's vehicle was burned, so badly, that the vehicle identification tag melted right off from the car's dash-board. This made it very difficult for us to identify it. We had to call in the Michigan State Police crime lab from Bridgeport for a positive identification. This took some time.

"There are several other identifying markers on an automobile, but they are all more difficult to locate. Luckily, there was a serial number stamped on the engine's block, which did not melt away. It is definitely your mother's car, There is, however, no sign of your mother with the vehicle. We are very sorry about this."

The room was deafeningly silent.

I remember thinking, *They found her car, but she is not with the car. So where is she?* This all took some time to absorb. This was very disturbing news. Chief Guigear continued.

"We will now need to speak with each of you, individually." With that announcement he stood, opened the door, and stepped aside. We were escorted deeper into the police station, and shown to separate interview room to be interrogated independently. I don't recall the name of the detective who was assigned to question me because a veil of numbness had descended over me.

⋅⊱─⊰ ⊱─⊰⋅

"Please state your full name for the record."

"Address?"

"Will you please state where you were on the afternoon of July 2, 2003."

Thinking back light-years, I recalled being at my cottage. Why didn't I insist on Mom coming?

"Can anyone confirm this information? I will need their names and phone numbers."

"When did you last see your mother?"

Then I flashed back to the last time I saw her, at Mary's daughter Erin's high school graduation open house, just a week ago. I remember her looking so small, sitting there with an uneasy wistful smile.

"Where do you live?"

"Occupation?"

"What kind of vehicle do you drive, sir? License number?"

And then I thought about their description of the charred remnants of Mother's vehicle, where it was located, and how long she'd been missing already. This did not look good.

"Do you own a firearm, sir?"

"Have you ever been arrested?"

"Please keep us informed of your whereabouts, as we will be needing to speak with you further," the detective said sternly, granting me my leave.

Answering all his questions as best I could, it dawned on me that I was being interrogated as if I was a criminal. Then I had to remind myself that they *had* to do this, because they had to eliminate me as a suspect. But it felt different.

We were escorted back to the break room after being questioned, and Chief Guigear rejoined us.

"We will be mounting a full-scale investigation of this incident and will keep you updated with information as it becomes available. We will be in contact with you. Thank you again for coming in," he said as he escorted us to the back door.

I now recall that moment, that place, and his announcement of Mother's car being discovered destroyed just as I recall the day when President Kennedy died and where I was when 9/11 happened. This was the most significant marker in my life.

After leaving the police station, while still in shock, we gathered back at Mother's trailer. Once there we tried to explain to Tim and Patty everything that had transpired over the past few days during their absence. Being the eldest, Tim wanted to reexamine the things we had already done and he questioned our doings as only the oldest child would do to younger siblings.

So now our first assumption, searching for Mom and her car based on the belief she had become disoriented on her way to the doctor's office, had proved incorrect. Something ominous had happened. Where was our mother? The entire city of Flint would now become our search area.

She could be anywhere.

Anywhere at all.

The News is Out

SOMETHING TERRIBLE HAD happened. Mother's car was found completely destroyed, but we still didn't know where she was. And now I realized that finding her alive might not be likely.

⋆⊸═◉ ◉═⊷⋆

After receiving the devastating news from the police we returned to Mother's trailer. We all felt numb but we couldn't just sit and wait for something to happen. We had to do something, figure out what to do and formulate a plan. Mike, Tim, and Patrick were dispatched to spend the rest of the day driving and searching for Mother, only now, without a vehicle to look for; it would be an entirely different kind of search. Mary and I stayed at the trailer fielding phone calls, and Patty cooked.

"Things don't look good, do they? Mom's eighty years old, and this has been such a nasty stretch of stormy weather," I said.

Mary nodded in agreement; some things are understood without saying.

We could not yet speak what we felt, but we knew that precious time was running out—and already gone. Strangely, time seemed to be moving at lightning speed and in slow motion at the same time. We were numb, in shock, and only operating on adrenaline. It was an emotionally draining day, and when evening mercifully came we parted, going back to our separate homes to deal with grief in our own ways.

⋆⊸═◉ ◉═⊷⋆

The next day, Monday morning, we discovered that the press releases we'd sent out were received. The story of Mother's disappearance began to hit the media, and all three of the local television stations called asking for additional information and requesting interviews. *The Flint Journal* also called wanting more details.

Some of the more ambitious reporters just showed up at Mom's mobile home to photograph the blue trailer at 311 Loyalist Lane, reported as, "The last place the missing elderly woman was seen alive." They were eager for news about the mysterious disappearance of eighty-year-old Dorothy Murphy, and we were anxious to get the news out to the community as soon as possible. Mother's home quickly became the official command post, where we democratically took turns giving interviews to the media, sending out search parties, and fielding phone calls.

Angie Schramski, the statuesque blonde news anchor from our local ABC affiliate, Channel 12, was conducting an in-depth interview on the lawn of Mom's trailer when an odd serendipitous connection was discovered. While discussing Mother's disappearance, and her blue Buick being destroyed behind Mr. Lucky's Nightclub, she recalled actually seeing Mother's vehicle while it was ablaze. The television station just happened to be located directly across the street from Mr. Lucky's, where Mother's car was found on five days earlier. The weather camera captured the thick black smoke as it was billowing from the car-fire burning behind the nightclub, and the station sent a news crew to investigate. After their arrival they videotaped the Flint Fire Department hosing down the blazing vehicle—our mother's Buick.

This invaluable bit of videotaped footage was then patched together with that day's interview to make the story into one seamless news item. That evening we all gathered around the television to watch the six o'clock news, and for the first time we witnessed Mother's Buick being destroyed by the raging fire. It was a chilling image. Mom always kept her tank full, and that car really blazed. That vehicle was totally engulfed in flames and left obliterated, with nothing remaining but a colorless, tireless chassis. It even melted parts of the cinder block building that it was torched behind, severely damaging the structure.

The story of her disappearance was definitely out there now, and suddenly more people began to just appear, offering their assistance. We gladly accepted. Flint was still a dangerous place, so we teamed up the volunteers into groups of two or three before sending them off to search areas not previously canvassed.

People wanted to support us in any way they could, and Mom's little-old-lady friends, who could not help search for her, sent food. Massive amounts of delicious home-cooked food began to miraculously appear. It was like the miracle of the loaves and fishes, when big hot-dish casseroles, chilled potato salad, colorful Jell-O salads, frosted-sheet-cakes, brownies, beanie-weenies, and whole Honey-Baked hams magically arrived at the trailer/command post.

And each evening a familiar ritual played out as our family, friends, and the generous volunteers would rendezvous at Mom's trailer to catch the six o'clock news, read the newspapers, and eat communal meals. And there was always more than enough food to go around. Bless us oh Lord, and these thy gifts.

·⊷⊷ ⊶⊷·

Late in the evening, after finally returning home, I was totally spent, because these past few days had been extremely exhausting, long, and stress filled. When home at last, alone with my thoughts, I knew that time was running out, and for the first time since she vanished I broke down and cried. I couldn't cease the tears. The realization hit me solidly that something dreadful had happened, and I knew my mother would not be coming home alive. She was gone. I sensed it, I knew it, and I grieved it.

·⊷⊷ ⊶⊷·

The following morning I awoke sobbing, as I would for many mornings to come. I could not control the crying, so I just let it happen. Then I would pray to God for the strength to go on another day, collect myself, shower, shave, and put on a brave face. We had many things to do.

Thirty years earlier, following our dad's early, untimely death, Mother demonstrated a great deal of strength. She was not emotional or weepy at all; she got up and did what she had to do. There were no complaints, or questioning why.

She just did it, calmly. And now we, her children, were expected to do nothing less.

On the French provincial nightstand next to Mother's bed was her always-opened Bible. It was Mary who first noticed the verse that Mom had marked and pointed it out to us. "Do not fear for me for I am in a far better place. Although turmoil may brew all around you, you will find comfort, and rest. Fear not." We shared a quiet moment in reflection and offered up a prayer while huddled in Mother's bedroom.

And from that night on, my sleepless nights were over, and I could peacefully slumber once again.

Truthfully, mom was never one to be physically, or emotionally, affectionate. We knew we were loved, but she never was one to speak it. She didn't praise unless she thought it well earned and deserving; she set the bar very high. Mom demonstrated her love through her actions, but it was difficult for her to say, "I love you."

"You guys know what?" I said. "I got this unusually mushy greeting card from Dort the week just before she disappeared, and I kept it, because it was so unlike her. The card said, 'I am very proud of you.' And, she signed it with, 'I love you very much, Love Mother.' She's usually not mushy like that."

To me, those few words spoke volumes.

"She sent me a card like that, too," Mary said. "Me, too," Mike confirmed. And then Tim added, "I got a card like that too." Somehow it seemed as if she knew she was leaving us, and this was her way of saying good-bye. When I received her card I considered it significant, so I kept it. Now I realized that this would be the last communication I would ever receive from my mom. "I love you, and I am proud of you." What more could I possibly wish to hear?

And even now, as I am telling you this, years later, I am weeping.

Not knowing where Mother was became the worst part. Nearly an entire week had passed without any word from her or any updates from the police. I wouldn't allow myself to wonder "what if" or be over-come with fear, grief, or despair. Mother wouldn't allow such thinking. Instead we decided to take action—pray, but take action—by making phone calls, contacting the media, handing out fliers, cooking, mowing the lawn, searching, doing anything but sitting and passively waiting for something to happen.

We felt *compelled* to search for Mother. It already seemed that way too much time had been lost. On shows such as *Cold Case Files* and *Without a Trace*, they claimed that the first twenty-four hours are the most critical in a disappearance, and we had already lost those precious early hours; they were gone before we even knew she was missing.

Not hearing anything back from the police for so long, we did not believe that anyone beyond our immediate family felt the same sense of panic or urgency that we were experiencing or taking Mother's disappearance as seriously as it should have been taken. It was quite apparent to us that something ominous had happened to her. She would not have vanished on her own like this.

⸻

Seven days after her disappearance, on Tuesday, July 9, 2003, we were asked to reappear at the police station for another meeting. We tried to brace ourselves for what may be more devastating news. Instead, we were greatly comforted when we met with Detective J Diem, a quiet, slightly southern -accented member of the Mundy Township police force. She had joined Mother's investigation.

Detective "J" knew our mother from teaching a Citizens Patrol class that Mom had attended a few years back. We'd all heard Dort tell stories about "J" countless times. She knew our mom was sharp and that she would not just "go off like this." Detective J would take this disappearance most seriously.

At last, we felt we had an ally in this investigation.

On Tuesday morning, July 9, 2003, Chief Dave Guigear began the briefing. "Thank you for coming in; we may have some additional news for you. It now appears that the dark blue, late-model vehicle that was used for a drive-by shooting last week, in the city of Flint, could possibly have been your mother's. This shooting happened on Tuesday; the second of July, the same day that we assume your mother disappeared. It appears the two incidents may be linked."

Perhaps it wasn't a coincidence. Mary's instincts about that news clipping may have been correct.

"The victim of the drive-by shooting is currently hospitalized while recuperating from the two gunshot wounds sustained in the incident. He is being questioned to determine if there is any connection between his being shot, your mother's car possibly being used in the shooting, and her disappearance."

We desperately hoped this shooting victim could tell us something, anything, because she had been missing for an entire week now, and each day brought more panic. But at last there was a glimmer of hope, a thread to hold on to. Maybe he knew something, such as who shot him, why Mom's car was used, or anything else that could possibly lead us to her.

"We're now working in conjunction with the city of Flint's police department, because the vehicle was discovered inside the city limits. We are paying particular attention to the timing of this shooting, and your mother's vehicle being found ablaze behind Mr. Lucky's Nightclub, because the two incidents appear to have happened within just minutes of each other. We are hopeful that something will break soon."

"We are still trying to figure out what the motive for the shooting is. But as of now, it appears to be nothing more than a lover's triangle that has gone wrong. And it may be entirely possible that the young man was shot by a jealous rival. But why his rival may have been using your mother's vehicle, and what this has to do with her, is still unclear."

•‑━◉ ◉━‑•

This small bit of news encouraged us, and we returned to Mother's trailer/command post to resume our searches. Today our brother Mike, his buddy Todd, and his brother, Brad, were taking canoes down the Flint River to search the riverbanks. They would be starting below the downtown dam, near the college, and traveling all day, going several miles downstream to Flushing.

Volunteer searchers were now driving and canvassing the more secluded areas of the city, where one might go to dispose of a body. During daylight hours we would search through abandoned houses, old deserted factories and vacated industrial sites. Along the Flint River empty factory parking lots were now sprouting young forests, and trash-strewn, overgrown fields held secret homes encampments. But we searched them, because finding our missing mother was our sole purpose now.

Work and personal life, as we once knew them, came to a halt. This search was our job. After reporting to Mom's mobile home command post each morning, we sent out updated press releases, gave interviews to the media, and coordinated the ever-expanding searches to include those areas that had not been canvassed.

We knew it was not likely we could find her on our own. We needed help. By networking we reached further out. First we filed a report with the Center for Missing Adults, a national database registry for missing grown-ups. Then we contacted Crime Stoppers, a national network that works to solve crimes by broadcasting local news segments. Quite often a cash reward was offered for helping to solve the crimes detailed in the segments.

We were desperate for any news of Mother whereabouts, but it never came. Her body was never found. Meanwhile Mother's mysterious disappearance became the lead story on the local news programs, and our white-haired mom's smiling face was becoming familiar to many people in the city. I truly believe that nearly everyone in the greater Flint area who owned a television or radio, or read the newspaper, had heard the story.

·→═◉ ◉═◄·

It was our brother Mike first brought up the possibility of visiting a psychic for insight into Mother's mysterious disappearance, and by now we were becoming desperate for news, and anything that could possibly help us find her was being considered. None of us would discount any source of information, no matter how obscure, if it led to Mother.

We were all receptive to the suggestion, so Mike made the arrangements. Our spiritual adviser would be Dianna O'Grady, and her suburban strip-mall office had trendy rock crystal formations, scented candles, a trickling fountain, spacey ambient music, and smelly Nag Champa incense scenting the air. Our rather large entourage was immediately recognized, and we were escorted back to a somber room, where even during the midday sun it was dark and meditative.

Tim and Patty, Mary, Mike, and myself were present. Mary's friend Lori Munger also joined us to take notes and be an objective observer. Diana breezed into the room and smiled pleasantly. She was pretty in a retro-hippie way, around thirty, with long and straight blond hair. She wore a white cotton embroidered peasant top, faded bell-bottom jeans, and huarache sandals. She appeared very fit.

"Welcome. It is most unusual to have this many people in one session, but welcome, everyone."

Mike stepped forward to introduce us and explain the circumstances of our visit, as well as some of the events of the preceding week. Lori, our observer, was coiled up in the corner sitting in a purple chair, tightly clutching a blue ball point pen, and ready to spring into action recording the psychic's every word on her yellow legal pad.

"Let me begin by saying how sorry I am to all of you," Dianna said. "I'm so sorry this has happened, and I will do my best to help you find the answers that you seek." Closing the blinds even farther, she lit the scented candles, dimmed the overhead lights, closed her eyes, and sat quietly for some time.

"Yes, I can see your mother now," she eventually began. "But…this is rather odd, she is…holding up an apple for me. She is showing a red apple. Does this mean anything to any of you?"

Opening her eyes, and looking rather surprised, she scanned for any signs of recognition. No one responded to her query.

"This seems to be quite important to her. She keeps showing me this red apple. But wait…I can…I can see…I can see where she is now."

The sacredly hushed room silenced even further, and we all leaned in closer.

"She is somewhere that is familiar to her, somewhere that is not too far from her home. It appears to be some sort of a clearing, a circular clearing, one that is a dumping site. And there are grass clippings here, and leaves… brush piles. Dead bushes are lying about. I can see water…and I can hear water. It's moving water. It is nearby…but it's dirty water, not clean. And there is some sort of tower…for radio…or TV maybe."

"Does your mom have some sort of stomach trouble, because I'm feeling intense discomfort in the midsection?"

Again she opened her eyes and scanned the room, looking for any sign of confirmation. After an uncomfortable lengthy silence, Mary offered, "She has acid reflux disease."

"No that's not it; it's more like, she is holding her stomach…like she is in intense pain. Does this make sense to anybody?" Dianna made circular motions with her hands around her central core. "It's like her stomach area hurts. Like, she has been punched or kicked in the midsection?"

I found this speculative vision disturbing. Was this my worst fear being confirmed, was she just guessing, or could she actually feel something?

"I am feeling intense discomfort in the midsection. And I see a shoe, just one shoe, a tan shoe. There are three people here, and someone with long, dirty, stringy hair. Does the name Moses mean anything to you?" Again, there was not a response from anyone.

"Make sure that you pay attention of your dreams from now on, because your mother may be trying to contact you through your dreams."

⋅⊷▱◉ ◉▱⊶⋅

She made a few other remarks but did not say where Mother was located, or if she was alive or dead. She didn't take out a map, point to a location and say, "Go search there." The information that we were desperately seeking was not revealed to us. After making an offering for her services, we departed.

On the drive back to mothers, each of us gave our insights into the clues that Dianna presented, but the apple thing puzzled us all, and no one seemed to know what that meant; it seemed to be very important to convey.

Rounding the corner toward Mom's trailer, we could see a large assembly of media people camped outside, and as soon as we exited the car they all descended upon us. "Is it true that you've just been to see a psychic? Who was it? What did they see? What did they say? Did they say where your missing mom is?"

Facing the reporters, I said, "Please respect our privacy in this matter. This is a private and personal family matter that we do not want to share with the public."

Then we quickly went directly into the trailer and closed the door behind us, shutting them out.

→══◎ ◎══←

The very next day, in big bold print, the front page of *The Flint Journal* read Psychic Gives Tips, as Hunt for Missing Mom Goes On.

→══◎ ◎══←

We were quickly learning that the media held a double-edged sword. It could cut both ways. We were now being portrayed as crackpots, kooks, and seeking counsel from Dionne Warwick and her Psychic Friends.

When I Was in Distress You Comforted Me

THERE ARE THINGS you cannot possibly do on your own; it takes the support of an entire community.

•→═⊙ ⊙═←•

Two more days somehow crept by without Mother being located. There was no further word from her, or about her, and very little significant new information coming from the police since they had found her car. But a strong sense of community had formed around us and this mystery disappear- ance, and we were being supported by our extended family, friends, and the community, and it helped us push on.

Jerry Parsons and his family had been friends for many years, and they thoughtfully initiated a reward fund. Donations were collected and an account was grown that was to be exchanged for credible information leading to Mother's discovery.

Todd and Heather, close friends of brother Mike, initiated a website for information sharing and to post words of consolation to the Murphy family. Rob Burden, another friend, kindly assembled an online phone bank for calling in confidential tips and information to the reward fund, which was then, linked to the police agencies.

Patty Hogan, a dear friend from my college days, suggested that attend to our spiritual needs and then arranged an afternoon service. She belonged to the same church as Mother, Holy Redeemer Catholic, and graciously made the necessary arrangements. The prayer service was scheduled for 4 p.m. on Friday, July 11, 2003, a full nine days after she disappeared. With Mom having a large family, and the four of us having many friends, we expected the service to be largely attended. But when the media shared the time and location on the evening news, we expected the crowd to be substantial.

This service was not an actual funeral, but it was our family's way of indirectly acknowledging that we believed our mother was gone. I believe that we felt this to be true, but could not yet speak it.

Father Bill, the parish priest, was young, hip, energetic, and well-liked. Early in this ordeal, he visited us at Mother's to help us begin our long journey, and he bonded with us over pizza and beer. Sadly he was vacationing, so a young training priest, Father Gregory, would be officiating in his absence. Meeting before the service, we selected the Bible verses and music, choosing the Twenty-Third Psalm, the Song of Saint Francis, and one contemporary song, "I Can Only Remember," as performed by Mercy Me.

The large modern suburban church filled to capacity with family, friends, church members, and the greater Flint community. Some of the local media outlets that we had previously solicited to help inform the community about Mother's disappearance were there as well. Pulling into the parking lot, we could already see their television broadcasting trucks and film crews assembled.

Our family solemnly walked in as one unified group and sat down, entirely filling the front pew. Then the media people, with their cameras rolling, swarmed in immediately after us, invading the sanctuary of our service. Apparently they were hoping to witness the breakdown of the grief-stricken family, and just in time for airing on the six o'clock evening news.

We viewed their intrusion as a most unwelcome violation and kindly requested that they remain outside the church. They instead chose to stay on and continue filming. Mary's sturdy son, Ryan, who had just returned home from a tour of duty in the army, looked splendid fully dressed in his Ranger's uniform. Rising from his seat, he marched over, stood in front of them while silently staring them down, and kindly escorted them back outside to the parking lot for the duration of the service.

All four of Dorothy Loraine Lee Murphy's children, and all four of her grandchildren, were seated in the front pew of her church. Several of her ten siblings sat in the rows directly behind us. Scriptures were read, singing filled the air, and communion offered to "those of you who are Catholic and in good standing with the Church." The high-strung trainee priest made that point abundantly clear. After communion, he pontificated at some length about saving the souls of sinners, hellfire, and damnation, but not about our mother or her life, as he never knew her. And the service was ended.

But then, after this service was ended, the most spiritual, moving, and uplifting phenomenon of my life occurred. As the exit hymn, "The Song of Saint Francis," was played, the congregation did not quickly flee church, as most loyal churchgoers do. Rather, they stayed.

Forming a long line, they began to walk up the center aisle, coming to the front pew where we were seated. One by one they appeared with their arms opened wide, they hugged us, lovingly shared words of comfort and consolation with us, and many of them cried with us, too.

Tears rolled down my face as a continuous stream of caring people appeared to embrace us, cry with us, share condolences, and give words of comfort. Each embrace seemed to lift a share of our burden, and in exchange they gave us their love and support, strength, and prayers. In all of my life I've never felt such a humbling yet uplifting and moving experience, or such an outpouring of love and support. This impromptu prayer service was one of the most profoundly moving spiritual experiences of my life.

The generous gifts of love we received that day would have to carry us through the dark days that were still to come, for this journey was not over yet.

I felt recharged by this outpouring infusion of love, but completely spent. I knew it was hard enough to lose a parent in the usual way, but this vanishing was much worse than a death. Not knowing where your loved one was, and what you were dealing with, required a great deal of faith.

When the last condolence was given, and the prayer service was ended, I needed a quiet moment to collect myself before rejoining the others. Stepping outside to have a smoke, I found a cloistered garden bursting with midsummer's bloom. Inside the intimate retreat my friend Mike was hiding, having a cigarette, and patiently waiting for me. For those who don't know who he is, we were once romantically involved. We are now close friends. Mike is smart, very tenderhearted, and still quite handsome—only now in a mature Richard Gere way.

"How you doing?" Mike said, exhaling a lungful of blue-gray smoke. "Was a nice service."

"Yes, it was nice; moving, and sad. I feel spent; wrung out like an old dish rag," I said wiping my eyes with the back of my hand, lighting a cigarette, and taking a good long drag.

"It'll be all right. Some day this will all be over, you know."

"I sure hope so, because these have been the worst days of my life. I'm exhausted. You know, no one has come right out and said it yet, but we feel that she's gone."

"Yes, I think there are a lot of other people who feel that way, too. There was an awful lot of weeping going on during that service."

"I'm sorry that you had to sit with my friend Bette and console her. Is she all right?"

"Yeah, she's fine. She's on the other side of the church smoking with her sister, Donna."

"I don't know what were going to do, Mike. I think this service was a good idea, but I won't be able to rest until we find her."

"They'll find her. You'll find her. It will be all right. Now come here," he said, and he opened his arms wide to comfort me. I fell easily into the familiar warmth of his reassuring embrace.

"I hope you're right, and that this will all be over someday soon."

"It will. And when it is, you'll have to write the story, because no one will believe it."

"You think that's a good idea?"

"Yeah, I do. And when you do write it, I have the title for you."

"Yeah, and what would that be?"

"Missing Mom."

"That's good, Mike. Thanks. We should probably join the rest of them pretty soon. But first, I want to thank you for being here for me during all of this. I can't tell you how much it means to me."

"You just did. Now come on, let's go face the music."

⋯⊷⊜ ⊜⊶⋯

For the most part, my family didn't know who Mike was, or what he truly meant to me over the past twenty-some years. I supposed they knew he was part of my inner circle, but they didn't know how significant he was. That was mostly my fault, because for many years I dealt with my gayness as the army did. They didn't ask, and I didn't tell. Consequently, for thirty years there was a big pink elephant standing in my living room, and nobody ever talked about it. That was just the way our family was. As children we were constantly told by our dad that children were supposed to be seen and not heard. You don't say.

⋯⊷⊜ ⊜⊶⋯

Ten days had passed since Mom vanished. The police had nothing new of significance to report. Waiting for some-one else to do something just wasn't in our nature. And all though we believed the police were doing everything they could, we still felt compelled to continue searching. We were sensing the strong primal urge to find our mother, bring her home, and bury her, and we could not rest until that happened.

Having another family meeting, it was decided to conduct an organized ground search next, to help locate Mother. So we wrote more press releases and notified the community, made the necessary phone calls to the authorities, and networked while preparing for our next event.

Nearly three weeks after she vanished, on Sunday, July 20, 2003, volunteers were asked to assemble at the west Flint Meijer store, just down the road from Mom's trailer park, to help search for her. The store graciously gave us permission to assemble in the parking lot by the garden center, and it also kindly provided us with cold bottled water for the volunteers, which was most appreciated, as we were experiencing an extended stretch of unusually hot and horrible weather.

In the mad rush to prepare for the search, the section maps needed for the volunteers were not copied. We made a last-minute dash to Kinko's, copied, and then delivered the maps back to the assembled anxious crowd. We were disorganized as hell, but felt as if we were doing something. To make this manageable we decided to limit our search to areas close to Mom's home and the routes between her trailer and her doctor's office in Flushing. We purposely excluded most of the city of Flint.

Around two hundred people arrived to help search, and many of those faces were familiar to us. Family members, friends and acquaintances, church members, an entire Boy Scout troop, neighbors, coworkers, friends from high school days, and many complete strangers turned out to help us.

The sweaty, restless volunteers were called to order via bullhorn. First we expressed our gratitude to all of them for their assistance, and explained how the search was to proceed. We also acknowledged and thanked Chief Guigear, Detective J Diem, and the other members of the Mundy Township Police Department who graciously volunteered to help us on their day off.

Before the crowd departed, Mr. Kaylor, a family friend, led us in the recitation of the Lord's Prayer. Then he read a poem to the crowd that Mother always kept on her bedside table.

Safely Home

I am home in Heaven, dear ones;
Oh, so happy and so bright!
There is perfect joy and beauty
In this everlasting light.
All the pain and grief is over,
Every restless tossing passed;

I am now at peace forever,
Safely home in Heaven at last.
Did you wonder why I so calmly
Trod the valley of the shade?
Oh! But Jesus's love illuminated
Every dark and fearful glade.
And he came Himself to greet me
In that way so hard to tread;
And with Jesus's arm to lean on,
Could I have one doubt or dread?
Then you must not grieve so sorely,
For I love you dearly still:
Try to look beyond earth's shadows,
Pray to trust our Father's Will.
There is work still waiting for you,
So you must not idly stand;
Do it now, while life remaineth—
You shall rest in Jesus's land.
When that work is all completed,
He will gently call you Home;
Oh, the rapture of that meeting,
Oh, the joy to see you come!
Priest of the Sacred Heart Monastery

Hearing that poem read, more than a few of us blotted away tears, and had a moment.

→⟩═◉ ◉═⟨←

Before the search commenced, Chief Guigear pulled me aside and spoke frankly with me. "Dan, do you think you are really prepared for what you may eventually find?"

In fact, it was something that we had indeed tried to prepare ourselves for.

"Yes, Chief Guigear, but you have to understand, we feel compelled to keep looking, because we want her back. We assume that she is gone by now, but we have to keep looking."

"I understand, Dan. But have you ever seen a dead body, or smelled one?"

Our family felt as if God himself sent us Chief Guigear. Throughout this ordeal, he, Detective J Diem, and the rest of the people in his department had quickly gained our trust and admiration. We believed they were doing every-thing within their power to find our missing loved one. Still, we were impatient.

⇥⊙ ⊙⇤

The bullhorn blared and suddenly volunteers started departing, scattering in every direction simultaneously. Patty Hogan, Bette, and I stayed behind in the parking lot command post to coordinate searchers, make and receive phone calls, and smoke cigarettes, lots and lots of cigarettes. We were disorganized as hell, but at least we felt as if we were doing something to help find Mother.

It wasn't storming when the search started, but shortly thereafter the sky unzipped, dumping a brief but thoroughly drenching downpour. Steam was ac-tually seen rising from the blacktopped parking lot as the rainy puddles instantly evaporated.

⇥⊙ ⊙⇤

For nearly two hours, soggy, muddy groups of people arrived back to report their findings, and when the last group checked in, Mother had not been found. We did, however, have several complications resulting from the search. Aunt Phyllis slipped on a muddy rain-soaked embankment and then slid into a drainage ditch, badly breaking her ankle. Luckily, Rob Herrick, another friend of the family, was helping us with the search. He was also a Michigan state trooper and sent her directly to the hospital. There were a couple of other minor bumps, but nothing too serious.

Through this trying ordeal we learned who our friends truly were, and we discovered that we were truly blessed with many friends. Tommy Taylor, a longtime friend, tromped through muddy fields in the rain while dressed in Gucci loafers and a splashy silk shirt. His searching party included Kate and Tom, and their friends Linda and John.

Bless all of the souls who helped us search that day. They cared enough for us and our mother, to show up on a stormy Sunday afternoon and help us look for her.

⊷⊨◉ ◉⊨⊷

Another week went crawling by following the ground search without any additional news coming from the police. In the meantime, we had other personal business to attend to. Our next scheduled event was a small informal service, as an acknowledgment to our immediate family and a few close friends that Mother had passed away.

The Sunday after the search was a breezy day, clear with blue cloudless skies. We assembled, at Mary's church, Saint Joseph's, in Gaines, Mi. Their meeting hall was a small pole barn, painted a bright cerulean blue, that was setting in a freshly mown, sweet-smelling hayfield. A small collection of family members and a few close friends gathered together to remember Mother, and pray for, and comfort each other. I was seated with my family, and comfortably tucked between my close friends Mike and Linda.

The church's deacon, Sister Ann, directed the simple service, and we were very pleased, because Mom just loved her. We were certain it was reciprocal. The Twenty-Third Psalm was recited, and a couple of Bible verses read, and then we sang one of Mom's favorite hymns, "The Old Rugged Cross." After, there was a brief sharing of personal memories, and brave Debbie Russell stood and spoke first.

"I really enjoyed playing Scrabble with Dorothy, and I liked her motherly ways."

Laughing, Sister Ann replied, "You should know better than to *ever* play Scrabble with an old lady. You can't possibly win."

We laughed, because laughter was always welcome. It was a cool and soothing tonic that helped to ease the ever-present tension. This gathering was not a tearful event like the formal church service. It was our family's private nod to the understanding that our loved one had passed away, and a much easier service to get through. This was one more event in what was becoming a journey, an odyssey.

When the service was ended, there was a potluck supper, with everyone bringing a dish, or three. A small group of family members and friends attended this service, but there was enough food present to feed a small country. Food being shared communally was a bonding activity throughout this ordeal.

⋯⟫⊚ ⊙⟪⋯

We were encouraged in the days immediately following the acknowledgment service, as massive search and investigation efforts were being undertaken.

After receiving several reports of an unusually odd offensive odor emanating from the Thread Lake area, the Michigan State Police sent their team of scuba divers and cadaver-seeking dogs to investigate the murky lake and its surrounding wetland areas. This neglected body of water was close to Mr. Lucky's Nightclub, where Mother's car was found destroyed. And it was, to my mind, a likely place to "stash a body," because the neighborhoods surrounding the lake were severely deteriorated. Most of the homes were long ago abandoned, with many debris-strewn vacant lots along dead-end streets that terminated at the lake.

A daylong search did not discover a body, and we were again deflated.

⋯⟫⊚ ⊙⟪⋯

The week after the dive team conducted the search, the Michigan State Police helicopter was dispatched to aerially scan Flint, with the pilot paying particular attention to areas surrounding Mother's home and those extending downstream and west toward Flushing. The aerial search did not find a body, but it was obvious to us that massive efforts were being undertaken by the investigators to find Mother.

She still was not found. But what was being accomplished was more things being checked off from a very long list of possible places to search for her.

·•)═⊙ ⊙═(•·

Later that week we sent out another round of press releases, because we wanted to keep the story alive, and this time we were simply requesting that the area residents search around their homes and surrounding property for any sign of Mother.

Before each new search we held out hope that Mom would be found, {dead or alive} and after each search that was conducted without finding her we felt deflated. So we paused, rested, prayed, reassessed, and planned for the next event.

Three Weeks Gone

THE FLINT JOURNAL'S July 21, 2003, front-page article summed it up best: No Clues, No Closure.

Three weeks had passed, Mother had not been found, and we weren't sure what to do next. Tim, Mary, and Mike checked back into their respective workplaces. Because I was self-employed I had more flexibility with my schedule, and I'd previously cleared my calendar for the entire month of August, so I stayed on to coordinate the command post. We all still felt that this search was our number one priority. However, all the other realities of life still remained, such as taking care of children, paying bills, and doing laundry—the demands of a long-neglected home and work life.

This week proved to be painfully slow without any news of any kind, but thankfully there was another diversion, because the annual Lee Family reunion was scheduled for Saturday, July 26, 2003. This was Mother's family, and our branch of the Lee family, the Lee-Murphy's, had volunteered to host the reunion last year, before all this happened. Mom was the matriarch of the family, so we were planning to host the reunion and also have a surprise eightieth birthday party for her; but that plan had been changed.

Having another family meeting, it was democratically decided to still host the event. Really it wasn't too large a task. Many relatives offered to assist us, and it was always a potluck event anyway. For the past several years it had been held at the Burton Eagles clubhouse, just outside Flint. The Aerie had two baseball diamonds and several horseshoe pits, plus swings and playground equipment for the kids. There was also a play-ground for the adults, as a cash bar was available.

We enjoyed normal socializing again, and attending an event that didn't have to deal with the disappearance; it was comforting. A time for grieving, a time for enjoyment, and a time for family; it was even permissible to stop worrying and relax. Family bonds took on more importance than ever, and this was Mom's clan assembling for their yearly powwow—and yes, there was some Indian blood in their line.

The Lees were prolific people. Mom was the eldest of a family of ten. We had nearly fifty first cousins alone. And while many of our family members expressed their sympathies to us; we were not here for consolation. This was our annual gathering of the clan and we were here to visit. Even Aunt Phyllis arrived, still hobbling on crutches, recovering from the broken ankle she suffered during the search.

Uncle Max led us with a meal blessing before the feasting began, because no Lee gathering would be complete without massive quantities of food. After the dinner Cousin Angie's homemade vanilla custard ice cream, made from Grandma's rich and heart-stopping recipe, was a tradition and treat. After the onslaught of eating there were games of white elephant bingo, old-timers vs. youngsters baseball, and plenty of catching up to do.

I had not shared much of my private life with my extended family; there were only a few relatives whom I felt close enough to. To most I was a fifty-year-old bachelor, and a long time ago they'd quit asking when I was getting married—because either they figured it out, or my life preference did not much matter to them. There was no one significant in my life right now anyway.

Now that we were entangled in this disappearance, my gay friends stepped forward, and they were accepted and even embraced. My friend old Linda was ever-present throughout this tragedy, and adopted by the entire family. She was always there to lend her support. A friend indeed.

When my friend Tommy Taylor brought his famous butterball cake to the trailer, he was immediately adopted into the family as well. Tommy was big and blond, and a colorful character with larger-than-life hair, too much bronzer, too much cologne, and too big of a heart to match. Too much was never enough for Tommy. His decadently delicious cake was devoured, and his promise to deliver an equally charismatic carrot cake was met with a chorus of cheers. I realized that my family accepted my gay friends as equals, no judgments made.

My family did not really know my close friend Mike Putman, partly because he didn't want that to happen, and also because I did not include them in that part of my life. They may have noticed that this handsome man was with me at every event during this odyssey, but they didn't know that he was one of the most significant relationships of my life, because I didn't share that with them. Even though we had not been intimate in many years, he still held a significant place in my emotional life, and he was there for me.

⋅⋅▷══◁⋅⋅

The weeks following the reunion went excruciatingly slowly, but thankfully, our briefing with the police brought us a bit of encouraging news. They told us there was a possible witness to the vehicle arson, and she provided the detectives with a detailed suspect description. This was the first solid lead that we had received in weeks, an eyewitness.

The observer reported seeing a short, heavyset, thirty-something black woman with closely cropped hair and wearing a yellow knit shirt, black jeans, and dark sunglasses emerge from behind Mr. Lucky's, around the same time as the noxious black smoke was seen billowing from the burning car. An artist's composite sketch was made of this woman and released to the media.

At last we had another thread. That made two.

⋅⋅▷══◁⋅⋅

Nearly a month had passed since I had been home, and I needed to go to my cottage badly. I definitely needed to take a break, but I also needed to take care of many things. When I suggested we could use a break, it was unanimously approved. We could all spend the weekend at my place, rest, relax, and try to restore some sense of normalcy. That was important now. Plus I could also tend to my laundry, the month's unopened mail, lawn mowing, and the some of the other chores that had been dropped since this ordeal began.

The weather gods were most cooperative, granting us exceptional weather that allowed for peaceful solitude, quiet, and communion with nature, which would help to heal our weary souls. All during the weekend the eternal flame of the campfire never went out, thanks to Patrick, our resident Boy Scout and pyromaniac.

⋯⊨◉ ◉⊨⋯

Because Mother's torched vehicle was found inside the Flint city limits, the Flint Area Narcotics Group (FANG) was now part of the search team. They helped canvass the areas surrounding Mr. Lucky's, along with the Mundy Township police. Going door-to-door, they handed out fliers with the new composite sketch and asked if anyone saw or heard anything, and they also mentioned that the reward was well over ten thousand dollars now.

More anonymous tips continued to be phoned daily into the phone bank, which had now been rerouted and taken over entirely by the police department.

⋯⊨◉ ◉⊨⋯

Confidential information received from our weekly briefings with the police would not necessarily make it into the media, or even leave the police station. Behind the scenes investigations were ongoing, and they were not prepared to share that information with the public yet. While considerate of our wish for closure, they kept us abreast of any developments they thought necessary. It was evident to us that they were still very hard at work with this case.

The police now tell us they were fairly certain now that it *was* Mom's car used in the drive-by shooting in the Carriage Town neighborhood of Flint on the same day she disappeared. The timeline suggested that it was possible for it to be used in the shooting, driven across town to Mr. Lucky's, ditched, and then torched. They were now looking for definitive proof.

Most likely, the woman whom the eyewitness described leaving the flaming vehicle would have some connection to the story as well; they were following up on additional leads and trying to locate her for questioning.

Knowing that we were desperate for news, resolution, and especially Mother's recovery, the chief was very measured with his words. While he was sensitive to our need for closure, he made sure not to give us any false hope. He evenly said, "We are, once again, questioning the man who was injured in the drive-by shooting, but he does not seem to have any connection to the rest of the story. However, we will not discount any facts."

As More Time Passes

MORE OF THE headlines appearing in the local media outlets featured articles about elderly people being abused, raped, scammed, and murdered. Senior citizens were now becoming terrified because they were now being targeted, caught in the crosshairs of this new wave of violence, and the local media was only fanning the ever-growing flames. The national news reaffirmed their justified fears when Flint was, once again, designated as the most dangerous city in America.

As these other stories took the front page, interest in Mother's case waned. An woman in her eighties was found murdered in her Flint home, and an elderly man was found slain on his farm west of Flint after inviting two young women over for an intimate tryst. An eighty-year-old woman was found raped, beaten, and robbed in her own home. And other seniors were falling victim to money scams, robberies, beatings, and the unthinkable: abuse at the hands of their family caregivers.

While we were truly sympathetic to these other cases, we did not want people to forget that our mother had not been found yet and that we were still searching for her. Keeping the short-minded public aware that Dorothy Murphy was still missing remained our job.

·>≡◉ ◉≡<·

Mother was baptized as Dorothy Loraine Lee, the first child of ten born to Mark and Lena Verona Lee of Marion, a small farming village in north Michigan. My great-grandparents started the fertile Lee homestead. After they timbered the wooded wilderness they built a small log cabin where they lived out their remaining years. Now the cabin is a heap of decomposing logs lying in the over-grown orchard that separates the old farmhouse from the big red, hip-roofed barn.

The last of the virgin timber had already been harvest -ed from the country-side by the time Mother arrived. By then the glacially carved rolling hills were being cleared of the tree-stumps and rocks with dynamite and teams of strong horses. Now those rich clay hills supported prosperous farms with large fami-lies of fair-haired children raising corn, soybeans, wheat, oats, and fat herds of contented cattle.

They were hardy people; they had to be to survive those difficult times. In its prime the Lee family farm held 165 acres of softly rolling hills that were inter-mittently dotted with patches of woods and had a crystal-clear stream traversing through the far-corner lowlands. The family was considered quite prosperous for Depression-era people, because they always had plenty of food. That was considered well-off.

During the worst of the Depression, Grandpa Lee, Mom's dad, left the fam-ily farm and traveled all the way to Flint to secure work. Eventually he found employment in the DuPont Factory, on the banks of the Flint River, and that's how our branch of the Lee tree ended up living in Flint.

Grandma Lee and the ten kids ran the farm while he was away. Mom, be-ing smart and ambitious, wanted to shake the manure from her shiny shoes as quickly as she could, and she sought a very different life for herself, far from the one she knew on the farm. At the tender age of eighteen she left home and moved to Flint; joining our grandpa who was working in the DuPont factory. The year was 1941. We had just entered the Second World War, and women were needed in the plants for the war effort. Our little mom joined the war effort and became a regular Rosie the Riveter.

While working in the plant she saved her money, attended the Baker Business School, and after graduating was employed as a secretary at the Gillespie Insurance Agency in downtown Flint. She remained there until she married our dad, at the advanced age of twenty-eight.

Before Mother married she cultivated a glamorous side, and one that her own children never saw or even knew she possessed. She purchased a fur coat or two and a trousseau of fine bone china, silver serving pieces, and cut Waterford crystal. We never saw these precious items because she kept them tucked away for safekeeping, hidden inside a musty old wooden barrel in the cellar. They were never used until I was grown, because according to her, "They were too good for you kids to use and break."

Dorothy finally found herself a man, and married. Most folks just called Dad Joe. He was baptized as Joseph, and his family called him Leon. He was known as Red to his buddies from the navy because of his Irish setter red hair. We never knew this, but our parents met in a bar. An old family friend shared his recollection of their initial meeting, because he was there. Joe Oulette was a child-'hood' friend of Dad's, and they quite often bonded over beers and boiler-makers. Now, Joe claimed that it went down this way:

"Well, yer mom and Marge Bishop worked together, in the Du-Pond plant. Marge wasn't much to look at, ya know, but she sure was a whole lotta fun, and they was real good friends. Well, this one night they was up ta John's Bar, on nort' Saginaw Street, and I was up there with yer dad. Well… yer folks met dat night and day really hit it off, if ya know what I mean."

"I'm pretty sure dat your dad took yer mom home dat night. They was real hot for each other. But they wasn't able ta get married for a few years yet, because yer Dad was sent to Ko-re-a, ya understand. And that was after he'd already served four years with the Navy in WW Two."

Joe had retired from the accounting position he'd held for thirty years at Buick's main office. He was a small-framed, nervous man, French with a large hook nose and thick Coke-bottle glasses. He smokes a lot, squints quite profusely, and blinks an awful lot, too. It's probably a facial tic. Ruth, his wife of fifty years, passed away last year. They stood up for our parents at their wedding and were Mary's godparents. Believe me; Joe's insights into our parents' early life before we children came along were cherished, because our folks never told us *these* kinds of incriminating stories, ever.

Pictures we found buried deep inside Mom's cedar hope-chest revealed a beautiful and glamorous young woman whom we scarcely recognized, and that was when I realized she must have envisioned a very different life for herself than the one she lived with us. It appeared that she fancied a much more glamorous life than the one she lived with us, one that was more like the manufactured Hollywood ideal of the day.

While many of the neighborhood mothers worked in the auto shops or the factory offices, ours chose to stay at home and be a full-time wife and mother because she thought that it was important work. She was good at it; she'd already helped raise nine siblings before we came along and had the good instinct to know when to be there and when to retreat. Mrs. Murphy did not raise any idiots.

⋯⊷⊚ ⊚⊶⋯

Even though her trailer was now serving as command central it still was her home, and it appeared just as tidy as when she resided there. We still mowed the lawn, watered the scarlet geraniums she planted in the white plastic planter by the front door, vacuumed the raspberry shag carpet, gathered her mail, and paid the bills.

Seeing Mother's unmade bed was a daily constant reminder of her continued absence to me, so I quietly remade it. Her fancy cream colored French-provincial bed wasn't disturbed again until many weeks later, when Detective J Diem collected some of Mother's personal items so her DNA could be extracted for forensic identification. Her bed-sheets and pillowcases, toothbrush, hairbrush, and a pile of discarded tissues from her bedside waste basket were carefully bagged, tagged, and removed.

Detective J went about her tasks very professionally and with great deal of respect and sensitivity. But handing Mom's possessions over for DNA testing brought home, once again, the sobering realization that she would most likely never be coming home alive, and these items would be used to identify her body if it was ever found.

All around Mother's home were reminders of her genuinely deep faith. And now prayer was an integral part of our search protocol. Mother's church, Holy Redeemer, kindly placed this message upon its roadside marquee: PRAY FOR MISSING DOROTHY MURPHY. It was a touching gesture that made us realize that not only we, her family, were missing and grieving her, but many other people were as well. An entire community was still watching the story intently.

⊶⊷

After a month of repeatedly being in the media we were now being recognized. People would point at us and whisper, "Those are the kids of that missing old lady." Some people—with genuinely good intentions—said some truly stupid things to us, and we came to realize it was part of the experience.

Crazy people just came out of the woodwork, attracted to all of the commotion. While some claimed they saw Mom in their visions and were content to report to the phone bank anonymously or write to the website, most kooks were not that highly functioning. Seeing Mother's trailer on the news, with the address displayed, they decided to just drop by and pay us a little visit.

But we were familiar with crazies; we had loons in our own family, mostly on the Murphy side. Still, we felt compelled to listen to everyone and everything, because however odd or obscure, it could possibly lead to Mother.

Phone bank messages were still being fielded and followed up by the police, and they shared what they thought was pertinent. No ransom note was ever received; no further news of Mother ever surfaced, period. We kept track of Mom's finances and knew there was no activity in her bank account, checking account, or credit card either. The police were monitoring those accounts as well.

⊶⊷

We did receive one rather unusual tip that I will share with you. A long-distance search group of clairvoyants from Fairbanks Alaska contacted us directly, and reported that they had "good feelings" about an area just south of Flint. They suggested that we investigate the Lahring Road area, near the city of Fenton. Of course, we felt compelled to do so.

On a rainy weekday afternoon, Nancy Brown, and I, along with a handful of friends, repeatedly drove up and down the entire length of that muddy road. We walked every inch and took every trail that splintered from it, sloshing through puddles, mosquito-filled woods, and hip-deep grassy fields. It made for a good day's walk but proved fruitless. In retrospect, how could people from Fairbanks,

Alaska, see all the way to Flint? But, as I said, we felt compelled to follow up on every lead no matter how odd or obscure.

⭢▬◉ ◉▬⭠

As more time trickled passed our hopes grew dimmer. Well over a month had passed since Mother vanished. The realization that she was no longer with us became stronger and stronger. We no longer hoped to find her alive but we very much wanted to find Mother's remains, bring her home, and lay her to rest with our father.

Well Over a Month Gone

WELL OVER A month had passed. At this stage of the disappearance we were still searching for Mother, but it wasn't nearly as urgent or organized as it once was. For the most part we'd given the search over to the police but still remained hyper vigilant, and the constant need to be on high alert was still there. I felt I had to be ready to immediately respond to the ever-unfolding developments of this case. It was almost impossible to stop constantly monitoring my surroundings, aware of what was happening, and who was there.

We all continued to look for Mother; her disappearance consumed most of my waking thoughts and many of my dreams at night. We all searched, but it was brother Mike who kept the vigil long after the rest of us quit. Night after night, he and his trusty dog, Mojo, drove in his big red Jeep and quietly searched.

⤙⟡⟡⤚

One of Mother's brothers, our Uncle Gerald (pronounced gare-ald), suggested hosting a fundraiser and raise more money for the reward fund, because sweetening the pot might entice someone into saying something. And since our uncle volunteered to take care of everything, we could not refuse his generous offer. But we were certain that it would never be held, because we were sure Mother would be found long before the event was supposed to take place, more than two weeks away.

⤙⟡⟡⤚

Somehow two more weeks managed to crawl by without any significant news in Mother's case, and the day of the fundraiser arrived. Saturday, August 16, 2003, six weeks after her disappearance, the fundraiser was held. The Buell Lake Patio and Pub, was a large family-friendly bar well suited for such an event. It was located way out in the country just across the road from shady, picturesque Buell Lake.

Uncle Gerald, Aunt Shirley, and the rest of the family did a great job finding something for just about everyone. There were swing sets, playground equipment, and an inflatable jump room for the little kids, dunk tank for the older kids, and horseshoes for the really old kids. The spacious patio bar had a big old dance floor, and for entertainment there was a swingin' country band featurin' Kelly Lee, Cousin Todd's wife, as their lead singer.

Uncle Donnie, Mom's second-to-the-youngest brother, pit-roasted and donated an entire pig for the event, and when it was served with the many generously donated side dishes, it made for one massive potluck supper. And for dessert there was another entire table filled with delicious homemade sweets and treats available—just help your-self.

At first the weather looked shaky, but the sun eventually came out, and so did the citizens of Flint. It was truly surprising how many people attended. I was afraid they were becoming weary of our events by now, but I found I was mistaken when people started arriving in large groups, and some of these folks I had not seen in thirty or forty years. There were fifty-year-old kids from the old neighborhood, friends from our high school days, and people we knew from work. It was more like a community-family picnic. Also in attendance were several of Mundy Township's finest, including Detective J Diem and Chief Guigear along with his lovely wife.

The Chinese and Dutch auctions held such treasures as colorful handmade patchwork quilts, hand-crocheted Afghans, and other handiworks that were kindly donated by our elderly aunts and crafty cousins. Generous people also donated services, such as facials, haircuts, car washes, artwork, beer mirrors, new merchandise, and white elephant treasures, with them all going to the most generous bidder.

The fundraiser was a success, and it also provided a much-needed break from the constant stress and worrying, because being on high alert all the time was becoming taxing, exhausting, and eroding. A picnic with the family and good friends, having a few laughs, plenty of good food, and even a couple of beers, was just what we needed. Plus over four thousand additional dollars were raised and added to the reward fund, which now contained nearly fifteen thousand dollars. We were certain that this large amount would entice someone into giving us the information that we were so desperate for.

Once again, the outpouring of support from friends, family, and community uplifted us, and thankfully once again media people were covering the event to help keep Mother's story alive. It had been quite some time since Mother's story was in the news, but overall our media campaigns had been quite successful, and by now practically everyone in the state had heard of our mother's disappearance. Reports were given of the story making it all the way down to Florida, most likely because many Michigan residents retired there.

⋅⊶⊚ ⊚⊷⋅

The doldrums of August descended upon us after the fundraiser was held, and nothing was happening at all. There were not any other events scheduled, and things slowed to a dead calm. Most of the tasks we were doing for Mother's case could now be completed after working hours, so we pretty much resumed our work lives as best we could. I found it difficult to fully concentrate while at work, because my mind was often elsewhere, and I was worried that I should be "out there," working on the case instead.

When our father died, at fifty-seven, Mother took over everything, and she was amazingly strong. I don't recall seeing her shed a tear. She simply got up and did what she had to do. It could not have been easy becoming a widow at fifty-five with an eleven-year-old son to finish raising, but she did an excellent job. To quote Mother, she "clamped right down on Mike, a couple times," maybe even more than with us older children. But much was expected from him, because he had to step in and fulfill many of the roles that Dad once did, such as home maintenance, snow removal, yard work, and companionship.

Not knowing where Mom was, was the most difficult part about this extended purgatory period

Days passed, then weeks passed, and now two months had passed. While we understood that we might never find her alive, we did not completely surrender that option yet. Some people would still say encouraging things to us, such as, "Don't give up hope, she might be found alive in some basement somewhere." But deep down we felt differently. In our hearts we sensed she was gone.

In the interim we did what we could, such as continuing to write and mail hundreds of thank-you notes and attend the weekly briefings with the police. During after-hours gatherings at the closed station, Chief Guigear would update us with the week's developments.

"Leads are currently being pursued, which we believe are starting to go somewhere," he told us. "Persons of interest are being questioned, and now someone is being extradited and flown to Flint for questioning."

Those were all encouraging leads, but nothing specific was happening that they could share with us. I'm certain they could read both the anticipation and the disappointment in our faces as the days, weeks, and months passed without Mother being found or any significant news about the case.

But it was obvious to us that they were doing something, because storage boxes containing the files containing depositions, questionings, interviews, and other materials collected thus far relating to the case began to fill the conference room where we held our weekly meetings.

We felt certain that someone saw something, someone knew something, and that something might give soon, especially with the reward fund nearing fifteen thousand dollars. But truthfully, at this point, we just wanted our mother back, no questions asked.

Summer is Over

NEARLY THREE MONTHS had passed, Mother had not yet been found, and summer was over.

This year the Labor Day weekend was spent at my cottage with the entire family in attendance. We all needed a break, because the past months had been extremely stressful, and this secluded place was good for restoring the soul.

As family tradition dictated, the eternal flame of the campfire never went out all weekend. The proud tradition of pyromania was once again being passed from father to son, and our resident Boy Scout, Patrick, was now becoming the family's fire keeper. All weekend long he spent his time collecting piles of wood, chopping it into smaller pieces, and getting blisters doing it. Plus he was no longer content to share in our communal fire; he wanted his own campfire, at his own campsite. He was growing up.

Dad definitely carried the gene for pyromania, and as children we had some hellacious fires, big blazes with flames so high they licked the starry northern sky. Dad passed the firebug gene on to Tim, and now he was proudly passing it to his only son. Wood fires cooked most of our meals. We liked the acrid smell of the sooty smoke. When gathering around the campfire at night we would talk and share stories and be content to quietly stare at the dancing hypnotic flames.

Memorial Day was the unofficial start of summer and it was always busy with new beginnings, such as getting the lawn furniture out, seeding the vegetable garden, and getting the window boxes planted with their colorful annuals. The Fourth of July, being the zenith of summer, was busy with picnics, fishing, swimming, fireworks, and attending the big parade. But Labor Day, in contrast, was the unofficial end of summer, and it was quite often anticlimactic, cool and rainy, a time for reflection.

⋅⊱⊰⋅

The week following Labor Day went extremely slowly. I tried to resume my old life. I even tried to socialize again, but I was not able to fit into those once-familiar routines because so much was still left unresolved. There hadn't been any significant breaks in Mother's case for quite some time.

During most of this period I felt distracted and could work for only short periods, because my concentration was still primarily focused on the disappearance. My life was still permeated with an ever-present and heightened awareness, always listening, constantly searching, and thinking primarily of the case. Limbo, as the nuns described it to us children, was the in-between, a perpetual state of waiting. This period certainly felt like limbo. It was faith, prayer, and the support of family and close friends that got us through.

Solidarity with my siblings helped immensely. We were going through this traumatic ordeal together, and together with each other's support, we would get through this. But we were experiencing "high-alert fatigue." Stress can be debilitating. This strange disappearance was becoming a lengthy, stressful journey, an odyssey, a series of events that were all interconnected and played out in front of an entire community. This kind of compounded stress could slowly erode your strength if you let it.

I'd finally reached the point where I would not wake up in the morning sobbing, but I still jumped, startled at every sound. Each time my cell phone chimed its annoying electronic tones I'd startle. That damned ringtone became permanently etched into my brain. I heard it everywhere, all the time, in movies, on television, and even in my dreams. The past three months had taken their toll.

⋅⊱⊰⋅

Initially the grandkids were frightened when their grandma suddenly vanished. They were justifiably afraid that these bad people who did this terrible thing to their grandma still had her address, keys, purse, and phone book, so they could learn where she lived, where they lived, and they feared that some act of retribution may be visited upon them.

But there was never any contact from her abductors—if she was abducted. There was never any activity in her financial accounts either. It appeared that the people responsible for her abduction were not seeking anything further from her, or from us.

Perhaps it was the circumstances of this case that so deeply touched an entire city—an eighty-year-old grand-mother disappearing—but somehow this terrible tragedy reaffirmed that a strong sense of community still existed here. I feared it had vanished from Flint a long time ago. We knew we were not in this battle alone. The good people of our home -town stepped forward, donating their time, energy, money, and resources to support us and assist us with our search.

⇥◉ ◉⇤

We were now approaching the third month since Mother had vanished. The police told us this was one of the most unusual cases they had ever experienced. The majority of cases such as this had some connection to close personal friends, acquaintances, or family members. As of now, the only connection to our missing Mother seemed to be her vehicle—and we assumed that most of the evidence therein—was destroyed by the intentional fire.

⇥◉ ◉⇤

During the first week of September the case began to percolate once again, because the drive-by shooting investigation was producing more related leads.

When the ballistics report was finally returned to the chief, he shared this bit of news with us. "The blue sedan that was used by the shooter, in the drive-by-shooting in Flint, was confirmed to be your mother's vehicle. We know this, because the bullet casings that were retrieved from the shooting were compared to the ones that were found intact inside your mother's car, and they were a perfect match."

"Consequently, the victim of that shooting is being questioned again, and more extensively. We are asking why he was targeted and whom he thinks was shooting at him. The un -likely story of the lopsided love triangle is being more closely examined, and this line of interrogation has subsequently led to a couple of persons of interest, They are being questioned."

Finally it felt as if something was brewing. The tide was turning and momentum was building, and at last it was beginning to move in our direction. We could sense that the police were on to something that may at last bring results. We could feel it. Thank God.

Since she had vanished, I had thought about Mother and the case continually, and we didn't want the city of Flint to forget that she was missing either. So Mike suggested we should all meet again to paint the concrete monolith on the corner of Twelfth Street and Hammerberg Road that is called "The Rock." This windowless bunker of a building sits just around the corner from the Chevy truck plant on Van Slyke Road. Standing very close to the road and Southwest Academy high school, it was often used as a message board. Usually these scrawled messages were happy birthday wishes, sports team shoutouts, and similar salutations.

Saturday, September 16, turned out to a clear blue cloudless morning. Our mission was to paint a message informing the public that Dorothy Murphy was still missing and we were still searching for her. Uncle Gerald and Aunt Shirley, Mary, Erin and Ryan, Mike, Tim, Patty, and Patrick were all in attendance. Ryan's girlfriend, Darci, and their Grandma Darlene were also there to lend a hand.

Being a painter, I always had plenty of partially filled paint cans sitting in the back of the truck going unused, so we put them to work. Everyone grabbed a roller, paintbrush, or spray can and went at the wall. Pale pink, periwinkle blue, soft green, terracotta, and warm black paints made it look quite colorful. The billboard looked great, and we even managed to have fun in the process.

When finished the billboard had Still Missing in big black letters at the top, and under that was her birth date and the day that she went missing. It looked quite nice, and we were proud of our artwork. But two days later, the billboard we so lovingly painted was replaced with Happy Birthday Barb. This was just a busywork project anyway, to keep the family bonded and feeling that we were doing something useful and at the same time keeping the story alive.

On that very same Saturday, after returning from painting The Rock, we found another article in *The Flint Journal*. It had been a very long time since there was any news.

Chief Guigear held a small afternoon news conference, where he'd made an announcement.

There was a possible suspect in Mother's case.

This was huge news for us, *huge.*

Thankfully the chief shared this bit of news with us a couple of days before releasing it to the media. Although he couldn't give us anything specific, such as a name or motive, he was upbeat and encouraging, and we were elated with this positive revelation.

Thank you, Jesus.

Another Thread * Some Family Ties

THE POLICE HAD a possible suspect, who was yet unnamed. They had verified that the bullet casings retrieved from the drive-by shooting location matched those found inside Mother's vehicle. The two events were now definitely connected.

It was unimaginable that anything could have survived that raging inferno. We viewed the decimated chassis in the police impound yard and watched the car while it was blazing on TV. The inferno was so intense that it melted the paint away. All four tires were burned off, the windows gone, and none of the interior—seats, carpeting, or upholstery—remained. It was simply a burnt-out, windowless chassis sitting on four rusting rims. But those bullet casings somehow miraculously survived that fire.

⋆⟞◉ ◉⟝⋆

Mary took charge of dealing with the insurance company and submitted Mother's vehicle loss claim. The Hartford Insurance Company, as written through AARP, insured her new Buick, and they wanted to know what an eighty-year-old {white} woman was doing at a predominately black—and notorious—after-hours nightclub. Consequently the entire sordid story needed to be explained over and over, to person after person, for them understand the circumstances of our loss, and to start processing the claim. Without having a certificate of death, many items of business could not be settled at all.

During all of this turmoil, we received an astronomical bill from Complete Towing, and they wanted to be paid this huge sum for towing the burned chassis to the police impound, and storing the rusted remains. The destroyed vehicle was still being held by the Flint Police Department as evidence of a crime that was still under investigation, and we didn't even have possession of the vehicle. But they were still billing us. For all we cared they could keep the worthless ruins because there was nothing left to claim, but we still needed to resolve this dunning matter.

Some days it was difficult even going to the post office or shopping, because we'd run into people who wanted to express their concerns. Many wanted to know the hows, whens, wheres, and whys. We did our best to answer their queries, but we often didn't have answers to the questions ourselves. People who were truly connected to us had heard the sordid details long ago, but more distant acquaintances would still make odd and awkward inquiries, such as, "Did you look in the trunk of the car?" and "Did you look under the trailer?" Those two questions were just a couple of the most frequently asked. And yes, we looked there, first thing. Thank you for asking.

->==◉ ◉==<-

During this week's briefing it was revealed that a specific line of questioning that Detective J Diem had been following was now going somewhere. Although the police couldn't share anything specific, they were optimistic about this new development and encouraged us to stay hopeful be-cause something would break soon. They told us an extradi-tion was forthcoming, and someone was being flown to Flint for further questioning. This was important news, and it was a long time coming. We ached for resolution.

At last a third thread to grasp…

->==◉ ◉==<-

Feeling energized after this week's briefing, we left the police station and went next door to the Rankin Family Restaurant to have a bite to eat and catch up with each other. During our dinnertime conversation, brother Mike said he had something to share with us. He had a dream, as Dianna the psychic had predicted.

→⊫◉ ◉⊨←

"Last night, Dort appeared to me in my dream. It was really freaky, because she immediately started cussing me out and scolding me. She was wagging her arthritic old finger at me, and saying, 'What is taking you so long to find me?' and 'Why haven't you done that yet?'"

We all burst out laughing, partially because of the story, but mostly because his humorous dream was explained while imitating Dort's nasally sounding voice, which we'd all been known to do from time to time. It was so like Mother to be impatient and demanding, and knowing that made us laugh even more.

"Have any of you guys had dreams like that?" Mike inquired. We all laughed again, because we loved his story-telling, and any moment of levity was greatly appreciated. And incidentally, none of the rest of us reported having Dort cuss them out in their dreams.

→⊫◉ ◉⊨←

Some Family Ties

These bios are included at this point to help you become familiar with the members of my family, and share some aspects of their lives, that are separate from the disappearance.

→⊫◉ ◉⊨←

Tim was born the eldest son, and he arrived just thirteen months ahead of me, making us unofficially Irish twins. Many people thought we were real twins— and they usually thought I was the older brother. Being the first to arrive, he got all the good genes, such as never having a cavity in his head and having a full head of hair, while I had teeth pulled at age three and have turned totally gray while slowly balding.

Tim is quite different from me in many ways. He is mechanically inclined, whereas I am mostly artistically motivated, a left brain/right brain distinction. He was a mechanical engineer at General Motors, and I'm an artist. Even as children we had different interests and friends. But Mother always said she could tell our same-size laundry apart because Tim's clothes had grease on them while mine were spattered with paint.

Tim was more interested in sports and competitive games, as well as hunting and fishing, and he would often do those things with our dad because they shared those common interests. He married his high school sweetheart, Patty, but in reality she was always part of the family because we'd known her all of our lives. Patty and I started school together and had our first communion and confirmation together as well. She's smart, funny, quick to laugh, and always seems to have some-thing to say; plus she loves to shop, cook, and decorate, and is quite fond of wine. These are all good things. We get along quite well.

They had two bright children who were born ten years apart, Aimee was the first, and she was independent and nearly perfect as a child. She never got dirty, was very self-directed, and practically raised herself. Now she is working on raising her parents properly. This summer she is finishing a law degree and engaged to be married next fall. We're all very proud of her.

Patrick, her younger brother, is a Boy Scout. He is also quite fond of fishponds, bonsais, and anything to do with railroads. He is still a work in progress. He and Tim share many traits and interests, such as pyromania, camping, and cross-country running. Patrick started running in middle school, and Tim began to jog right along with him. Tim discovered that he liked it very much, and to this day they run together, side by side.

Tim began taking evening classes in woodworking and set up a wood shop in his garage, where he now makes fine furniture, mostly more cupboards to hold Patty's ever-growing collection of dishes, because she has a real jones for dishes. He's also made lovely end tables, shelves, chests, cabinetry, and two sturdy Adirondack chairs for my cottage.

·>⊨◉ ◉⊨<·

Baby brother Mike is nearly twelve years younger than me. Consequently we grew up in the same home but practically in two different generations. I began college the year he started kindergarten. Mike was bestowed with Irish charm and good looks, too. He was well liked in the neighborhood and school, and is truly blessed to have so many good friends.

It's a shame that he had so many hard knocks so early in his life. At eleven he witnessed Dad having the massive heart attack that ultimately took his life, and at twenty-eight his lovely fiancée, Nattily, was killed in an accident shortly before they were to be married. We still believe he will find someone special and happiness.

A few years back he purchased a GM home in the historic Mott Park neighborhood of Flint. These solidly built homes have slate roofs, plaster walls, and hardwood floors throughout. Curving cobblestone streets surround a central park containing a golf course and a stream. Mott Park can easily be called a Catholic ghetto, because many of its residents belong to the Saint John Vianney Church, which is located in the heart of the neighborhood.

Mike shares his comfortable home with Mojo, his super-cool, sleek black, mixed-breed dog. Their comfortable place has an open-door policy, with everyone being welcome. For many years now he has worked for Federal Express, and it seems to agree with him; he's made many friends there. All and all, he seems to be happy and well adjusted.

Mary Ann is the only daughter and she was our dad's pride and joy. There is a genuine sweetness about Mary; she is kind and truly considerate of the needs of others. I truly don't believe there is a soul on earth who would have a truly bad thing to say about her, and that's quite an accomplishment for an IRS employee. She is pretty, in the Irish way, with bright blue twinkling eyes, milky-white skin, wavy auburn hair, and a healthy blush in her rosy cheeks. My friends often comment on how nice she looks, and how truly sweet she seems to be.

Mary married her high school sweetheart and produced two smart and beautiful children, Ryan and Erin. They were quite young when their parents divorced, but Mary did an excellent job of raising them on her own. Taking charge of her life, she grew, blossomed and prospered. She is my personal hero, and always does the right thing.

Her oldest, Ryan, had just finished a tour of duty in the army, with the Rangers and returned home. He is a very bright young man who is planning to attend the University of Michigan in the fall. He dated his childhood sweetheart, Darci, since they were fourteen, and we expect that marriage and grandchildren are not that far off.

Miss Erin, his younger sister, is a blue-eyed, blond-haired cutie. She recently graduated from high school, near the top of her class, just a week before Dort disappeared. She was also planning to start college in the fall, too, and earning a master's degree in early childhood development. We wish her the best.

                            ⊷⫸ ⫷⊶

I am Daniel, the second-born son, and the author and narrator of this book. Up until now I have been an artist. For the past twenty years, since 1988, my home has been a quaint lakefront cottage that is nicely nestled on four wooded acres fronting picturesque Canfield Lake. Located just outside the Victorian harbor town of Manistee, in northwest Michigan, my century old home was once Grange Hall that was converted into a residence.

I am a 1976 graduate of the University of Michigan, where I earned a bachelor of fine arts degree. Currently I am single and share my life and cottage with Miss Kitty, my fierce tortoise-shelled cat. It is a good life.

The Search is Over

NEARLY THREE MONTHS had passed since Mother disappeared, and life had taken on a different sense of normalcy. The weeks following Labor Day were peculiar, but that peculiarity had now become the new normal. That new reality meant trying to turn off the hyperawareness mechanism, stopping the constant searching, trying to have a normal life, returning to work, and even socializing again. I found that difficult, because I was constantly worrying that I should not be frivolously wasting time visiting, and be out searching or doing more for the case instead.

We realized that the detectives were steadily making progress, but we were so impatient. Where was Mother? Why was this taking so long? We had no idea at the onset of this ordeal that this would be such a lengthy, on-going nightmare. What if we didn't find her? What would we do if this nightmare never ended? How could we go on with our lives having this kind of unfinished business?

·→=◉ ◉=←·

During this week's meeting with the police they seemed to be more energized, leading us to believe that they were pursuing the correct leads with their investigations. They now inform us that the "person of interest" who was extradited to Flint a few weeks back had been questioned and this line of inquiry had subsequently generated new leads. This was encouraging news, but still nothing was specific. But bit by bit, we could feel the momentum start to increase, and begin to move in a positive direction.

⋆⇥◉ ◉⇤⋆

By now it was now nearing the end of September. I had not been home since the Labor Day weekend, and it was long overdue. I needed to check on my former life and home again, and recharge my battery as well. Fall was coming on strong. You could feel the coolness in the air, and many tasks still required completion before winter once again reared its ugly head. The leaves needed to be raked, screens removed, the old storm windows washed and reinstalled before it got too cold, and lots of seasonal items needed to go into safe storage for the winter.

Usually a long weekend at the cottage would relax and restore me, because the natural world is good for my soul. But somehow on this weekend I felt uneasiness, an odd restless sensation that I just could not shake. Here I was at the most peaceful place I knew, and I was still restless. It was hard to concentrate on any specific task and I managed to accomplish very little real work. Even a long walk on Lake Michigan's deserted shore could not shake the unsettling sensation I felt.

Looking forward to a long relaxing weekend away, I had arrived at the cottage early on Thursday afternoon. But by Friday afternoon, before the weekend even began, I felt so restless that I repacked my suitcase, locked the house up, and headed back toward Flint.

After I'd driven half an hour west of Manistee, I pulled into a small roadside park on the scenic Pine River, parked, turned off the truck, and sat quietly for some time; gazing at the crystal blue ribbon of a river as it meandered through the scarlet and amber fall foliage dotting the high-banked hills.

A great big truck abruptly appeared out of nowhere and rumbled across the graceful silver bridge, interrupting the pristine quiet. But the peace was once again quickly restored as the big rig vanished over the next tree-covered hill, with the only sound remaining being a lonesome whippoorwill's call echoing through the river-chiseled canyon.

Suddenly the cell phone chimed, interrupting the peaceful panorama. I stared at it and watched it vibrate as if I were both waiting for the call and dreading it at the same time. I answered on the fourth and final ring.

"Dan?"

"Yes."

"Ah, Dan, this is Officer Joel Grahn, of the Mundy Township Police Department."

"Yes. Hello, Officer Grahn."

"Ah, Dan, there's been a discovery here, in Flint Township today. We have found a, a body… And we believe that it may be your mother."

I don't recall the rest of the conversation. I only remember hanging the phone up and sobbing. When I was sufficiently recovered, I resumed my trip to Flint to join my family.

That evening we once again gathered on Mom's big flowery couch to watch the six o'clock news. Tonight's lead story on all the local television stations was the discovery of decayed human remains in a Flint Township neighborhood. Encamped news crews were relaying a live feed from the discovery site, which was located in a suburban neighborhood less than a mile from Mother's former home.

As we watched the story unfold, we all prayed that the remains, as they were being called, were those of our missing mother. But we would have to wait until Monday for the official results. That Sunday we all attended church together and prayed that our long ordeal would finally be coming to an end.

→≡◎ ◎≡←

Investigators from the Michigan State Police forensic laboratory in Lansing were called to the discovery site to scrutinize the scene and supervise removal of the remains, which were sent to Flint's Hurley Medical Center, where they would be autopsied.

On Monday morning, September 29, 2003, police officials called a news conference where they confirmed that the remains discovered last Friday in Flint Township were indeed those of Dorothy Lee Murphy. Her obituary follows.

Murphy, Dorothy L, of Flint age 80, died in Flint. A Memorial Mass will be celebrated at 11 a.m. Friday, October 3, 2003, at Holy Redeemer Catholic Church, 1277 East Bristol Road in Burton. Father William F.

Weigher officiating. Those desiring to may make their contributions to the American Heart Association. Visitation is 2–9 p.m. Thursday at the Swartz Funeral Home at 1225 West Hill Road, Flint. A vigil service will be held at 8 p.m. Thurs- day evening at the funeral home. Visitation will be held at the church from 10 a.m. Friday until the time of the Memorial Mass. Mrs. Murphy was born in Marion, Michigan, on March 2, 1923, the daughter of Mark and Lena Lee. She married Joseph L. Murphy on June 21, 1952. She was a member of Holy Redeemer Catholic

Church, the Altar Society, and the Altar Guild. She was also a member of the Rosary Guild at St. Luke's Catholic Church, and the Burton and Pierce Senior Centers. She devoted her life to the service of others. She was a Secretary, wife, mother, grandmother, the Lee Family matriarch, and oldest of ten children. Surviving are three sons, Timothy L. and wife Patricia M., Daniel L., and Michael M.; daughter Mary Ann Deering; two granddaughters, Aimee Cain and Erin Deering; two grandsons, Ryan Deering and Patrick Murphy; sister Jean V. and husband Elin Reid; six brothers, L.J. and wife Evelyn Lee, Max and wife Elaine Lee, Charles and wife Sheron Lee, Gerald and wife Shirley Lee, Donald and wife Phyllis Lee, Dean and wife Mary Lee, nephews, nieces and great-nieces and nephews too numerous to mention. She was preceded in death by her husband, Joseph L., December 9, 1977, her parents, and two brothers.

At Long Last, a Funeral

THREE MONTHS HAD passed since Mother was taken from us, but thank God we now had her back. Now it was October and summer was a distant memory. A chilly and miserable drizzle started to fall on the day they discovered Mother's remains, and it continued dribbling for two days afterward, turning the skies the steely gray of winter and stripping the trees of what was left of their dead brown leaves.

Immediately following Mother's recovery there was another flurry of activity, because we could finally have a memorial service, funeral, and perhaps even a burial some day. After accomplishing all that, we could apply for a death certificate to settle her meager estate. We also hoped to find some peace in our lives now, and maybe justice someday.

A large media presence covered the removal of Mother's remains, with many of the reporters staying on while the surrounding area was searched extensively. For the next three days, thirty volunteer firemen, several police officers, and a crew of Michigan State Police forensic technicians, along with their cadaver-seeking dogs, combed the area for evidence.

Personal effects found with the remains were identified as belonging to Mother. Her dentist had provided a complete set of dental X-rays, and they were compared with the teeth of the remains and that helped confirmed that the body was Dorothy Murphy. Next her remains were sent to the state forensic lab in Lansing, to be examined further, in an effort to determine the cause of her death. We suspected a DNA profile would be completed at some point to positively confirm the identity. Consequently, Mother would not be returned to us for an extended and indeterminate period of time, if ever.

A media presence covered the exhumation at the discovery site, and another contingency was sent to 311 Loyalist Lane, Mother's home, where they awaited comment from the Murphy family. By now we understood if we did not address them they would create something to fill up their pages and screens that may or may not be entirely accurate. Consequently we wrote a brief statement to appease them.

⊷⊶

Press release, Monday September 29, 2003

Today the Murphy family has received official confirmation that the remains discovered on last Friday, September 26, 2003, are indeed those of our mother and grandmother, Dorothy Lee Murphy. Our family is greatly relieved by this disclosure, and plans for a funeral will be forthcoming. It is also our wish to have our mother returned to us, so she may be laid to rest with our departed father, Joseph L. Murphy.

The family wishes to acknowledge all the efforts made in our mother's behalf and thank those who helped search for her and who have generously donated to the reward fund. We also wish to thank our family, friends, and the community for their love, kindness, and support.

We wish to specially acknowledge the Mundy Township Police Department, who spearheaded this investigation, and in particular Chief Dave Guigear, Detective J Diem, and Sergeant Joel Grahn. This case is still being investigated. We hope to someday find the persons who are responsible for murdering our mother, and see those persons prosecuted to the fullest extent of the law.

⊷⊶

Footnote

I thought I'd share this bit of information with you, because you may find it interesting. I know I did. First of all, the site where Mother's remains were found was eerily close to what Dianna, the psychic, had described. Mother's little tan orthopedic shoe was the very first thing they saw, and that solitary shoe would lead them to her remains. One tan shoe, as Dianna foresaw.

Secondly, this place was familiar to Mother because she'd driven by there thousands of times. The River Forrest, River Oak neighborhood and apartments, where she was found, were less than a mile from the home where she'd lived for more than twenty years, as also noted by Dianna. Quite surprisingly, her remains were hidden in plain sight, lying out in an undeveloped wooded section of a suburban neighbor- hood just five hundred feet from several nice homes.

Thirdly, this paved but undeveloped street concluded in a circular dead end cul-de-sac, much as she'd envisioned. A cell-phone tower is not very far away. This homeless street was located quite near the Flint River, a dirty and yet moving body of water, as she also foresaw. Over the years this aban-doned street became a dump site for trash, garden waste, debris, and brush, as she had described.

She also predicted that three people were involved, and apparently this lover's triangle had three principals. As of now, however, there seemed to be no connection to Moses, or an apple, at all.

·•⊨◉ ◉⊨•·

Assembling back at Mother's home, we held another family meeting, where it was unanimously decided to have a funeral, of sorts. Even if we did not have Mother's body, the urge to bury her, now that we had found her, was of utmost important to us.

Once again we discovered that Mother was *pre*-prepared. She'd previously preplanned and prepaid for her own funeral, at the Swartz Funeral Home in suburban Flint. The day before the memorial service we met with the home's staff to discuss the details, and this was going to be a most peculiar service, because there wouldn't be a body to embalm, casket to fill, hearse to drive, or even a burial.

To represent Mother at her memorial service, we would use the same photograph we employed throughout the entire search. Posed against a lavender background, she wore a mauve dress; her smile was crooked and unsure. Her snowy-white hair was permanently waved, and rose-tinted glasses framed her pretty face. This photo was greatly enlarged, placed in an ornate silver frame, and set upon an easel.

Music for the service was selected, and once again we included the song "I Can Only Imagine" as performed by the group Mercy Me. We also chose to have the Twenty-Third Psalm read, and selected the other verses and prayers that would complete the service. We did our best to respect Mother's wishes, considering the peculiar circumstances. These were uncharted waters.

⋅⊶⊷⋅

The Swartz Funeral Home is a large, formal, two-storied, neoclassical building dressed with dark brown brick. Out front is a long impressive portico of white Corinthian columns, creating shelter for their patrons. The second-floor visitation rooms open to a balcony flanked by the white wooden spindles of a gracefully curving spiral staircase. Hanging in the center of this grand lobby is a massive shiny brass chandelier, with many curving arms. It softly radiates a rosy glow onto the mauve moiré, damask wallpapered walls. It is most impressive by Flint's standards.

As was the current trend, we put together visual display boards that were covered with our family photos and memorabilia for visitors to look at during the service. Old photos, her best rosary, and some of her favorite jewelry were used as a pictorial representation of her life. Discussions easily sprang from the boards, because pictures have a way of taking you back to the best times of your life. "Did you see that picture...and, oh my God, did you see the photo where... and look at all that hair!"

Flower arrangements started arriving, and they continued to be delivered until there was nowhere left to place them. Many people knew, and perhaps some read in the paper, how Mother loved her flowers. The reception room was heady with a floral perfume. She surely would have balked at all the money being wasted on them and blushed at all the fuss being made about her. But I secretly imagined that she would have loved watching her final reception and beamed with pride at being rewarded for a life well lived. Blessed be the humble.

The largest room of the memorial chapel was given to us, along with an overflow room that could be opened to accommodate more people if needed, and it was definitely needed. When arrangements for her service were televisized we expected a large turnout. But we underestimated and were inundated.

It was peculiar seeing in one place all the people who represented the different parts of Mother's life and our lives as well. There were people from neighborhoods we lived in forty years ago, our coworkers, church members, friends, and even strangers. They all came to say good-bye to Mother.

Father Bill, or Reverend William Weigher, conducted Mother's visitation service. Keeping the service simple and light, he spoke of her eighty good years of life and her achievements, and not about her death. It was an uplifting sermon. Afterward he led the overflow crowd in the recitation of the Rosary. No tears were shed, because this was more a celebration of Mother's life. We'd already spent three months dealing with her death.

One more step completed. Thank you, Jesus.

⋅➤⋗ ⋖⋘⋅

The next morning, Friday, October 3, 2003, a full three months after her passing, a Mass of Christian Burial would be celebrated at Holy Redeemer, and Father Bill would again officiate. And once again, it was to be another unusual occasion without a body or casket. Mother's photograph would again represent her, and this time for her funeral.

⋅➤⋗ ⋖⋘⋅

After the visitation was ended I was much too wound up to go home and sleep, so I stopped to visit my friend Bette. During our lengthy conversation we discussed what an ordeal this odyssey had been, and how pleasant the evening's memorial service was. Then Bette remarked that she had something she wanted to share with me, if I wanted to hear it.

⋅➤⋗ ⋖⋘⋅

"Do you want to know how your mother died?"

I was caught completely off guard by her question, so I thought for a moment before replying. But before I could respond, she continued. "I had an appointment with Dr. Lloyd today, and during most of my visit we discussed your mother. Did you know he attended her autopsy at Hurley?"

"No, I didn't."

"Well, he was there, and that's how he found out how she died; he shared that with me."

"Really?"

"Yes, he did. Do you think you want to know?"

After thinking for another moment, I replied, "Yes, I think it's usually better to know what you are facing. But I just don't know if I want to hear it right now. Tonight."

"I understand. OK. Well, you just let me know when you do want to know."

"All right, you can tell me."

"All right, well, you'd better sit down. Brace yourself, because you know this won't be good."

"Go on."

"As you know, you, your mother, and I see Dr Lloyd. During my visit he explained, in the strictest of confidence, you understand…it was a gunshot that killed your mother."

"Oh dear God," I said, gasping for breath.

"Are you all right? Do you want me to continue?"

"Yes," I said, still catching my breath.

"He learned this through the autopsy, you under-stand, but he could have learned it through the grapevine at the county jail, because he is their physician, too."

"Wow."

"I know."

"Oh dear God. The poor thing; she must have been scared to death."

⋅→▌◎ ◎▌←⋅

I tried to absorb this devastating news, but this confirmed that our mother did not just disappear. She was taken against her will and murdered. It pained me to the core of my being to think that someone hurt her and she suffered before she died. She must have been terrified. I would not share this terrible news with my family until after the funeral.

⋆⇒● ●⇐⋆

Friday morning, October 3, 2003, turned out to be a lovely fall day, sunny but cool. The church slowly filled with people while I waited outside, visited with the last few stragglers to arrive, and hung out with the socially outcast smokers trying to squeeze in a few last desperate drags from a cigarette before entering the church. I asked God for the strength to get through the service, and went in.

The hushed tones of reverent conversations echoed throughout the modern suburban church as all four of her children and her four grandchildren were escorted down the center aisle to the front pew. Many of her brothers and her only sister were sitting in the rows directly behind us. Patrick sat next to me, and he looked so grown up in his gray flannel suit, already as tall as I.

The organist began playing, the congregation joined in singing, and Father Bill read the chosen scriptures. I tried not to cry, but I couldn't cease the tears that automatically began to flow. I became totally lost in my grief, unaware of the outside world, and found myself bawling uncontrollably. My body heaved, and snot bubbles flowed from my nose as I wept for the terrible months of unknowing, the long journey it took to finally find her, and the suffering she surely must have endured at the end.

Many others were weeping as well, even the deacon. How terribly sad and tragic it was to lose a loved one in this way. But this was, after all, the appropriate time and place for grieving. Patrick was sitting next to me, and he tried his best to comfort me by rubbing my back and sooth me with words of consolation as I bawled. And after I'd filled both of the handkerchiefs I had with tears, he kindly offered me his. I was truly touched at his kindness, I shall never forget it.

With God's grace we made it through the funeral.

Father Bill ended the service by extending an invitation to everyone to join our family at the church's family-life center, just across the parking lot, for a lovely luncheon being put on by the ladies of the church, Mother's dear old-lady friends. Once again the miracle of the loaves and fishes was duplicated to feed all those hungry people, and food was shared as communion by the loved ones of Dorothy Murphy.

Time Marches On

THE WEEKS FOLLOWING Mother's memorial service and funeral were extremely busy. Now that her remains had been found we could finally receive a certificate of death and begin to settle the business of her estate. Much was still left to be settled, such as what to do with her home, clothing, bank accounts, insurance policies, and all of her personal possessions. As anyone who has dealt with the aftermath of a loved one's passing knows, it is necessary to go through every item in the person's home, examine it, and determine its destiny. Everything was removed until all of her worldly possessions had been dissolved.

Meeting as a group, we made all these decisions democratically. Each item was examined, and whoever wanted something could have it; if not spoken for, it was given to the Saint Vincent de Paul. Her three closets full of clothing were given to the Women's Shelter of Flint, so others could use them. Over a very busy weekend her home was entirely cleared out, and it was not too overwhelming a task because she'd already weeded out many excess items and really had few possessions left.

All of her business affairs were in excellent order as well. The important papers pertaining to her estate were stored in a safe-deposit box, and all her accounts were jointly owned, so there wasn't a need for probate. For the most part, Mother never really discussed her business with us, and I was truly surprised to learn how few assets she possessed.

After emptying Mother's home, it took over a year to finally sell it, but in the meantime we continued to pay the lot rent and keep it maintained, and each time we'd mow, or pick up the mail was another reminder of her absence.

⋯⟩═◎ ◎═⟨⋯

We continued to have our briefings with the police, but now they were held at their request, at the Flint Township Police Department headquarters, because they were in charge of the investigation now. Mother's remains were discovered within their jurisdiction, and this has placed Detective Mark Schmitzer as the new lead investigator for the case. We found him to be a bit gruff, formal, and detached, and we didn't feel the close bond we had with Chief Guigear and his team, but ultimately felt that he was very competent and doing everything to continue advancing the investigation.

November brought on an early winter. Fresh snow was accumulating daily, and staying put. Fresh news was accumulating in Mother's case, too. For one, the "person of interest" was now considered the suspect in the case. Detective Schmitzer and his people were hard at work taking depositions and serving warrants for searches. They led us to believe they were making steady progress.

⋯⟩═◎ ◎═⟨⋯

Thanksgiving took on a new meaning that year when we all gathered at Tim and Patty's home in Flushing for our annual celebration and meal. We certainly felt Mother's absence, because this was the first year without her and her traditional green Jell-O layered salad. But we were even more thankful for everyone who was gathered this year, and especially for having Ryan safely returned home from the service. We appreciated our family bonds even more now.

⋯⟩═◎ ◎═⟨⋯

One of the other tasks remaining was to disburse the reward fund. The police informed us that it was a young man from Consumers Energy who accidentally found Mom's remains. We believe he found her, accidentally or not, so we gifted him with the majority of the reward. A small portion was set aside for the Mundy Township Police Department, because we wished to acknowledge our

appreciation for everything they did. We considered them to have accomplish
-ed the lion's share of the investigation.

⊷⊷⊛ ⊛⊷⊷

Early December brought additional news in Mother's case, and this was *huge*. But
we learned this information by reading an article in *The Flint Journal* instead of
hearing it from Detective Schmitzer's office. A suspect was going to be named,
arrested, and formally charged with Mother's murder. The person who had been
previously referred to as the "person of interest" was the culprit. And most surprisingly, we discovered it was a woman. A young woman was being charged
with Mother's murder.

⊷⊷⊛ ⊛⊷⊷

Six long months had now passed since Mother's abduction and murder, as we
could now officially call it. Although we felt progress was being made in the case,
it was strangely deflating during this period. The holidays can be trying, even
during the best of times, but celebrating the first Christmas without a loved one
is the most difficult of all.

⊷⊷⊛ ⊛⊷⊷

We now knew for certain that Mother did not just drive off the road somewhere
after becoming disoriented. She was taken from us—against her will—and murdered. And whereas we originally wanted to have her returned, dead or alive,
with no questions asked, we now wanted justice for her. We now wanted to have
a trial, see prosecution, and have the person who stood accused of taking our
loved one's life pay for her crimes.

But we would have to wait until August of the next year, 2004, for the trial to
be held. Ms. Kimberly Angenette Morgan, a thirty-three-year-old single woman,
would stand trial and officially be charged with murdering Dorothy Lee Murphy,
our beloved mother.

A Burial

MOTHER'S REMAINS WERE taken from Hurley Medical Center's autopsy suite and sent to the Michigan State Police lab in Lansing, where they were to be examined to determine the *cause* of her death. At first we were told they would need them for an indeterminate period of time, and then the story changed. We were informed she might never be returned to us. We formally protested their decision in the strongest terms possible, and stated that we absolutely wanted our mother back so she could finally be buried. After spending three long months searching for her, we absolutely needed that "closure."

Luckily the forensic examiner relented and decided that we could have her remains returned when they completed their investigation. Mother was returned to us late December of 2003, and we had another family meeting, where it was unanimously decided to have her remains cremated, and when her ashes were returned we would have a small burial service.

⋆⇒⊜ ⊜⇐⋆

On a miserably gray December morning a handful of family and a few close friends gathered in the New Calvary Cemetery to ceremonially lay Mother to rest. Blowing snow pelted us as we huddled together on the snow-covered hillside, where our mom and dad would once again be reunited after being apart for twenty-five years.

As we stood shivering, Father Bill conducted the short internment service by reciting a burial prayer and saying a few carefully chosen words of consolation; it was much too miserable for more of a service. A few bouquets were placed upon the icy frozen ground and we quickly departed.

This mock-burial service was mostly ceremonial in nature, because Mother's ashes would actually be interned in the spring when the ground thawed. At that point we would also amend their headstone to include the date of her departure—but not today.

Today, following the graveside service, we attended Mass as a family, and afterwards met at the Golden Gate Diner for breakfast. Although the service was primarily ceremonial in nature, we felt it was absolutely necessary for us, and it was another step completed in what had turned out to be a very long journey. But we were not finished yet.

⋅⋙══ ══⋘⋅

At our next briefing the Flint Township's detectives explained that they were doing their best to build a solid case and bring it to trial. Our job now was to be patient and let them do their jobs. From now on we would be notified and updated as they thought it necessary.

⋅⋙══ ══⋘⋅

On January 14 of the following year, 2004, another article appeared in *The Flint Journal* stating that the accused, Ms. Kimberly Angenette Morgan, was going to undergo a mental competency exam as requested by her court-appointed attorney, David J. Goggins. The detectives told us not to worry; this was simply part of the judicial process, because she needed to be deemed "of sound mind and body" to stand trial. But it was exasperating to think she could possibly try to escape prosecution by being declared mentally incompetent, or some other fast-handed legal maneuver.

⋅⋙══ ══⋘⋅

Six months had now passed. Seeking justice for our slain mother was still in the forefront of my mind, but in the meantime life had become somewhat more normalized. We resumed our private lives and went back to work, with each of us coping as best we could. But I still remained vigilant, and not yet able to turn off the high-alert mechanism, because darkness entered our lives and deep shadows had been cast. My view of the world had been permanently altered, and life would never be the same.

⋅→▸━◉ ◉━◂←⋅

Shortly after the new year, we were contacted by Lisa Jaworski, who informed us that she would be our court-appointed liaison and help us navigate from the policing and investigative agencies into the judicial arena. She strongly advised that we all attend Victims of Violent Encounters (VIVE) meetings. These "meetings" were in reality group-counseling sessions where the families of crime victims could discuss their feelings with other victims and a trained therapist. Certainly there were many concerns that one would have after such an unforgivable act of violence had been perpetrated upon a person, a family member, or a loved one. I understood the need for such a program, especially here in Flint, the most violent city in the country.

We all attended the first few classes together, as suggested. Group was conducted by a graduate student of psychology and held weekly at the First Unitarian Church. Truthfully, it was rather difficult for us to open up and share our feelings, because we weren't raised to be that way. As children we were always expected to be seen and not heard. During the first session, all my sweet niece Erin could do was silently weep, because she was too emotionally overwhelmed to even speak. The rest of us participated as best we could; it was a difficult subject to discuss, and the wound was still fresh, barely scabbed over.

These weekly groups were usually quite small and often we were the only attendees. I thought this was rather odd, because the classes were free and this city had such pervasive violence. Hearing others discuss the violence committed against them and their traumatic losses was not therapeutic to me. It was only further confirmation that the world was a dangerous place. But in reality, discussing Mother's death *was* helpful.

We were more fortunate than most of these other people because our family, friends, and community were providing support, and that helped immensely. I considered myself very fortunate to have a strong supportive network of friends to talk and share my feelings with. It had never been too difficult for me to communicate that way. And luckily I had a close friend who was a retired therapist and great listener, too, and she also helped me cope with this trauma. She also managed to attend every event we had throughout this strange ordeal.

Thank you, all of you.

One thing I did not know before being tested by this traumatic event was the inner strength that I possessed. And I believe we all gained strength through supporting each other. Mom was always very strong, and she expected nothing less from us children.

Her faith was strong, too. The first thing you saw when entering Mom's home was the painted resin plaque next to her door that read, "Lord, there is nothing that You and I cannot face today, together," and she believed that. I believe that God, prayer, and the support of family, close friends, and community were what helped us get through this ordeal.

We were not finished yet.

The Ball is Rolling

WE WERE LEARNING more of the facts concerning Mother's case, but usually this news was found by reading the information in the paper. For instance, the person of interest, who is now identified as Ms. Kimberly A. Morgan, was extradited from Nashville, Tennessee, to Flint to be questioned about defacing a vehicle and destroying other personal property belonging to an ex-lover.

When she allegedly committed those violent acts, Ms. Morgan violated the restraining order, was charged with that offense, and extradited to Michigan. She was being held in the Genesee County Jail awaiting trial. During her incarceration she was questioned about breaching that PPO, and also asked about the lover's triangle she was reportedly involved in.

Kimberly was incarcerated throughout the Thanksgiving and Christmas holidays while waiting for her court appearance. Apparently she felt lonely during the holidays, because she did a little talking. She chatted with her many transient cellmates, the religious volunteers who regularly visited, and even to the jailhouse guards. I guess chatting broke up the boredom of being incarcerated. We were told she even had a few lengthy conversations with the detectives, all at her request.

We were told that Ms. Morgan fancied herself as being smart. In fact, she thought herself smarter than most. I suppose she requested these meetings with Detective Schmitzer thinking that he was a country bumpkin and she could talk her way out of her troubles. His manner was quite unassuming, and nonthreatening, and apparently she felt comfortable talking with him. During these lengthy chats she felt comfortable enough to confess, and not just once, but twice, and on videotape both times. Maybe what the nuns told us was true—confession is good for the soul.

⋅⊹⊫◉ ◉⊣⊹⋅

The official arrest warrant for Ms. Kimberly Angenette Morgan was issued in early January 2004, and she was charged with eight counts. Arraignment was scheduled for April 20, 2004.

⋅⊹⊫◉ ◉⊣⊹⋅

The period between January, when Ms. Morgan was charged, and April, when she was to be arraigned, became another excruciatingly long stretch of time. After this arraignment was held, we would still have to wait until August 26, 2004, for her actual trial, and that was more than eight months away.

⋅⊹⊫◉ ◉⊣⊹⋅

As previously mentioned, we did not learn about Ms. Morgan being charged with Mother's murder from the detectives working on the case. Instead, we learned this information by reading it in *The Flint Journal*. The public was informed at the same time as our family. The article's author stated that he had "inadvertently" obtained this information by reading it in a court document, and then wrote the article for the public's enlightenment.

After that article was released, we wrote *The Flint Journal* and the author of the article, to inform them that we felt slighted by this information being issued in this way, and would appreciate being told about such personally pertinent news before the general public was notified, if that was possible. The response was less than apologetic. In essence, the writer claimed that he was just doing his job.

⋅⊹⊫◉ ◉⊣⊹⋅

During the eight months between when Ms. Morgan was charged and the trial, many things were happening behind the scenes. Many capable people were carefully constructing Mother's court case. Now several jurisdictions were helping the prosecution to build a winn-able case, including the detectives from Mundy Township, the city of Flint, Flint Township, and the Michigan State Police. The FBI was also involved at one point.

During this interim the charges against Ms. Morgan were also amended, and instead of facing eight counts, she was now accused of ten offenses, and they are: open murder, felony murder, carjacking, kidnapping, armed robbery, assault with intent to murder, arson, carrying a concealed weapon, firearms possession by a felon, and felony firearm.

It was difficult for me to comprehend how anyone could hurt our little mother, let alone kill her. She was eighty years old, stood barely five feet tall, and hobbled because she was plagued with arthritis. Even more difficult to comprehend was that the person accused of committing these crimes was a woman. Mother's murder did not appear to have anything to do with money, gangs, or drugs.

Kimberly wanted Mother's car.

⊷⊶

There was still much to know, but we were steadily learning more, although usually by reading it in *The Flint Journal.* To further sensationalize this already strange story, the newspaper ran another article on January 7, 2004, and it stated that Kimberly Morgan used Mother's car in a drive-by shooting where she was targeting an Alan Johnson, the current boyfriend of Ms. Morgan's, lesbian, ex-lover.

Kimberly Morgan, her lesbian ex-lover, and her ex-lover's boyfriend were the three principals involved in this twisted love triangle. Mother's accused murderer was a jealous lesbian, which only added another salacious detail to the already strange tragedy.

We were now told that the story given to police, by the man who was shot in the drive-by shooting, was that he had no idea who was targeting him, or why. It appeared that might be true. We initially thought that the story about his being shot by a jealous rival as part of a lover's triangle sounded far-fetched. But we are now learning that this may be true, and from what we could gather, Mother was seemingly just collateral damage.

That same article stated that Ms. Morgan was stopped in Indiana for speeding, questioned for twenty minutes, ticketed, and then released. Fortunately this traffic stop was videotaped and it provided police with a plausible timeline that could place her in the Flint area on July 2, 2003. Quite unbelievably she was nearly apprehended while fleeing Flint after committing her crime spree, but the ticketing officer had no idea what Kimberly had been up to before he stopped her.

This same article also stated that Morgan "accidentally" shot our mother—three times. She shot her twice in the eye and once in the chest. Again, this was a totally devastating revelation, and we had to learn this by reading it in the paper. The autopsy intimated that Mother died from a gunshot wound, but we didn't know that she was shot three times until it appeared in *The Flint Journal*. Once again, thank you for your continued sensitivity.

⸺◦≡◦ ◦≡◦⸺

On April 20, 2004, all four of Dorothy's children and their families attended the district court preliminary exam, and this was the first time we saw in person the woman who stood accused of killing our mother. I did not anticipate seeing a short, plump, and well-groomed woman. I imagined someone larger and thuglike, darker and more menacing. She was quite short, maybe five feet tall at the most, round and thick-hipped with a low center of gravity. She had chocolate skin and big, warm brown, protruding cow-like eyes that blinked profusely.

This woman did not appear to be dangerous at all. Her manner was detached, unemotional, but very much self-contained. She did not look like a low-life murderer. There were no visible scars, tattoos, or needle marks. In fact, we learned that she grew up in the same respectable suburban neighborhood where Mother's remains were found, giving her a squarely middle-class upbringing. She attended the same suburban high school that Mike and Mary graduated from, and we were told she attended college.

⋆⇛ ⇚⋆

Another *Flint Journal* article stated that Ms. Morgan had previously served time in federal prison for robbing banks, and once again we are learning the facts by reading them in the paper and not from the authorities. She was convicted of robbing three banks and had served a total of forty-one months for committing these crimes. She was indeed proving to be no angel.

But it all seemed so senseless. There seemed to be no rational reason for Mother being abducted and murdered, if just for the purpose of obtaining her vehicle. Certainly, she would have given the car away rather than being killed.

⋆⇛ ⇚⋆

The five months between the arraignment and trial were very busy. Many of our anxieties were being alleviated because we'd finally found, recovered, and buried our mother, someone was being charged with her murder, and a trial was forthcoming. Life could stop its retrograde motion and begin to slowly return to some sense of normalcy.

But Murphy's Law would once again be placed into motion when, later that summer, in late August, I would be turning fifty, and that was right when the trial was scheduled to get under way. Plus we also had an upcoming wedding, as Tim and Patty's lovely daughter, Aimee, would be marrying her beloved, David Czacherowski, in early September—on Labor Day weekend—and that would also be occurring during the trial. This was shaping up as a very busy summer indeed.

To the Courts * Little Shoes

OUR BRIEFINGS WITH the police ended, and now our court-appointed liaison, Mrs. Lisa Jaworski of Crime Victim Services, was keeping us updated with all information pertaining to the court case. Lisa was very personable and greatly assisted our understanding of and navigation through the judicial process. We were becoming familiarized with names of the people and workings of the court system.

→⊙ ⊙←

Our first official notice from Crime Victim Services stated that a preliminary exam was scheduled for April 20, 2004, in Genesee County's 67th District Court, and we all attended this exam. The Honorable John L. Conover presided, Attorney David J. Goggins defended Kimberly A. Morgan, and Prosecuting Attorney Arthur A. Busch argued his case. During this exam, the prosecutor clearly proved that ten crimes had occurred and it was most probable that Ms. Morgan had committed them. In essence, he showed there was probable cause, and the case moved on.

→⊙ ⊙←

The next notice from advocate Lisa's office was for an arraignment scheduled on May 3, 2004, in the Genesee County Circuit Courthouse. Here Ms. Morgan was formally charged with committing these ten crimes. During this phase, a defendant may plead guilty, not guilty, or stand mute. The amount of bail bond is also examined, and the judge explains the defendant's rights.

At her arraignment, Ms. Morgan was represented by attorney Carol Jaworski, and she pled not guilty to all ten charges. No bail was accepted, her rights were explained, and the case moved on.

Shortly after Ms. Morgan's arraignment, and after having Mother's case for only a few weeks, the Prosecuting Attorney's Office experienced an internal shake-up. So Prosecutor Busch stepped down to spend more time with his family, and it was decided - by all parties concerned, that Assistant Prosecutor Mrs. Karen Hanson would oversee the case and bring it to trial. We were all happy with the decision.

On July 15, 2004, a pretrial conference was held in circuit court between the prosecuting and defense attorneys. This meeting was held privately inside Judge Geoffrey Neithercut's chambers. We did not need to be present, but we were there. This informal meeting was held to determine if both lawyers were pre-pared and if the case should continue proceeding toward trial, or if a plea agree-ment could be reached. No plea was entered, no bond accepted, and both parties continued moving toward trial.

We did not need to, but we faithfully attended every single appearance, be-lieving it was our duty to represent Mother. Most of the steps taken so far were perfunctory and necessary to ensure that justice existed for all parties. The mo-tions provided another chance to study the unassuming woman who stood ac-cused of murder. Examining her closely, I tried to see the darkness that must surely be there.

Our next notification from Crime Victim Services was a change of defense notice. Another court-appointed attorney was now representing Ms. Morgan, bringing the total to three. David J. Goggins was representing her at the initial exam and arraignment, and then - for a brief interim period, Carol Jaworski (by the way, no relation to Lisa Jaworski of Victim Services) represented her. Later we were told that Ms. Jaworski did not have experience handling capital cases, and she was replace by Philip H. Beauvais III. He would bring the case to trial. We were told that he was very competent and would make sure to dot every i and cross every t.

→─◉ ◉─←

July 2, 2004, was the first anniversary of Mother's disappearance. In some ways it seemed impossible that an entire year had passed since she disappeared, and in other ways it seemed as if an eternity had transpired. There were still times when I forgot she was gone and tried to phone her, and then remembered that she was dead and hung up. So on this infamous day we all met at Mom's church for a Mass that was donated in her honor. Many Masses were given to us. In early March we celebrated a Mass for her eighty-first birth-day, in early May we honored her on Mother's Day, and on June 21 yet another Mass was offered to commemorate the summer solstice, and also our parents' wedding anniversary, or, as our dad liked to call it, "The longest day of my life."

→─◉ ◉─←

On July 22, 2004, another circuit court pretrial was conducted. Judge Neithercut presided, and attorneys Hanson and Beauvais attended this private meeting, which was held in a courthouse conference room. Their consensus was that their cases were ready to present, and they wished to continue proceeding toward trial.

→─◉ ◉─←

On August 13, 2004, another circuit court pretrial was held inside Judge Neithercut's chambers. This private meeting was as an informal conference held between the two attorneys to determine if the case was ready to move toward trial, or if it could be settled by a plea agreement. Their consensus was to continue proceeding toward trial.

⋆⊶❁⊷⋆

Everything seemed to be on track and we had nearly reached our trial date, but there were a few more bumps along the way. The next notice informed us about a private meeting, which would be held in Judge Neithercut's court, on August 17, 2004. Therein defense attorney Mr. Beauvais put forward his motion to throw out both of the videotaped confessions, and petitioned to have a change of venue, and move the trial to another location. He argued that the areas extensive news coverage involving Mother's case may have unwittingly influenced many potential jurors. We were incensed at his audacity, on both counts. The judge denied both of these motions, and the case again moved forward.

⋆⊶❁⊷⋆

Our next notification from advocate Lisa's office was the announcement of Mother's actual trial. The trial of the People of the State of Michigan versus Kimberly Morgan was scheduled to commence on August 24, 2004, in Circuit Court Judge Geoffrey Neithercut's Courtroom.

⋆⊶❁⊷⋆

In the eight long months spanning the time between the arrest and trial we tried to keep ourselves busy. Many tasks were accomplished, including closing Mother's accounts, settling with the insurance company on her claim, and dissolving Mother's estate. Finally we sold her modular home, and believe me; we were relieved to have it purchased, because it was a constant reminder of her absence.

And in the meantime we waited, took each succeeding step, and chugged our way through the judicial process.

Little Shoes

Dianna, the psychic, envisioned one tan shoe. The first thing that the man noticed, before he found Mother's remains, was one little tan orthopedic shoe. That single shoe, lying by the edge of the road, was what led him to Mother, who was lying in the woods just a short distance away.

Those little shoes would be difficult to fill.

During the prolonged purgatory-like period between when Ms. Morgan was arrested and her trial, more news had "leaked out." An article was written by Paul Janczewski in the Wednesday, March 24, 2004, edition of *The Flint Journal*, and it bore this unusual headline: Elderly Slaying Victim Told Attacker, "I'll Pray for You."

By reading this article we learned that Mother's kidnapper drove her around the city of Flint for over thirty minutes before killing her, where enough time elapsed for them to have extended conversations. This was disturbing news. Mother's ordeal was prolonged. I had prayed it would have been short and painless.

Ms. Morgan had plenty of time to let Mother out and not take her life in the process.

I can't imagine the torment Mother went through, being worried, scared, terrified. But it seemed she had other thoughts, because the article quoted Mother as saying to her kidnapper, "You look desperate; are you leaving me here?" And her last words spoken on this earth showed compassion toward her executioner: "I will pray for you."

Mother did everything one is supposed to do when in an abduction situation. She related to her kidnapper, and empathized, but that did not help her live one minute longer.

It made me weep to read those words. "I'll pray for you." She did not plead for her life; instead she spoke words of kindness to her tormentor. She truly lived her faith, and she seemed prepared to die. I believe she knew her time was near.

When I try imagining what I would do -- in such a situation, I seriously doubt that I would pray for my executioner. I'd most likely plea for my life to be spared, and for my own deliverance.

My friend Bette gave me comfort when she said, "Most people have to wait for three days to get into heaven, but your mother's entrance was swift, immediate, and glorious." I'd like to think that.

In early November, when things quieted down a bit, we visited the spot where Mother's life was taken. This was nothing more than a dead-end street and dumping site, but we considered this place significant to Mother's story. The debris was cleared from the spot where she once laid, and a basket of tulips, hyacinths, and daffodil bulbs, that were gifted by a dear friend, Donna Turnage, were planted.

We didn't want this desolate spot to become a shrine but we wished to somehow acknowledge that this ground was special to us, because this was where our Mother's life was taken. After planting the flower bulbs, another gift of a small resin angel was placed upon the memorial site as we said a few prayers and remembered Mother.

The following spring brother Mike revisited the River Forest site, where they found mom, once again. He reported that the flower bulbs were coming along beautifully, and that something even more remarkable had taken place. Large white morel mushrooms were springing from the spot where Mother's remains were discovered. Their appearance was unusual, because they normally don't grow in recently disturbed locations. They prefer instead to live in mature, undisturbed woodlands.

Mom absolutely loved eating morels. As children we would tromp through the north woods with her and Grandma Lee and pick bags full of the tasty gourmet morsels. Finding them growing on Mother's death site was most unusual indeed. Mike picked the mushrooms and brought them to our family meeting. Those earthy mushrooms were rinsed of the heavy clay soil from which they sprang, patted dry, floured, seasoned, and then fried to a rich golden brown in pure melted butter. Then we salted and devoured the meaty gourmet treats, and thought of Mom.

Later that spring the gifted spring flowers bloomed in profusion, with soft rosy pink hyacinths, vivid red tulips, and bright sunny yellow daffodils pushing their way through the newly greened grass that had started to grow there. The flowers and dainty angel made the site look less like a muddy dump site and a bit more like a proper garden and memorial.

That same spring Mother's remains were interred with our father, so we would then visit them both at the cemetery. But this deserted dumping place held its own importance, because of one little shoe. I will always make note of this spot when passing on this side of town, because it is a significant piece of Mother's story.

Our Day in Court * Trial Day One

SUMMER ALREADY PEAKED—YOU could feel it in the air—and it was quickly rounding the bend toward fall. We were experiencing one of our last lovely warming spells before winter began pushing its ugly way back in. Clear blue sapphire skies were cloudless, but that definite cooling tinge meant fall was here to stay.

Well over a year ago Mother disappeared, and now her murder trial was about to commence. As far as I was concerned, this case was the only thing going on in my life now, and everything else came to a complete halt; my work and personal life could resume after this trial. And I truly believed that my brothers and sister felt exactly the same way.

Before the trial I was a wreck. I'd even stupidly started smoking again that past year, after having a fourteen-year hiatus. But at the time I really didn't much care, because it gave me comfort and something legitimate to do during all the waiting. Outside the courthouse I waited until the last possible second, puffed away mightily, and extracted every last drag of precious smoke I could inhale before emptying my pockets in preparation for being scanned, x-rayed, and searched for weapons by the courthouse security guards.

The trial had not yet started, but we were already being recognized as "the family of the old lady who was killed." The courthouse staff seemed sympathetic to our unusual case and accommodating to the large groups of family and friends and the media presence that came along with us.

It certainly seemed like a long time since Mother disappeared, but we were finally in court and facing her "alleged" killer. Timothy (and Patricia), Daniel, Mary Ann, and Michael—all four of Dorothy Lee Murphy's children—were seated in the front row to represent her and see justice served in her name.

All four of her grandchildren were here as well. Ryan and Erin were seated with their paternal grandmother, Darlene Deering, and Aimee and Patrick sitting behind their parents. Throughout the trial my loyal friend Linda De Groat sat on the bench next to me. Mom's sister, our aunt Jean, and Uncle Elin sat with Aunt Shirley, Uncle Gerald, a few cousins, and a couple of friends of the family. The remaining seats were filled by a few detectives and police officers who worked the case.

This impressive and recently restored historic courtroom was intimate but grand, small and lovely. A dark walnut wainscot covered the lower four feet of the walls, and it was dressed with formal chamfered wood panels the same rich warm brown as the floors, chairs, and massive carved benches of the jury box.

Covering the entire wall behind the judge's lofty bench was a floor-to-ceiling mural. This pastoral scene was painted in a rather romantic style, depicting Flint during its early years. A tanned and chiseled American-Indian man was trading animal hides with a buckskin-clad white settler. A sparkling blue ribbon of river weaved through a lush green landscape dotted with wispy whites. This noble red man's painted pony was weighed down with furs as he stood watching their exchange against an expansive back-drop of painterly blue sky. The majestic mural conjured an image of Flint that I never imagined, but it also provided something beautiful to look at during the pauses that would inevitably occur during the trial.

Scooting in the door at the very last minute were two uniformed officers and *The Flint Journal's* acerbic court reporter. For well over a year this case had been in the media, and many people still wanted to know the details.

You could feel the low-frequency buzz coursing through the courtroom while awaiting the judge's appearance. Soon witnesses would be called to give their sworn testimony concerning who did what, when, where, and how, to draw a clear picture of how this surreal drama was playing out. Giving testimony during the trial would be a witness to the arson, the drive-by shooting victim, the defendant's ex-lover, and even our sister, Mary. Specialists would give their expert insights in the fields of arson, forensic anthropology, DNA, and ballistics.

State Police officers from Michigan and Indiana would give their sworn testimony, as well as those from the city of Flint and Flint and Mundy townships.

Details pertaining to how Mother died, what led up to it, and other facts not previously known to us would be forth-coming as well. I tried to prepare myself for these inevitable disclosures, determined to see this final step through.

Toward the back of the courtroom sat a quiet, and well dressed older black couple, and they stood out. I thought they might be Ms. Morgan's parents and introduced myself. This surely could not be easy for them either.

→━━◉ ◉━━←

The courtroom was seated and awaiting the judge as early morning light came filtering in through the tall north-facing windows. The deep-set windows were flanked by heavy mossy-green velvet draperies that were a bit fussy but still appropriate for a courtroom predating the Civil War. We watched as the bailiff adjusted the wooden blinds to let some natural light filter in but still keep the distracting world obscured.

* There was an unusual coincidence I would like to share before trial commences. Our brother Tim was notified to report for jury duty for Mother's trial. What were the odds of that happening? Of course, he was dismissed for having a good enough excuse. Meanwhile fourteen other jurors were selected the previous day and instructed of their duties for several hours.

With the jurors selected, approved, and instructed, the official trial of the People of the State of Michigan (including us) versus Kimberly Angenette Morgan was ready to start at any minute. Originally eleven people were slated to give testimony or share expert advice during the trial, but that list had grown to include twenty-six names.

The felony complaint listed ten counts in all:

1. Homicide, open murder
2. Homicide, felony murder
3. Carjacking
4. Kidnapping

5. Robbery—armed

6. Assault with intent to murder

7. Arson—personal property

8. Carrying a concealed weapon

9. Felon in possession of a firearm

10. Weapons felony (use of a firearm in the commission of a crime)

Two long, dark, and heavy wooden tables sat opposing each other in the galley directly in front of the judge's bench. He sat upon an elevated platform, high above all the others. Representing the people was Assistant Prosecuting Attorney Mrs. Karen Hanson. She was a tall, sturdy natural blonde with spunk.

On the opposing side, the defendant, Kimberly A. Morgan, would be seated at the defense table with her attorney, Philip H. Beauvais III. He was a tall, trim, and conservative man who wore a plain gray suit and gold wire-rimmed glasses; he was probably a Protestant and Republican, too. Appearing to be in his early fifties, he had thick dark hair that was showing telltale touches of silver at the temples.

A heavy wooden door opened at the back of the courtroom, to the left of the judge's bench, and then a large-framed man dressed in a crisply pressed khaki uniform emerged. Shuffling behind him was Kimberly A. Morgan, with her leg and wrist chains clinking and clanging as she went.

Mr. Beauvais rose as she approached and they shared a few secretive words. The officer of the court extracted a large noisy ring of heavy keys and removed the handcuffing restraints on her wrists and the leg chains binding her ankles, and she sat down.

Again I studied her round face for any telltale clues that she might give, because now we were closer to her than we had ever been, maybe just ten feet, close enough to smell the pomade in her closely cropped wavy hair. Sensing us scrutinizing her, she twisted her torso and turned her back to us. Staring straight ahead, she blinked quite often but made eye contact with no one.

From the very back of the courtroom we heard the jury room door creaking open. Turning, we watched as the newly selected jurors were escorted out by the bailiff and then seated in two long benches directly behind the prosecution's table. For the first time we viewed the jurors. I hoped they'd take their duties seriously.

This was a diverse group. Some appeared to be suburban types, dressed in nice clothes like those one would wear to church. One colorful young man definitely stood out, because he looked more like a radical skateboarder, dressed in gangster-style baggy shorts and a vividly colored, flaming-designed, short-sleeved silky sport shirt. A soul patch rode on his cinnamon-colored chin, and I'd bet he had tattoos some-where on his body, too. There were equal amounts of women and men, with a wide range of ages and colors.

All eyes were focused forward anticipating the arrival of the Honorable Judge Geoffrey Neithercut. His name was a familiar one, because he had conducted many of the pretrial motions for this case and had also been a well-respected judge serving on the bench in Flint for a great many years.

Opening Statements, Prosecutor Hanson

THE BAILIFF STOOD, stiffened, and then bellowed, "All rise for the Honorable Judge Geoffrey Neithercut," and the entire courtroom stood in unison. Briskly walking in, with his black silk robe trailing behind him, the judge hopped up to his bench, sat down in his big black leather chair, pulled his half-lens glasses from the top of his shiny bald head, and started reading from a foot-deep stack of mail piled upon his desk. While reading mail, he completely ignored the overflow crowd of spectators in the courtroom.

The bailiff bellowed once again, "All be seated." With a wind-making whoosh, the congregation simultaneously sat back down. Prosecuting Attorney Hanson rose and confidently walked over to the front and center of the court to assume the podium.

◆━━◉ ◉━━◆

"Your Honor, before we begin we have filed an amendment to the charges, to have them changed from a charge of open murder to a charge of premeditated murder. That the defendant did, deliberately, with intent to kill and premeditation, kill or murder Mrs. Dorothy Lee Murphy."

"So noted," said the judge, while still going through his mail. "Would the jury please stand to be sworn in," he added without ever looking up. The jury was sworn in, and after receiving their solemn oath, the judge gave them a nice hour-long fatherly talking-to and explained their many duties. When finished, he turned toward the prosecutor and said, "Mrs. Hanson, please begin your opening remarks." Pulling his glasses back down from his head, he returned to reading the mail.

⸱⸱⊷◉ ◉⊷⸱⸱

"Dorothy Murphy didn't deserve to be in this at all. That's a statement made by the defendant, on January 4, 2004, to Detective Schmitzer.

"The judge has read you those charges, and we will be proving those charges during the trial. This case may seem complicated to you, but if you pay attention you'll see it's really not complicated. It all comes down to one thing, that the defendant wanted her lover back, Savannah Liddel. Testimony will show that she and Savannah broke up. She wanted her back. She would do whatever it took to get that.

"Testimony will show that she drove back from Tennessee to get rid of Alan Johnson, Savannah's current fiancé. Dorothy Murphy, an eighty-year-old woman, was in the wrong place, at the wrong time.

"We'll hear testimony that on July the second of 2003, the defendant, Kimberly Morgan, did carjack and kidnap Dorothy Murphy. She put her in the backseat of her own vehicle, drove her out to Flint Township, to a place that was known to the defendant, because she used to live in that area. She got her out of her car, walked her at gunpoint into a wooded area, and shot her two times in the face and once in the chest, after Dorothy had just said to her, 'I'll pray for you.'

"The defendant then got back into Dorothy's car and drove to the city of Flint, where she waited. She waited for Alan Johnson to get off from the bus.

"You'll be hearing from Alan Johnson, that he got off the bus a little after five on July the second, at the corner of Grand Traverse and Third Street. As he walked toward Grand Traverse and Fourth Street, he noticed a blue car sitting over on the corner. He'll tell you it wasn't unusual, because it was a drug area, high-crime area, sometimes cars just parked there.

"He'll tell you that as he approached the curb on Fourth Street, the car pulled out in front of him, blocking his way. He'll tell you that wasn't unusual. Sometimes people wanted to sell drugs, or something. He turned to walk around the car, and then he got shot in the stomach. He'll tell you that he ran across the street to a vacant lot that had brush in it while trying to get away from the car, and as he was running, someone in the car chased after him, and was shooting at him.

"Alan will tell you at that point he was shot again, in the shoulder. He'll tell you that the shooting continued as he was running through the streets of the city of Flint, that this car was chasing him, and shooting at him, and obviously trying to kill him.

"Alan will tell you that he doesn't have the best eyesight, but from what he could see, in the distance, it appeared to be a young black male with short hair driving the car. He'll tell you that he hid behind a house and watched as the car crept around the corner, till he heard sirens coming. Then he ran to the party store across the street, where an ambulance came and took him to the hospital.

"You'll hear from Officer Terry Lewis, who responded to the drive-by shooting scene on the corner of Grand Traverse and Fourth Street. He found a spent shell casing there. Minutes later he responded to a vehicle-fire call, behind Mr. Lucky's bar on Lapeer Road in the city of Flint, about four miles away from where Alan Johnson was shot. He will tell you that he arrived on the scene of the burning vehicle and found an emblem from a Buick vehicle on the ground."

"You'll hear from Fire Investigator Kathy Taylor, who will tell you that she went to the car and that, while investigating inside the car, she found a burnt purse. Inside that purse was a credit card that was half-burnt and a spent shell casing."

"You'll hear from Ron Ainsley that those shell casings were sent to the crime lab, and that those casings matched, that they came from the same gun.

"Ronald Johnson, a person who knew both the defendant and Savannah Liddel, will tell you, on July 2, 2003, in the late morning, he was driving by the Walgreens on the corner of Dort Highway and Atherton Road, where he saw the defendant. He said that she crouched down into her black Probe, as if she tried to hide from him.

"You'll hear from a Simone Callahan, who was parked in the apartments across the street from Mr. Lucky's, and she saw someone walking from behind Mr. Lucky's. She saw smoke was coming from behind there, and this person was wearing a yellow shirt. She gave a description to the Mundy Township Police, who made a composite sketch of that person, and you'll see that composite sketch.

"An Indiana trooper will be coming in to tell you that later that same night, on July second, he stopped the defendant in her Probe and she told him that she'd just come from Flint.

"Sergeant Joel Grahn will come in and tell you that he was the investigator in the original missing persons complaint of Dorothy Murphy, and that complaint led him to her car, that was burnt, to Alan, to Savannah, and ultimately to the defendant. And he'll tell you how he went to Tennessee to search her apartment and the black Probe.

"Barbie Garrison, one of the defendant's friends, will be coming in to tell you that from July 2 to the end of July, the defendant called her numerous times. When she would call her, she'd ask if she'd heard anything about a missing old lady. Have you heard anything about a guy being shot? You heard anything about a burning car? When Barbie told her that there was a composite sketch of the person that was seen walking away from the burning car, she asked, 'Does it look like me?'

"Detective Mark Reaves will be coming in to tell you that he went to Dorothy's burning vehicle and investigated, he sifted through all the debris that was there, and he found another spent casing. And he found a burnt bottle of hand lotion in that vehicle under some of the debris. He will tell you that he sent that bottle to the lab, and a DNA expert will be here to tell you that it came back matching to Kimberly Morgan.

"Richard Gehring will tell you that on September 26, 2003, he was working for Consumers Energy in the area of River Forest Apartments in Flint Township, when he walked into a cul-de-sac where he found Dorothy Murphy's remains.

"Sergeant DuBuc from the Flint Township Police will be here to tell you that they processed the scene, and he'll explain about the stuff they found there. And he'll tell you one of the things they found there was a pair of prescription sunglasses that were lying next to those remains and there was a hole in the right lens of those glasses.

"Firearms expert Ron Crichton will be here to tell you that this hole is consistent with a bullet hole. There will be other people coming to testify during the course of this trial, to put the pieces together for you. Finally, you'll hear from the officer in charge, a Detective Schmitzer, who'll tell you about these statements the defendant made to him.

"The statements saying that, she did in fact go to the Walgreens, lay-in-wait, and then carjack Dorothy, kidnap Dorothy, and took money out of her purse. She drove Dorothy to a place that she was very familiar with, got her out of the backseat of her car, walked her into the woods, shot her in the face twice, shot her once in the chest.

"You'll hear from the detective that Kimberly told him, she got in the car and went to the city of Flint, where she waited for Alan. She shot Alan, and then she burned Dorothy's car.

"Ladies and gentlemen, these ten charges are here for you to consider. We've charged the defendant with those ten counts, and I will ultimately be proving those charges to you, beyond a reasonable doubt, during the course of this trial. We are confident that, after you hear all the testimony, you'll see all there is to see, and that you'll find the defendant guilty of all those charges.

"We'll talk about reasonable doubt, and we'll agree, that doubt without reason is the basic common sense that you all bring to this courtroom. Reasonable doubt is not beyond the shadow of a doubt, it is a reasonable doubt. Common sense. If you looked outside and saw that it was raining, you would know that it was raining outside. But there is also the circumstantial evidence. Evidence that means, if someone walks through that door, they are dripping wet, and they have an umbrella, you can infer that it is raining outside.

"We ask that you use your common sense, logic, and reasoning during the course of this trial. Please listen carefully to all the evidence that you'll be hearing. The details are very important in this case."

"The detectives are going to show that the defendant committed these crimes, and the steps she took to try and get what she wanted. Details show that she deliberated and she thought about what she was doing, thought about the choices she was making. Details will show you that her intent was to kill Dorothy

Murphy, and she intended to kill Alan Johnson. Details are going to show the planning and the premeditation of these crimes.

"Ladies and gentlemen, we're confident that after you have heard all the facts, that you will find the defendant guilty of all the charges that the defendant is charged with. Thank you."

Opening Statements, Defense Attorney Philip H. Beauvais III

ATTORNEY PHILIP H. Beauvais III rose and assumed the podium. After placing his papers upon it, he turned and walked over to stand in front of the jury so he could speak to them more directly and personally. He wore a white button-down shirt, plain gray summer-weight wool suit, and a matching nondescript tie. He appeared to be about fifty.

⋅⟫⟩⊙ ⊙⟨⟪⋅

"Ladies and gentlemen of the jury, as the judge introduced me earlier, my name is Phil Beauvais. I represent Kimberly Morgan, who is the defendant in this case. I know the judge has talked to you, and I am going to talk to you, at some length, about some of the tenets of our criminal justice system and what those entail.

"Something that the judge said, so many times yesterday that you probably got tired of hearing it, but you are gonna hear it again from me. Number one is this, the presumption of innocence. That's what makes our system different from any other system.

"When you listen to the witnesses, and you're viewing the evidence, you have to keep uppermost in your mind the presumption of innocence. Because, all through this trial Kim Morgan (just like a fervent preacher delivering a fiery sermon, he steadily raised his voice, turned and pointed to Kimberly, and his voice fell again upon delivering his words) is presumed to be innocent.

"Now, we ask you, the judge asked you, and I will ask you, whether or not you can presume her to be innocent all the way through the trial. Each and every one of you said, 'Yes. I can do that.' And we intend to hold you to that agreement.

"What I like to tell everybody is this, it's sort of like this. She is wearing a cloak all during this trial. That cloak says 'innocent' on it, because that's what the presumption of innocence is, from the start of the trial all the way through to the end. As you listen to all the evidence, you're listening with the presumption that she is innocent.

"Now, the burden of proof in a criminal case lies with the prosecutor. It doesn't lay with Kimberly Morgan (again he emphatically pointed toward her). *She* does not have to prove anything to you. She does not have to produce any witnesses. She does not have to testify herself *if* she chooses not to. She has the absolute right to *not* testify, and the right *to* testify, depending on what *she* wants to do. That's not something you can hold against her, because she has no burden in this.

"The burden is upon the prosecutor to prove guilt beyond a reasonable doubt. Now, reasonable doubt is a little different than it sounds, for people to apply this in their daily lives. Most of the time we don't apply any reasonable doubt. We don't say, because I have reasonable doubt I don't do something."

Grandly gesturing with his hands, Mr. Beauvais paced back and forth in front of the jury while making his points. "When we buy an automobile we take a look at it. We say, gee, I like the Buick, or I like the Chevy. Chevy's a little cheaper; But the Buick might be a little more dependable, depending on where you work. I still have reasonable doubt if whether or not my choice is the best choice. We can't do that here. Here, if you have reason to doubt, you only have one choice, and that choice is *not guilty*.

"Now, there's gonna be a lotta evidence here, a lotta witnesses, a lotta people are going to testify. Sometimes what you *are* hearing is as important as what you *don't* hear. The holes that are there, that your common sense tells you, gee, something should be in those holes and it's not there. That's reasonable doubt, ladies and gentlemen, and that's what you're going to hear in this case. Is there some holes in this case? Something that say's, jeez, that just doesn't add up.

"We're gonna ask you to do what you're supposed to do as a jury. Do your duty. Your duty is to listen to all the evidence, apply the presumption of innocence, do not make any decisions until you have everything together, and you go back to that jury room."

Turning quickly, he pointed dramatically to the back of the courtroom, to the jury room, and his voice rose once again.

"And in there, we expect you to come back with a fair and impartial verdict, that's all we can ask of you. We expect that will be a verdict of *not guilty* after you have listened to all the evidence. Thank you."

And with that remark he turned, picked his papers up from the podium, and went back to his seat next to the defendant.

Alan Johnson, Savannah Liddel, Simona Callahan Testimony

JUDGE NEITHERCUT LOOKED up from his paperwork and spoke. "In the case numbered 04-013968, the State of Michigan versus Kimberly Angenette Morgan, I hereby call the jury to order." Peering over his glasses, he scanned the courtroom. "Any persons giving testimony or witnessing during the trial, please leave the room now, so as to not be unduly influenced by the testimony about to be given."

Mary stood and left the room because she would be called as a witness. As she did, Ms. Morgan watched her leave. Sitting quietly and composed, she was dressed in a rebel blue-gray mock turtleneck knit top and slacks set, with clean white canvass slip-on shoes without any socks. Her hair was closely cropped, and she wore no makeup.

--- ◉◉◉ ---

"Please state your name."

"My name is Alan Johnson."

He was a tall professional-looking man somewhere around thirty, wearing a short-sleeved cotton shirt and tan chinos. He was blinking quite often as if his contact lenses were bothering him. The prosecuting attorney walked up to the podium to begin her questioning.

"Mr. Johnson, can you tell me where you were on July the second of 2003?"

"I was at work, at the Ennis Children's Center in Flint. I am employed there."

His remarks were delivered in a rather staccato manor, quickly sounding, as if he was irritated.

OK, Mr. Johnson. Tell me, how did you get to work that day?"

"I walked."

"I see, and how'd you get home?"

"I took the bus."

"Can you tell me what happened next?"

"Well, I got off from the bus at Grand Traverse and Third streets. I started to walk down Third Street, and then I noticed a car was parked on Fourth."

"Was that unusual, Mr. Johnson?"

"No, there were cars stalled or parked there quite often."

"Go on."

"As I approached Fourth Street I saw that this car had begun to move, and then it pull-t in front of me, and it tried to impede my progress. I tried to move around behind the car. I had on my sunglasses. I thought I saw a young black man inside. I thought he wanted to try and sell me some drugs, or something."

"OK, what happened next?"

"Well, the window went down, and then I saw a gun get pull-t, and I begun to run away from the vehicle. I was holding my personal organizer and a bag full of bars of soap that I dropped and ran. I was shot in the stomach. There were about four or five more shots fired, and I ran down an alley trying to get away. The car chased me down the alley, to a parking lot from an old grocery store. I went behind a tree to hide, as it was the only place. There was a big wooden fence, and a dog was barking on the other side of it. I think they tried to reload the gun right then, and then I heard sirens and knew the police were coming."

"Were you shot again, Mr. Johnson?"

"Yes. I was shot twice, once in the stomach and once in the shoulder." He was definitely perturbed now. "It was broad daylight and there was people out standing on their porches, just watching. I yelled at them to call the police. Then I got up and ran down an alley toward Mason Street. When I had got there, I saw the car again; it had come around the corner. It tried to run me over! Then it fishtailed and I got away. I ran into a field; the car stopped by that time. Then

I heard the police coming and the car drove off. I was shot in the shoulder and didn't even know it."

"Mr. Johnson, do you know a Kimberly Morgan? Can you point her out?"

"Yes."

"Mr. Johnson do you see her in this courtroom?"

Raising his right arm, he pointed at Ms. Morgan without looking at her. "That is her right there."

"May the record show that Alan has identified Ms. Kimberly Morgan."

"Yes," the judge said flatly.

"Have you seen her before?"

"Yes, at the Flint Public Library. This person approached me and told me who she was."

"What did she tell you?"

"She said that Savannah and her was having problems, and that they were working on them and trying to get back together. To tell you the truth, I was only listening because I have a daughter with Savannah, and she's involved. I was quite surprised to hear that Savannah was involved with a lesbian relationship. I didn't even know she was one."

"When did you start seeing Savannah?"

"A…March of 2003."

"When did you hear from Ms. Morgan again?"

"Well, I was dating Savannah when she got a couple phone calls one night that upset her. I answered the next call, spoke with her, and suggested that she come over and we could talk this out."

"Did she come over?"

"No."

"When you talked to the police, after you were shot, what description did you give them?"

"Possibly, could have been, young male, wasn't sure; could have a mustache, short hair, dark skin. I wasn't looking for a description."

"OK. What color was the car?"

"Dark blue, four-door, believe it was a Buick."

"Any doubt that this person was trying to kill you?"

"No! No doubt in my mind," Alan emphatically replied.

Mrs. Hanson handed a group of photographs to Mr. Johnson and asked him to identify them. He noted that they were the car used in the shooting, the street where he got off from the bus, the street where he was shot the first time, the fence where he was trapped, the vacant lot where he hid, an alley he was chased down, and the four-fold planner that he dropped while fleeing.

Mrs. Hanson asked that they be entered into evidence, and with Mr. Beauvais not having any objections, the judge flatly said, "Admitted."

⋅⊶⩴⦵ ⦵⩵⊷⋅

It was now defense attorney Beauvais's turn to question the witness.

"What day did this all take place, Mr. Johnson?"

"The second or third of July, 2003."

"Approximately what time was it?"

"About five-oh-seven, something like that."

Mr. Beauvais pressed Alan to clarify the difference between Fifth Avenue and Fifth Street, and Second Avenue, where he was shot, and Second Street, where he worked. He also asked what bus he took home. He truly was a stickler for details.

"Mr. Johnson, didn't you think the car was stopping for directions? Did you tell the police that you thought they were stopping you for directions?"

"Yes. Correct," Alan curtly replied.

"Did you then walk toward the car, and then the window went down?"

"Correct."

"Did you tell the police that you looked in and saw a young black man was the driver, in his early twenties?"

"Yes, I do believe that is what I said."

Mr. Beauvais was writing down notes. As he did, Alan volunteered, "People do ax for directions, but do not act in that peculiar a manner."

"Did you then say, 'This person had a nice haircut, dark complexion, and weighed approximately one hundred fifty pounds?"

"Yes, something like that."

"Mr. Johnson, would you please stand and lift your shirt to show the courtroom where the bullet entered your torso, turn, and show where it exited your back." Obediently standing, he lifted his shirt to reveal his lean brown torso, and showed where the bullet went "through-and-through."

"Thank you. You've claimed that you had seen Ms. Morgan on only one occasion, at the Flint Public Library. How long before this event would this have been?"

"About six months, I guess."

"How long did she talk to you?"

"About twenty to thirty minutes."

"You were shot again? Where?"

"In the shoulder."

"Where did this happen?"

"I don't remember. Not on the Fourth Street spot."

"Nothing further, Judge."

⟶◉ ◉⟵

Prosecutor Karen Hanson took the podium again. "Alan, do you know how Savannah and Kim's relationship ended? Was it peaceful?"

"No! It wasn't peaceful."

"Your Honor, this is hearsay!" Attorney Beauvais shot out of his seat, strongly objecting.

"Sustained," said the judge, flatly.

"I will rephrase that. Did Kim tell you, at the library, how well things were going between her and Savannah?"

"No."

"No more questions for this witness, Your Honor. I now ask that Savannah Liddell be sworn in."

Alan exited the witness chair, the lobby door opened, and a petite young black woman entered. Her straightened hair was neatly pulled into a fat black ponytail. She was attractive and dignified, well-dressed in a modestly tailored navy skirt and a crisp and neatly ironed white cotton blouse. She wore conservative gold earrings and minimal makeup.

-·)═● ●═(·-

"Please say and spell your name for the record," Mrs. Hanson asked.

"S, A, V, A, double N, A, H, L, I, double D, E, L," she said in a singsong manner.

"Do you work, Ms. Liddel?"

"Yes, at Mazel's, on Dort Highway."

"Is there a cross street there?"

"Yes. Dort Highway and Atherton."

"Are there any other businesses around there?"

"Yes."

"Where is the Walgreens, in relationship to where you work?"

"Right across the street, on the corner."

"OK...do you have any children?"

"Yes, two."

"Your youngest has Alan Johnson for her father. Is that right?"

"Yes. Alan is her father."

"What is your relationship with Alan?"

"We are dating."

"Did you know a Kimberly Morgan?"

"Yes, I do," she simply replied, clearly irritated at just being there.

"Please point out Ms. Morgan."

The witness nodded her head in Ms. Morgan's direction without looking at her.

"Savannah, how do you know Kimberly Morgan?"

"She was my ex-lover."

A buzz of whispering traveled through the courtroom like a stiff breeze.

"And when were you lovers?"

Savannah looked up, as if trying to recall. "I guess I met Kim July of 2000. We dated for a year."

"At any time did you live together?"

"Yes. We lived together as a couple."

"Was it happy, or was it violent?"

"Only verbal," Savannah answered, making a sour face and clearly annoyed at the question.

"When did you break up?"

"2001."

"Did you see her after this time? Did the defendant come to your home at any time, when you didn't want her to?"

"She started to vandalize my home, broke out my car windows, tried to kick down my door."

"OK…what did you do?"

"I called the police and got a personal protection order against her. She would call me at home, at work, on my cell phone, and harass me."

"I see. Were you working on July 2, 2003?"

"Yes."

"What time?"

"I believe about nine o'clock. I am not certain."

"When did you hear about Alan being shot?"

"They called me from the hospital. I couldn't believe he was shot."

"Did you end it with the defendant?"

"I ended it! She used to come to my house and work, harass me at my job," she said, clearly perturbed as her face darkened and scrunched up.

"Did she tell you she'd moved to Tennessee? And did you see her on the second of July, 2003?"

"I did not see her, that I recall, on that day."

"Did you tell her where Alan worked?"

"No!"

"At what time did she learn that you and Alan were together?"

"She learned that night when she called and Alan answered the phone. She kept calling and calling. I kept hanging up on her, and eventually I turned the phone off."

"Was she moody?"

"Yes. Sometimes she'd be all right, and then all of a sudden she would be like this whole other person. If things didn't go her way she got possessive, and things."

"Thank you, Miss Liddel. No more questions, Your Honor."

⋆⊶ ⊷⋆

Mr. Beauvais rose and assumed the podium, grasping it firmly with both hands.

"Miss Liddel, when did you first meet Ms. Morgan?"

"I believe that would be 2000, of July."

"And how was it that the two of you connected?"

"We met through a mutual friend, Tawana Houston."

"When did you became more than friends?"

"I guess that was July." She seemed to think quite hard before replying, "I guess…it was July."

"So it started quite quickly?"

"Yes."

"When did you start seeing Alan Johnson? You have a child with Mr. Johnson, don't you? How old is that child?"

"The girl is two."

"Where do you work?"

"Mazel's Outlet Store, on Dort Highway."

"Did you and Ms. Morgan move in together?"

"Yes, we did."

"And there was this child, by Alan Johnson? Any other children?"

"I have three children altogether."

Mr. Beauvais continued to write things down while asking each question. Ms. Morgan leaned her elbows on the table, propping up her head and appearing to be quite bored with the whole thing. Mr. Beauvais asked a few more tedious questions, and then announced, "I have no more questions for the witness."

⋆⊶ ⊷⋆

"Stand and stretch!" Judge Neithercut said, surprising the restless jury. They obediently stood and stretched while waiting for the next witness to appear. A couple of minutes later a young woman was escorted into the courtroom and seated in the witness chair. The prosecutor resumed.

⊸⟩═◉ ◉═⟨⊶

"Please state your name, and spell it for the court record."

"Simona Callahan," stated the young black woman, probably not yet thirty. She was tidy but casually dressed in an oversize blue T-shirt and black jean slacks.

"Let me take you back to September 3, 2003. Were you in the area of Mr. Lucky's Nightclub on Lapeer Road, in the city of Flint? Anything unusual happen?"

"I was comin' down Lapeer Road, and I look to my left and I seen this dark smoke comin' from behind Mr. Lucky's, and I seen a female walkin' from behind there and go into the apartment complex parking lot across the street."

"Do you recall what that apartment complex is called?"

"Green Ridge Apartments."

"And where is that in location to Mr. Lucky's?"

"Across the street."

"What did you see this person do then?"

"I pull-t into the building, parked, an' was just looking over there. She was just comin' from in back of there, comin' through the street, an' then she walk behind the apartments, an' walk right pass the van I was sittin' in."

"Can you describe that person?"

"About my height, hair was cut short, curled at the top, short on the sides, had on some dark shades."

"Did you give the police a description they could use in a composite sketch?"

"Yes."

The courtroom door opened and Detective Schmitzer appeared. Mrs. Hanson walked back to meet him. After having a small exchange, they both returned to the courtroom. The detective took a seat at the prosecutor's table, and that was where he would remain for the duration of the trial. Mrs. Hanson resumed her place at the podium.

"Thank you for your testimony, Miss Callahan. I have nothing further for this witness, Your Honor."

Mr. Beauvais stood and quizzed the witness at some length about what side of the street she was on and her recollection of the facts, and then she was dismissed.

Sergeant Joel Grahn Testimony

Prosecutor Hanson stood, resuming her place at the podium. "I request that Sergeant Joel Grahn be admitted as the next witness."

I immediately recognized the police officer as he walked in. He was the man whom Mary and I placed the second missing persons report with, on the Fourth of July in 2003. Once seated in the witness chair, he was sworn in. He was a very sturdy man, with a thick flattop black haircut and a dark heavy mustache. Today he was wearing "street clothes," a navy blue suit, white shirt, and dark necktie. He appeared to be is his mid-thirties.

⊷⊷⊙ ⊙⊷⊶

Prosecuting Attorney Hanson asked the officer, "Would you please state and spell your name for the record."

"J, O, E, L, G, R, A, H, N."

"And what is your occupation?"

"I am a police officer, with the Mundy Township Police Department. I have been there since 1991, for approximately thirteen years now."

"During the early part of July 2003, were you involved with a missing person's investigation?"

"Yes I was, for a Dorothy Murphy."

"And did you get any leads as to Dorothy Murphy's whereabouts?"

"Not originally, no, we didn't develop any leads. It had not been broadcast that she had been missing."

"I'm handing you what is proposed as people's exhibit number one. Do you recognize who is in this picture? Who is that a picture of?"

Taking the picture, he examined it and then answered, "Its Alan Johnson. He is a victim of a shooting, near Grand Traverse and Fourth, in the city of Flint."

"OK," she said, retrieving the photo from the officer and walking it over to Mr. Beauvais. He had no objections, and it was shared with the jury and then entered into evidence as people's exhibit number one. "Were you involved with the investigation of the shooting of Alan Johnson also?"

"It was, in fact, learned, that the vehicle used in the drive-by shooting of Alan Johnson was indeed Mrs. Murphy's vehicle that was reported missing."

"Was that vehicle found, and where?"

"It was located in the twenty-three hundred block of Lapeer Road, in the city of Flint. It was burned completely up."

Walking toward him with another photograph, she asked, "Does this look like that vehicle you examined? And... why does it look yellow? The car was blue, wasn't it?"

"Yes, the vehicle was blue. It was burned severely in the arson, and it's yellowed now because all the paint burned off. It's oxidizing from sitting out in the impound yard."

"I move to have the photo entered into evidence as people's exhibit number two. Do you recall if there was anything recovered from that vehicle?"

"Yes, there was several items recovered. One of them was Dorothy Murphy's purse, her credit cards, and ID. And also, inside the purse was a spent .380 shell casing."

"Sergeant, at some point was a composite sketch made of the person seen leaving that vehicle?"

"Yes. During the investigation there was a witness, a person was seen walking away, across Lapeer Road, near the time of the burning of the vehicle, and that witness helped complete the composite sketch."

"I am handing you what is proposed as people's exhibit number three and asking if you recognize that."

"Yes, I do. That's the composite sketch completed by the composite technician, city of Flint police department, of the person the witness seen crossing Lapeer Road."

"Sergeant, was that sketch shown on television?"

"Yes, it was."

"And was Dorothy Murphy ever located?"

"Yes, she was located, in a cul-de-sac on River Oaks Drive, in Flint Township."

"Did you go to that scene?"

"Yes, I did."

"I'm handing you what has been proposed as people's exhibit's four, five, six, and asking you if recognize these. What are they?"

"Yes, these are the aerial photographs taken in the area around where Dorothy Murphy was located."

"Your Honor, I would like to enter these photos as people's exhibits four, five, and six, as evidence."

With Mr. Beauvais not objecting to them, they were then shared with the jury, and the judge acknowledged. "So entered."

"Officer Grahn, when speaking with the defendant, did you ever find that she had lived in this vicinity?"

"Yes. She lived in the River Forest Apartments, just one street over from there. The defendant told me herself that she once lived there."

"So you know Kimberly Morgan, and you had conversations with her?"

"Yes."

"Do you see her in this courtroom?"

"She is seated right there, in the blue shirt," he said while turning to the right and pointing a finger in her direction without looking. "I had several conversations with her."

"Did you in fact go to the defendant's current address, in Tennessee? And why did you go there?"

"I went there to execute a search warrant on her apartment in Nashville. Her apartment is a duplex -style residence. She was living in the front, and her black Probe was parked out front."

"Sergeant, I am handing you what is marked as people's exhibits seven, eight, nine, and asking if you recognize these and what they are," she said while passing them to him.

Accepting the photos, he closely examined them before speaking. "The first photo is of her apartment. The second is in her bedroom, of an entertainment center there. The third photograph is of her black Ford Probe, parked out front of her place."

"Now, Officer Grahn, I'm handing you a photo that is marked as exhibit ten, and asking if you recognize this."

"Yes, that's a photo of Dorothy Murphy's remains," he said, looking and quickly turning away. "Sergeant, is that the way you saw Dorothy's remains that day?"

"Yes. It was on September 26, 2003. I arrived around two o'clock, and I was there before she was removed."

The photo was shared with attorney Beauvais, who stood to address the officer. "Sergeant, I just want to ascertain if you saw the remains *just* as they are in this picture."

"Yes, I did. It was before anybody had removed them, or anything like that."

"I have no objections then."

"At that point the investigation becomes someone else's. Is that correct?"

"Yes."

The prosecutor handed him another photograph. "Now, when you went down to Tennessee, to the defendant's apartment, what did you find in the entertainment center that is pictured in that photograph?"

"There we found a Michigan license plate, hidden behind a shelf. Earlier that plate was reported missing in Michigan, and then later seen on the defendant's vehicle during a traffic stop in Indiana, on July the second, 2003."

"You indicated you also found a black Ford Probe down there. Is that correct?"

"Yes, I found the car parked out front of the apartment."

"And what, if anything, did you find inside that car?"

"Inside I found clothing, miscellaneous emergency equipment, shoes, and items like that. We searched the vehicle and then had it towed back to Mundy

Township. Inside were several items of clothing. One was the short-sleeved yellow shirt that was described by the eyewitness."

"Officer, I am handing you a bag and asking you to open it; please identify the item inside." She handed him the brown paper bag. The judge handed him a pair of blue handled scissors. Taking them, he opened the bag, looked inside, and handed the scissors back to the judge. "It's a yellow polo-style shirt. The same one we removed from the vehicle."

Prosecutor Hanson took the wrinkled yellow shirt and held it up for the jury to view. She then handed another brown paper bag to the officer. "What is in this bag? Please remove and identify it."

"This is the license plate recovered from her apartment, Two, David, one, David, one, seven." He then held it up for the courtroom to view.

"Your Honor, I would like to enter these items as people's evidence numbers eleven and twelve."

"So ordered," the judge said, never looking up.

"Sergeant, at some point in time, did you talk to the defendant about Dorothy's car and her remains?"

"Yes, I did. Originally it was a lead brought to us by a female named Savannah Liddel. And the defendant, during the course of the investigation, could not be eliminated. Originally she was thought to be in Indiana at the time of the shootings.

"Speaking with the defendant, she believed she was in the Flint area, but it was on the thirtieth of June; she was unsure of the date. After speaking to her at a later time, she recollected that she was in Flint on July first or the second. She was stopped by the Indiana State Police and received a speeding ticket, just south of South Bend. Afterwards I viewed a video of that traffic stop. It was learned at that time that she was, in fact, able to be in the Flint area at the time of the shootings, and she was headed south on I-69, going back to Nashville."

"OK. Thank you, Officer. Nothing further at this time."

Mary Testifies

T<small>AKING THE WITNESS</small> chair was our sister, Mary Ann. She was dressed in a two-piece blue crepe jacket and skirt ensemble. She looked professional, composed, but to me she looked nervous. Her recently highlighted hair made her appear suntanned, but in actuality her cheeks were red and flushed, indicating that she was stressed. Her little hands were neatly folded together and resting on her lap.

Judge Neithercut swore her in, and then Prosecuting Attorney Hanson rose to address her.

⋅⇒◉ ◉⇐⋅

"Could you say and spell your name for the record, please."

"Mary Deering. The last name is spelled D, E, E, R, I, N, G."

"And, Mary, do you know a Dorothy Murphy?"

"Dorothy is my mother."

"OK…um…how many sons does Dorothy have, and what are their names? And what about daughters, are there any other daughters?"

"She had three sons, Timothy, Daniel, and Michael. I am the only daughter."

"Does she have any grandchildren?"

"Yes, four."

"And where did your mother live?"

"At 311 Loyalist Lane, Flint, Michigan. That's in Mundy Township."

"Mary, I'm handing you what is proposed as people's exhibit number fifteen and I will ask you if you recognize this."

"Yes, it's a picture of my mother, Dorothy Murphy, taken about four years ago."

"Mary, at some point in time, your mother was discovered missing. Do you recall when that was?"

Speaking deliberately and slowly, Mary replied, "On July 2 I went to her house and I knew she wasn't there, but I didn't know if she was out playing cards or something. It was on July 3 that I discovered she had not been home the night before."

"How did you find that out?"

"I dropped off some stuff at her house on July 2, on the countertop. And I left a message on her machine. Um…the next morning I called and she wasn't there. I asked my daughter to stop on her way out of town, to see if the items I left on the counter were still there, and she called me and told me they were."

"Is that unusual?"

"Yes. It is not like my mother to leave town and not tell anyone she is leaving."

"OK… Do you know if your mother had an appointment on July 2?"

"She had a doctor's appointment in the afternoon on July 2. When I got there, on July 3, I pushed the play button on the answering machine. My message I left was still on there, and there was a message from the doctor's office, asking why she missed her appointment."

"Whaddya do at that point?"

"At that point I called my brothers. One was on vacation. Then I called the other two to ask if they knew where she was. I also called the senior center, the place where she played cards, to see if she was there. I called some of her friends, some of her relatives, and then I went home and called the police."

"Did you ever find your mother?"

"No," Mary said flatly.

"At some point in time, did you discover that your mother had been killed?"

Mary looked up, as if to recall, and then she began speaking slowly. "On Sunday the sixth, they called us into the police station. That's when they found her car. It had been torched. That's when we came to the conclusion that she was gone."

"What happened over the course of the next few months, if anything?"

"Intensive searches. We organized a community ground search to look for her. Sometimes people would call us if they had dreams, and my family and I would go and check. The family had a benefit to raise reward money, to come up with a reward fund, to come up with information."

"At some point in time, did you discover that your mother's remains had been found?"

"On September 27, we received a phone call that they found skeletal remains, and they thought that they were hers, but they would have to do some testing."

"Do you recall the kind of car Dorothy was driving?"

"It was a 1998 four-door Buick Century."

"And, did she usually wear any jewelry?"

"Yes... It would depend. Generally she wore a necklace...um, and generally wore a wristwatch. If it was a day that she was going to church, maybe a pin on her jacket, earrings, or something like that."

Mrs. Hanson approached Mary and handed her another package. "Mary, I'm handing you what is proposed as people's exhibit number fourteen, and I'll ask if you could open it. Do you recognize this?"

Mary, taking scissors from the judge, opened the package. Reaching inside, she removed the contents. "It's a wristwatch. It looks similar to an everyday watch that my mother had."

"You can put it back," Mrs. Hanson said. Retrieving the envelope, she carried it over to Mr. Beauvais. He examined it and had no objections, and it was shared with the jury and entered into evidence.

"Mary, I'm handing you what is identified as people's exhibit number fifteen, and asking if you can identify it as well."

Mary again cut the envelope open, removed the contents, and examined it. "Yes, this is the small aquamarine birthstone necklace that my mother wore."

Mrs. Hanson took the envelope and handed it to Mr. Beauvais. He had no objections, and it was shared with the jury and logged in.

"Mary, do you know what type of shoes your mother wore on a typical day?"

"Generally a leather lace-up shoe, like a walking shoe."

"What about sunglasses? Did your mother wear sun-glasses?"

"She had cataract surgery in May, and so she had to wear these large dark-colored glasses which fit over her regular glasses. They wrap around the sides."

"When was the last time you spoke to your mom?"

"On the evening of July 1."

"OK. I will show you what is proposed as people's exhibit number sixteen and ask you if you can identify this."

"This is the outside of my mother's house, on Loyalist Lane."

"Mary, how long did your mom live there?"

"About fourteen years, I think."

"Now, does she normally park in that spot shown in the picture?"

"Yes."

"You had mentioned that your mother was a religious person, is that correct?"

"Yes, it is."

"Mary, would it be common for your mom to tell people that she would pray for them?"

"Yes, if you told her you were troubled about something, or having a problem, she might tell you that she would pray for you."

"Thank you for your testimony, Mary." Turning to the judge, she said, "Nothing further at this time, Your Honor."

⋅⊷⊷⊷ ⊶⊶⋅

Attorney Philip Beauvais III rose and assumed the podium.

"Now, Mrs. Deering…um…does that car in the picture belong to anyone that you know?"

"Yes," Mary said. "It's the car of a friend."

"Your mother's car was a blue Buick. Is that correct?"

"Yes, it's a medium blue."

Mr. Beauvais was taking more notes; he was always writing things down. "Do you recall approximately when you called the Mundy Township Police to report your mother missing?"

"It was in the afternoon on July 3, 2003. It was a Wednesday."

"Your mother had a doctor's appointment that day. Is that correct? And why was she going there?"

"Yes, she had an appointment for a check-up on the Friday a week before, but had to reschedule because of a funeral. She was feeling like she had a kidney infection, and she was going to see her doctor that Wednesday, at two."

"Did you speak to her on this morning?"

"No."

"Your mother had cataract surgery and that's why she wore those dark glasses. Is that correct?"

"Yes, she wore the dark glasses over her eyeglasses when she went in the sun."

"I have nothing further," Mr. Beauvais flatly announced, returning to his seat.

⋅→══ ══←⋅

Mrs. Hanson once again assumed her place at the podium. "Mary, did your mother frequent the Dort and Atherton Road area?"

"There are a couple stores that she went to over there on a regular basis."

"I am sorry for your loss."

Turning toward the judge, she said, "I have nothing further, Your Honor."

⋅→══ ══←⋅

Mary was escorted down from the witness stand, and she rejoined us in the gallery. Mrs. Hanson turned to the court announcing, "At this time we call David Filmon to the stand."

I watched as Mother's neighbor was escorted in. I thought it rather peculiar to see him here now, because when we were encamped outside Mother's trailer for nearly three months he barely spoke a word to us.

⋅→══ ══←⋅

"Please say and spell your name, for the record."

"David Filmon, that's, David, F, I, L, M, O, N."

"Now, where do you live at?"

"I live at Chateau Torrey Hill, in Mundy Township; it's a mobile home park."

"OK. Do you know a Dorothy Murphy, and how?"

"As a neighbor, she lives, er lived, right across the street from me. We talked as neighbors do from time to time."

Approaching the witness, she handed him several photos. "Your Honor, I bring people's exhibits seventeen, eighteen, nineteen, and twenty. Do you recognize these photos, Mr. Filmon?"

"This is Mrs. Murphy's house, this is my house, this is her carport, and this is the street between."

"Did you see Dorothy Murphy July second 2003?"

"Yes. I was standing in the front bedroom of my trailer, which faces the street. It was just by chance that I saw her. I was opening a window on that morning and I saw her backing out, as I have seen her do so many times before."

"You're sure it was Dorothy, and she was alone?"

"There was no doubt that it was Dorothy, and she appeared to be alone. It was between eight thirty and nine o'clock, I would guess."

Mrs. Hanson thanked him for his testimony and took her seat.

⋅⇥⊜ ⊜⇤⋅

Mr. Beauvais took the podium, and discussed the photos of the carport, its proximity to his trailer, and where she parked. Then he announced that he had nothing further for this witness and returned to his seat.

⋅⇥⊜ ⊜⇤⋅

After a brief pause, the next witness was escorted in and then sworn in by the judge. Mrs. Hanson took the podium and began.

⋅⇥⊜ ⊜⇤⋅

"Please state your name and spell it for the record."

The next witness was an attractive, young, and light-skinned black man dressed in a nice navy blue suit. He wore thick eyeglasses, and his neat wavy hair is short.

"My name is Terry, L, E, W, I, S."

"And where do you work, Mr. Lewis?"

"For the city of Flint, in the police department."

"How long have you worked there?"

"Going into my seventh year."

"Were you working on July the second, 2003?"

"Yes, I was on second shift."

"Were you called to respond to a shooting on the corners of Grand Traverse and Third Avenue on July 2, 2003?"

"Yes, I did. Me and my partner, Brian Murfrey, found the victim, who was identified as Alan Johnson, apparently suffering from recent bullet wounds. He sat on a yellow park-ing bump in the parking lot of the Pickwick Party Store. It is on the corner of Third Avenue and Grand Traverse."

"Do you recognize what this photograph is; people's exhibit number twenty-one?"

"It appears to be Alan Johnson, the man who was shot."

"What happened to Alan after you got there?"

"Quickly, I got some suspect info from him as to what occurred, how he came to suffer from two gunshot wounds, and then he was transferred to Hurley Hospital."

"Did you investigate the area where he was shot?"

"After more patrolmen entered the scene, we informed them of the situation. Then we checked the Third and Mason Street scene, because it was evident that the spot where Alan was located was not the origin of this shooting."

"People wish to enter into evidence numbers twenty-one, twenty-two, and twenty-three." She handed the photos to the officer and he identified them as the original shooting scene, the secondary scene of the shooting, and the party store where Alan was found. They were shared with the jury and entered into evidence.

"Please explain these photos."

"About a block east from where the victim was found I found a witness and what appears to be a spent .380-caliber, semiautomatic shell casing, the victim's day planner, and a plastic grocery sack with what appeared to be soap and personal care items."

Handing a Ziploc baggie to the officer, she asked him to identify the contents.

"Yes, I recognize these items. This is one spent round and a shell casing; located in the area of Fourth and Grand Traverse Street." They were then entered into evidence.

"OK. After you got this call did you receive another call, Officer Lewis?"

"Yes, we did. A vehicle matching the description of the vehicle that was used in the shooting was located on Lapeer Road fully engulfed in flames."

"Did you respond to that scene? And what did you find once you got there?"

"We found the Flint Fire Department had all ready extinguished a vehicle fire, and it was the charred chassis of a midsized, four-door vehicle; could not make out the color of it because of the damage. I found the emblem for the vehicle. It was a Buick Century, four-door."

"What did you do with the evidence that you found at the shooting scene?"

"I collected that evidence, put it into envelopes, while not touching it with my fingers, and turned it over to IB tech Cathy Knight as evidence to be held for prints."

"OK. Nothing further at this time."

⋅⊷⊙ ⊙⊶⋅

Mr. Beauvais assumed the podium. "Officer Lewis, you said at that date you were working second shift. Could you clarify that to us laypeople?"

Looking at him rather oddly, he responded, "Second shift is late shift; it starts at three forty-five and runs to eleven forty-five."

"Approximately what time did you get this call?"

"To be specific I'd have to look at my notes to refresh my memory, but approximately seven hundred hours; 5 p.m."

"You say you went to the party store at Grand Traverse and Third, that correct?"

"Yes."

Attorney Beauvais then made another big spiel about the difference between the streets and avenues. He took great pains asking about the locations, and took copious notes. Officer Lewis responded patiently and accurately to all of his tedious inquiries."Did you get a description from the man that was shot by the shooter?"

"He said it appeared to be an African-American subject, approximately nineteen or twenty years, and average weight. He couldn't quite tell, because the person was over on the driver's side, and he was opposite. Shots were being fired; he was frantic while trying to run in the opposite direction."

Mr. Beauvais then went on to once more verify all the facts Mrs. Hanson covered earlier, belaboring particulars of the incident's location, vehicle description, and the evidence. After making more notes, he finally announced, "I have no further questions for this witness, Your Honor."

⋆⟞⟐ ⟐⟝⋆

Mrs. Hanson walked up to Officer Lewis and handed him a piece of paper. "Do you think that reviewing your notes may make it easier for you to remember the specific time you took that call?" she said while looking directly at attorney Beauvais.

After reading from the page, the officer glanced up, smiled, and confidently responded, "Yes, it was five-oh-eight."

"Nothing further, Judge."

⋆⟞⟐ ⟐⟝⋆

"All right. Court is now adjourned for lunch. We will resume at one thirty sharp," the judge said, quickly exiting stage right.

The jury was escorted out, the defendant was taken away, and the remainder of the courtroom filtered out. Collecting as a large group, we walked across the street to the Masonic Temple for lunch. Being much too wound up, I didn't have much of an appetite and only poked at my food. While dining we all discussed this morning's trial. Afterward Linda and I went outside to smoke as many cigarettes as possible before the trial's resumption.

Detective Mark Reaves Testifies

AT 1:33 THE judge sat with his glasses on his head, anxiously tapping his fingers upon his big desk and impatiently waiting for Mrs. Hanson to begin her questioning the next witness. Detective Mark Reaves, a Michigan State Policeman who was assigned to Flint's Violent Crimes Task Force, as already sworn in and seated. He was relatively short for a policeman. He appeared to be around my age, and his graying and thinning hair was cut into a flattop. Wearing a winter-weight wool tweed jacket, he fidgeted with the tie of his too-tight white shirt collar while waiting to give his testimony.

>⊨⊙ ⊙⊨⊷

Prosecutor Hanson finally began. "Detective, were you involved with the investigation of the missing person complaint of Dorothy Murphy?"

"Yes, I was involved in the investigation. I have been assigned to the Violent Crimes Task Force in the city of Flint for over three years now."

"Detective, did this investigation lead you to an Alan Johnson?"

"Yes it did. I investigated the scene of the drive-by shooting of an Alan Johnson in conjunction with Officer Terry Coon of the Flint Police Department. I visited the shooting scene on several occasions."

"Did you also investigate the arson of the vehicle of Dorothy Murphy?"

"Yes. I investigated the vehicle while it was at Complete Towing, on Dort Highway."

"Do you know where that arson occurred?"

"That investigation led me to Mr. Lucky's Nightclub, on Lapeer Road, in the twenty-six hundred block, Flint, Michigan."

"Did you also investigate the distance between the shooting scene of Alan Johnson and the arson of Dorothy Murphy's vehicle behind Mr. Lucky's?"

"Yes I did. It is between five and ten minutes' drive. MapQuest says it is two point four miles."

"Did you examine the vehicle at Complete Towing?"

"Yes. Because my police experience has taught me, you go back to where you believe the incident took place, and that's where you will find the most evidence. The most evidence to be found was in that car."

"And, did you find any evidence in that car?"

"Yes I did. In mid-August, myself and Detective Coon from the Flint Police Department went to that car. We put on sterile gloves and sifted through the ashes with our hands. At that time, I noticed broken glass down inside the driver's door, and I sifted through the right-hand passenger side of the car floor. I found what appeared to be a small off-white lotion bottle, partially burned and heated by the fire. I took it to the crime lab in Bridgeport, for DNA testing."

Mrs. Hanson approached the witness, handing him a photograph. "Detective, you recognize this?"

"Yes I do. That's a photo of the bottle I found in Mrs. Murphy's car, taken on August 29 of 2003. I sent that to the state lab in Lansing for DNA testing. First I had it sent to the State Police Bridgeport crime lab because that is our regional lab, but they were backed up, so I requested that it be sent to Lansing, to the state lab for DNA testing."

"Detective, I am handing you what is people's exhibit number forty-seven. Will you please open the manila envelope and tell me if you recognize it?"

Putting on blue latex gloves, he opened the sealed package and then carefully removed its contents using tweezers. It appeared to me to be a tube of Vaseline petroleum jelly with a screw-off top.

"Yes I do. This is the evidence envelope, and it contains the lotion container found in Mrs. Murphy's vehicle."

"Is that the lotion bottle you found under the insulation and ashes inside Mrs. Murphy's car?"

"Yes, it is."

"Your Honor, I would like to enter people's exhibit number forty-seven into evidence."

"Detective Reaves, did you find anything else inside that vehicle?"

"At a later search, in August 2003, myself along with Detective Joel Grahn from the Mundy Township Police screened the entire contents of that car. Whatever was left in the ashes of the car was screened several times."

"What else did you find?"

"Spent bullet casings, more glass, cigarette butts, pieces of carpet, and debris that was somewhat protected because some of the insulation from the ceiling fell on top of it, protecting it."

"OK. I am handing you people's exhibits numbered forty-eight and forty-nine and asking you to identify them."

"That's a picture of a trowel we used to sift the ashes, and a spent bullet casing."

"And, where was this found at?"

"Inside of Mrs. Murphy's vehicle."

"So, Detective Reaves, do you know who did this testing?"

"Yes I do, but she's Indian and I don't know how to say her name. I only know her nickname." The courtroom chuckled.

"Um…OK…now, during the course of your investigation did you discover where Savannah Liddel worked at, on July the second of 2003?"

"Yes, Mazel's."

Prosecutor Hanson handed him another photo and asked him to identify it.

Detective Reaves responded, "That photograph is the Walgreens store on the corner of Dort Highway and Atherton Road in the city of Flint, Michigan."

"Detective Reaves, please explain the proximity of the Walgreens store and the Mazel's store where Miss Liddel worked."

"It is literally just across the street."

"Detective, do you know a Kimberly Morgan? Please point her out to the court." Glancing across the courtroom, he nodded his head in her direction without ever looking at her. "She is seated to the left of her defense attorney."

"Sergeant, did you do any more investigation with Ms. Morgan, and what did you find? In fact, discuss that fact, that the defendant got a ticket in Indiana the night of July 2."

"Kimberly Morgan told me that she had been stopped, so I ordered an NCIC—that's a National Crime Investigation Report—which indicated that her number had been run in Indiana at a traffic stop. I watched the video of the stop that the Indiana State Police made on July the second, 2003."

"Do you recall the approximate time she was stopped?"

"Approximately...8:25 Indiana time. That's about 9:25 Michigan time."

"Did you at some point investigate where Kimberly had previously lived?"

"Yes I did. In years 2000 and 2001, she lived in the River Valley Apartments on Beecher Road, near where Mrs. Murphy's remains were found. She moved to Nashville, Tennessee, in 2002."

"Were you called to the scene when Mrs. Murphy's remains were found?"

"Yes. It was an undeveloped cul-de-sac in River Valley, on a street called River Oak Drive."

"Was the whole body found?"

"No."

"What was missing?"

"For sure, the skull and the upper jaw was missing. There may have been other smaller pieces missing, but I did not know about that."

⊷⊷◉ ◉⊶⊶

Wow. That hit like a ton of bricks. Her skull was missing, and we were just now learning this during the trial. Was it taken? Who took it? Is that what they were searching for during the three days after her remains were removed?

⊷⊷◉ ◉⊶⊶

Mrs. Hanson resumed. "Detective Reaves, do you recall if a DNA sample of the defendant was taken?"

"Yes I do. It was sent to the State Police crime lab in Lansing."

"Do you know if…um, the shell casings you found…what about those?"

"All the shell casings were sent to the Bridgeport crime lab for firearms investigation."

"OK. All right…I have nothing further at this time, Your Honor.

⋯�=◎ ◎=⟩⋯

"Let's take a twenty-minute break," the judge announced, pleasing the court.

The jury was escorted out. Afterward the rest of us trickled out. We could all use a break. Taking full advantage of this pause, Linda, Uncle Gerald, and I all went outside to smoke profusely. Exactly twenty minutes later the jury was escorted back in and seated, and the trial resumed.

Officer Thomas Dujovich Testimony

HERE IS AN observation I will share with you before we return to the testimony. The judge reminded me of the judge from the 1959 movie *Anatomy of a Murder* because he was all business but exhibited a folksy, common, and approachable manner.

Sitting back in his leather chair, he smiled warmly and addressed the jury.

"You're working in a video courtroom. If you'd noticed, there is no stenographer taking down the words. Instead, we have cameras placed in various locations around the room that are voice activated; they work off the microphones."

The next witness entered without an escort. He was a tall, slim, young officer dressed in a pressed khaki-and-brown uniform. "Please come right up here, Officer," the judge said, smiling and motioning for him to approach the witness chair.

⋅⟶◉ ◎⟵⋅

"Please say your name, and spell it for the record," Prosecutor Hanson said.

"Thomas, M. Dujovich. D, U, J, O, V, I, C, H."

"And what is your occupation?"

"I'm a state trooper with the Indiana State Police for eleven years now."

"Were you working as a trooper on July 2, 2003?"

"Yes, I was. From eight thirty at night till four thirty in the morning."

"Do you recall stopping a black Probe that night?"

"Yes I did."

"I am handing you what is proposed as people's exhibit number fifty-two and asking if you can identify it, please."

"Yes. It is a copy of a ticket that I turned into the court, it was given to a Kimberly A. Morgan."

"Does it state what kind of a vehicle she was driving?"

"Yes. She was driving a black Ford Probe, had a Michigan license plate."

"Now, do you see that person sitting in the courtroom? Can you point her out?"

The trooper turned in her direction and nodded. "She is sitting to my left."

"May the record reflect that the witness has identified the defendant."

"Yes," the judge acknowledged.

"Officer, in your car do you have a video recorder? You have it on that night?"

"Yes I did."

"Approximately how long was that stop, do you recall?"

"It was over a half hour."

"Did the plate on that car match the black Probe?"

"No."

"Did you talk to the defendant about that?"

"Yes I did. She stated that she thought the plate on her car was a Tennessee plate, but that someone must have changed them and replaced the Tennessee plate with the Michigan one."

"Um. OK? Did she tell you where she had been?"

"She said she was returning to Tennessee from Flint, Michigan."

"I'm handing you what is proposed as people's exhibit number fifty-three and asking if you recognize this."

"It looks like a copy of the traffic stop I executed."

"OK. Um...was the whole traffic stop recorded?"

The judge, chiming in, looked over his glasses directly at the prosecutor and asked, "Do you intend to play the whole thing?"

"Only part of it, Judge."

The video was projected on a large piece of whiteboard set upon an easel. The audio was rough, and the visual had quality poor. When it was finished, the judge commented, "It was difficult to hear."

"I had a difficult time hearing myself," Mrs. Hanson added, smiling pleasantly. "Do you recall the conversation going on between you and the defendant at that time? And do you recall asking her where she was coming from?"

"Yes, she said she was coming back from Flint. She said she'd left Tennessee the night before. She left from Tennessee, to drive to Michigan. What, I thought, was a long way to be driving for only one day."

"OK. Was there an issue about the plates and the registration of the vehicle?"

"The plates she had did not match the vehicle registration. It ended up being lost or replaced plates. I don't recall what the vehicle was that it came back to."

"OK. Nothing further, Your Honor," the prosecutor said in closing.

⇢═◉ ◉═⇠

"Trooper," attorney Beauvais began before even making it to the podium, "when you write a ticket and you put a time on it, is that the time you stop the person, or the actual time of the violation?"

"Actual time of the violation."

"And how long would it have been from the time you saw her doing eighty-five miles per hour to the time you stopped her?"

"Within a minute or two; I was sitting in a stationary position."

"Where, in terms of...what road were you on?"

"I-69."

"Where on 69?" Mr. Beauvais shot back, clearly perturbed.

"Forty-one-mile marker."

"Forty-one-mile marker means what? You're forty-one miles into Indiana?"

"Forty-one miles north of Indianapolis, and approximately one hundred and twenty miles south of the Michigan line."

"Does 69 end in Indiana?"

"Yes."

"Do you know what time it was that you stopped the vehicle?"

"Believe it was eight twenty-nine. That's what it says on the ticket."

"Now, eight twenty-nine—is that central standard time or eastern standard time?"

"I believe its eastern. For me now, its three forty-eight," he said while glancing at his watch. "So, you're an hour behind where we are. You don't use daylight savings time?"

"We do not."

"Now, you also heard Kimberly Morgan tell you that she had left the state of Tennessee the night before to drive to the state of Michigan."

"From what I heard, yes."

"And that she was in Michigan just long enough to pick up her car and come back. Is that what she said?"

"I believe it had something to do with getting the title," the trooper clarified.

"Nothing further, Judge."

Mr. Beauvais returned to the defendant's table.

⋄⟞⊙ ⊙⟝⋄

It was after five and the trial was coming to an end for the day, so the judge turned his big chair toward the jury members.

"Jurors, you are going to avoid the Lapeer Road area, around Mr. Lucky's, and also the Beecher Road area around where the body had been recovered. *Do not* speak of this trial while you're at home. Be back here tomorrow morning. Trial will resume at ten thirty, sharp."

⋄⟞⊙ ⊙⟝⋄

Then the judge popped out of his chair and disappeared into his chambers. The members of the jury were next escorted out by the bailiff and led back into their jury room. The defendant was placed back into her arm and leg restraints and taken away by the deputy. Afterward everyone else filtered out, ending the first day of the trial.

Whew.

The Second Day of Trial

BEFORE TRIAL COMMENCED we all assembled on the long limestone steps spanning the length of the courthouse. Linda and I were busy building up our nicotine levels, Tim was slurp -ing a huge tub of Coke, Mike was talking on his cell phone, and everyone else was visiting while enjoying the beautiful morning sunshine.

On August 26, 2004, at exactly ten thirty in the morning, we were all seated as the bailiff called the court to order. The defendant, Ms. Morgan, was already seated at the defense table, dressed in the same blue outfit she wore the day before. Today she had her torso twisted so her back was facing us, , a defensive posture she would maintain throughout the remainder of the trial. The jurors were escorted back in and seated, and then the first witness of the day was escorted in, seated, and sworn in.

⋅⊱⊰⊙ ⊙⊱⊰⋅

Prosecutor Hanson confidently assumed the podium. "Could you say and spell your name for the record."

"Richard Gehrig. G, E, H, R, I, G." He was tall, slim, and suntanned, a wholesome young man dressed in a yellow short-sleeved summer shirt with a fine check, and tan Docker type slacks.

"And what is your occupation?"

"I am a machine operator for Consumers Energy."

"Does that lead you to surrounding areas of Genesee County?"

"Yes."

"And were you working in the vicinity of River Oak Street on the day of September 26, 2003?"

"Yes."

"Do you recall approximately what time you were in the area?"

"Yes. It was about one thirty in the afternoon."

"OK. Um…" Mrs. Hanson walked over to the witness and handed him something. "I'll ask you if you recognize this photo. What is that?"

"It's a picture of a subdivision off from River Forest."

"And did you go to that location on September 26, 2003?"

"Yes."

"What, if anything, did you find there?"

"I found a body."

"Go on."

"At first I wasn't quite sure what it was. My first thought was that it was a deer carcass or animal bones. And as I got up closer, I recognized it wasn't. I knew what it was, but had to convince myself of what, exactly, I had found."

"OK…so, do you recognize this photograph as what you found?" she asked while flashing another photograph onto the screen. Thank God the viewing screen was tilted toward the jury, so we didn't have to see the picture of Mother's decomposing body and live with that disturbing image.

"Yes, that's the body I found," he said, looking at the photograph and quickly looking away.

"Does it look like it did the day you found it?"

"Yes," he replied without looking back to be certain.

"Nothing further, Your Honor."

⇥◉ ◉⇤

So this was the man who found Mother. Just like the jury, we were learning the story.

⇥◉ ◉⇤

Attorney Beauvais assumed the podium, shuffled his papers, wrote something down, and then began questioning.

"Curious, Mr. Gehrig, what were your duties that day in September?"

"That day in September we were installing some meters off from the Beecher and Dye area."

"Were there any houses over in the area where you found the body?"

"No."

"Were you looking for lines?"

"No, actually, we had finished up a job and we were on the way back from lunch; I had to relieve myself. From jobs done in that area before, I knew of a private spot where I could stop and go quick."

"You just happened to walk out and walk upon it, is that correct?" Mr. Beauvais asked, sarcastically. "Did you call the police?"

"I walked up on it and, and called my dispatcher, and had her call the police."

"What you did was call your dispatcher; that what you said? Did you touch anything?"

"No!"

"Thank you. Nothing further."

⋅⊱⊷◉ ◉⊶⊰⋅

Prosecuting Attorney Hanson began, "Your Honor, we call Ron Nelson to the stand at this time."

A tall and rather portly man with a ruddy complexion took the stand, wearing a heavy woolen tweed jacket. being late August, I thought that rather peculiar.

⋅⊱⊷◉ ◉⊶⊰⋅

"Please say and spell your name for the record."

"R, O, N, A, L, D, N, E, L, S, O, N."

"And what is your occupation?"

"I am a police officer with the city of Flint's police department. I'm assigned to GAIN, and that is a countywide auto-theft team. I work with stolen vehicles, and I've been with the force since 1977."

For over thirty minutes he described in great detail his examination and identification of the vehicle at Complete Towing. He explained that he identified the vehicle by locating a stamp on the engine's block. After finding that marker he called the Secretary of State to determine the owner's identity. "The car was registered to a Dorothy Murphy."

As usual, attorney Beauvais quizzed him at length about everything. Eventually he seemed to accept his explanations and returned to his seat.

⊷⟝⊚ ⊚⟞⊶

The next witness was shown into the courtroom and sworn in by the judge. Looking to be in her early forties, she was properly dressed in a trim navy blue suit and white button-down shirt. Businesslike, and attractive, she had a telltale smoker's cough, which popped up quite often during testimony.

⊷⟝⊚ ⊚⟞⊶

Assistant Prosecuting Attorney Hanson rose and took the podium. "Please say and spell your name for the record."

"Kathy, pardon, Kathleen Taylor."

"Please tell me what your specialty is, Ms. Taylor."

"I am a specialist with the State Police, in the Fire Investigation Unit. I've been there for three and a half years."

"And what is your area of expertise?"

"My job is to investigate fires, whether accidental or intentional. I specialize in house fires, vehicle fires, etc."

She went on to enumerate all of her training in these areas, stating that she was certified in each one. The court accepted her as an expert witness, after the usual objections and tedious questions posed by Mr. Beauvais.

"At the request of the Mundy Township Police I was directed to view the vehicle and determine the cause of the fire. Going to Complete Towing, I examined the vehicle on two separate occasions. After taking photographs of the torched chassis, I inspected the engine, trunk, and then the interior.

"I sent three samples from the interior of the vehicle to the State Police crime lab in Bridgeport for examination and determination of the substance found therein. A Keith Lambert examined those samples, and he discovered that gasoline was used as the accelerant to set the fire inside the front seat of the car.

"It was also determined that the front seat of the vehicle is the origin of the blaze, and the fire spread from there to the engine, backseat, and trunk. I determined this from the burn pattern. The cause of the fire was incendiary, started on purpose. This was an intentional fire.

"A license plate from Dorothy Murphy's car was located on the floor of the front seat, on the passenger side. Although badly burned and partially melted, it was still recognizable. Also found therein were the keys from the automobile, a key ring with three keys upon it, and Dorothy Murphy's purse.

"I carefully removed the purse from the vehicle, and inside was two credit cards, partially burnt but still recognizable as reading Murphy. Also inside was a gold spent shell casing, which was sent to the Bridgeport crime lab for testing."

"Thank you, Ms. Taylor."

Mr. Beauvais grilled the fire expert at some length about every, single, thing. He was a stickler for details; he asked for specifics about how she did all of her examinations.

Detective Russell Fries Testimony

THE COURTROOM WAITED for the next witness to appear, and while they did the judge turned toward the jury, sat back in his big leather chair, and began to entertain them.

"The beautiful mural you see on the back wall here behind me tells the story of Genesee County in the olden days; it was painted in 1927. And, if you didn't know the history of this place, way back in the old days we didn't have roads in Michigan, and the only way to get around was on the water."

At this point the witness appeared and the judge motioned for him to please step forward. He was sworn in and seated. The prosecutor took the podium and began.

→═◉ ◉═←

"Please say and spell your name for the record."

"I'm Detective Russell Fries of the Flint Township Police Department, F, R, I, E, S."

"Were you with the department in July of 2003, Detective?"

"Yes I was," he eagerly stated. He had the freshly scrubbed face of a choirboy, and the enthusiasm to match. You could almost see his tail wagging.

"OK. Were you also involved with investigating the shooting case of an Alan Johnson?"

"Yes I was."

"And, do you recall were there any search warrants requested?"

"Yes I do. There was a lot of technical information, and if you don't mind I would like to refer to my notes," he said, pulling out a very large brown folder brimming with papers.

"OK," Mrs. Hanson said. "And, what did you get search warrants for?"

"I obtained two search warrants. They were for two Nokia cell phones, two from AT&T, two from Cingular, and also for some prepaid and Quest calling cards."

"And, who did all those phones belong to?"

"Those phones were taken from the property room of Mundy Township; they were all the property of the defendant in this case."

"And, do you recall the defendant's name in this case?"

"Yes…Kimberly Morgan, my apologies," the detective said, blushing.

"OK. Did you ever have any direct contact with the defendant?"

"Uh…yes I did. There was one occasion, when I was seeking a warrant at the Genesee County Jail, and I saw Kimberly sitting down on a bench in the holding area."

"Do you see her in the courtroom?"

"Yes, she is sitting to my left wearing a blue top," he said without looking.

"May the record reflect the witness had identified the defendant."

"OK. So you got a search warrant and sent it to the phone company, and what happens next?"

"Um…the search warrant covers the telephone numbers. We also wanted to get any subscriber information, about outgoing and incoming calls. The telephone company provided that information to us."

"When you say subscriber, what do you mean?"

"Who the phone was owned by, billing address, etc."

"What did you do with this search warrant?"

"After the data was returned I took all of the inform-ation, it was several pages of information, and I put it into a Microsoft access program. That is a data-based program that lets you search by date, time, telephone number, where the calls were made, where the call came from, who it was made to, all the subscriber information, and the serial numbers of the phones. There are several different fields in all. That way I could sort out what was necessary to follow up on this case."

"Why did you do that?"

"Well, there were several phone numbers on there and we didn't know who they all belonged to. So we wanted to know who the suspect was calling."

"Will you look at this paper, please, and tell me what this is?"

"This information came from the search warrant. It is a total call analysis in this case. It shows Kimberly Morgan, who is located on the inner circle, making telephone calls to these people on the outside of this circle, which is on this line. Those are the numbers of calls that Kimberly Morgan had made, to those people.

"It includes a record of the calls made to Barbie Garrison's cell phone, to her residence, and to her son. To Savannah Liddel, to the mini-storage, to Genesys hospital in Grand Blanc, to Hurley hospital in Flint, to McLaren hospital in Flint, to Mr. Lucky's bar in Flint, and to the Arbor Village Apartments across from Mr. Lucky's. All of these calls were made between July 2 and July 27, 2003. Just to give you an example, she made forty-two calls to Barbie Garrison alone in this time frame."

"Please narrow down the time frame of the calls, particularly those made to the Ennis Children's Center, where Alan Johnson worked."

The detective dug deeper into his valise, found his notes, and read from them. "Calls were made on July 7 and July 8 of 2003. On July 7 calls made at 10:19 and 10:53 a.m. And calls number three and four were made on July 8 at 10:09 and 10:18 a.m. Mr. Lucky's calls were made on July 3, 2003, at 1:10 p.m. and July 3 at 8:30 a.m."

"And what about the calls to the hospitals, what date and time were those calls made?"

"Calls were placed to Hurley hospital on July 3, 2003, at 2:15 in the afternoon, and also on July 4, 2003, at 7:43 and 7:49 p.m. Calls were made to Genesys hospital in Grand Blanc at 7:51 p.m., and the Flint Osteopathic Hospital Campus on Beecher Road at 7:45 p.m. Calls were also made to the McLaren Medical Center at 5 p.m. These are all listed on my report. Also, on July 7, 2003, at 1:45 p.m., another phone call was made to McLaren."

"And what about calls to Savannah Liddel?"

"A call was made on July 27, 2003, at 9:13 a.m. And on July 27, 2003, at 9:14 a.m., that call lasting nine minutes and fifty-eight seconds."

"And, what about calls to Mazel's, where Savannah worked?"

"Calls were made there on July 7, 2003."

"No more questions for this witness, Your Honor."

⋅►╾◉ ◉╼◄⋅

Mr. Beauvais circled around and took the podium. Once there, he quizzed the witness in depth on many facts, such as, can you tell which calls were from cell phones or from calling cards? Detective Fries stated that he had four pages of calling card calls alone. Mr. Beauvais asked if there was any way to determine who it was who was using this calling card. Mr. Fries replied, "Yes." Mr. Beauvais then asked if a search warrant had been executed on Savannah Liddel's cell phone, and he pressed particularly hard upon this point.

"I will have to check my records."

While the detective searched his notes, the judge turned his attention back toward the jury. He sat back in his chair, pushed his glasses upon his bald head, and resumed his story right where he'd left off.

"Now, as I was saying, back in the olden days, they didn't have any roads in Michigan, and the people here got around by the water. The three biggest towns in the state were Detroit, because it was on the river; Mackinaw, because it was on the Great Lakes; and Saginaw, because it was on five rivers—the Tittabawasee, Saginaw, Cass, the Shiawassee, and the Flint rivers; they all joined at the Saginaw Bay.

"The traders all knew that they could trade with the Indians, the Ojibwa and the Chippewa, because they were at those places as they came down the rivers. Now, Jacob Smith was an entrepreneur, and he went up the Flint River to where the Indians crossed the river. That place is known as Grand Traverse Street now, and that is where they set up the trading post that is now Flint.

"This mural is the depiction of the first settlement. And it gives you something to look at while the detectives are sorting through their notes."

Seeing that the witness was finished with his searching, he turned back toward the courtroom. "You may proceed," he said, nodding at the witness and smiling.

"There was not a search warrant executed of Savannah Liddel's cell phone."

"Thank you. Nothing further, Your Honor."

Detective J Diem Testifies

I IMMEDIATELY RECOGNIZED the next witness as she ambled to the stand. Detective J Diem wore sensible black walking shoes, simple black dress slacks, white cotton knit top, and a jacket with a fine black-and-white hound's-tooth check. Thick black curly hair was pulled into a loose ponytail. Around her neck a detective badge hung from a brown braided lanyard rope.

⊷⟹ ⟸⊷

"Could you say and spell your name for the record."

"Detective J Diem. That is spelled as just the letter 'J.' And the last name is spelled D, I, E, M."

"And what is your occupation?"

"I work with the Mundy Township Police Department, as a detective. I've been with the department for seven years. I have been a detective there for two years, and I was a detective in Texas for two years before that."

"Detective, were you an investigator in the Dorothy Murphy case? And did you, in fact, follow up leads in that case?"

"Yes, ma'am."

"And, how many agencies were involved with this investigation, do you know?"

"The Flint Police Department, the Flint Township Police Department, the Mundy Township Police Department, and the State Police."

"Did you ever talk to a Savannah Liddel?"

"Yes, ma'am."

"Did you talk to a Kimberly Morgan, and, do you see her in this courtroom?"

"Yes, ma'am, she's sitting at the defense table, there in the blue turtleneck," Detective J said as she pointed toward the table where the defendant was sitting.

"Your Honor, may the record reflect that the witness has identified the defendant in this case." It was. Mrs. Hanson continued. "Detective, was Dorothy Murphy ever found?"

"Her remains were found," she clarified, "on River Oak and River Forest." Detective Diem responded very slowly, choosing her words most deliberately.

"Did you go to the scene?" the prosecutor asked while handing her photographs to examine. "And what do these pictures look like?"

"Yes, I did go to the scene, and this is a picture of the cul-de-sac where the remains were found."

"And do you recognize this picture?"

"Yes, ma'am, this is a picture of the remains," the detective said, glancing at the photo and then quickly turning away.

"Now, Detective, were any of her personal items found at the scene?"

Speaking very slowly and methodically, she answered, "She had a shirt, a pair of pants, a pair of shoes, a watch on her left arm, and a pair of dark glasses, eye protectors."

"Where were those glasses found in relationship to those remains?"

"They were under a bush, just south of the remains."

"I am handing you what is recorded as people's exhibit number fifty-nine and asking if you recognize that."

"Yes, ma'am. This is a picture of the eye-protector glasses, as they were lying at the scene."

"Detective, you said that is the way those glasses were lying at the scene, what, if anything...was unusual about those glasses?"

"Um, there is a hole in the right lens."

"Now, were those glasses sent to the crime lab?"

"Yes, ma'am. They were sent to see if in fact that hole in the lens was from a bullet hole, and to see if there was any trace evidence of lead or gunpowder."

"OK. Now, were you requested to take anything up to the lab for testing?"

"Yes, ma'am. I found out, through investigation, that the eye protectors were from Genesys hospital. That is where they were given to the victim. So I went down and got three pairs of those eye protectors, transported them to the crime lab, and then met with a Lieutenant Ainsley. We shot one pair of them, to compare, to see if the hole was the same, and it was."

"Thank you. No more questions, Your Honor."

⋅⇥═◉ ◉═⇤⋅

We just learned that Mother was shot directly in the eye. How cold-blooded.

⋅⇥═◉ ◉═⇤⋅

Mr. Beauvais assumed the podium and immediately launched into questioning. "Detective, what was your role in this investigation?"

"As an investigator...I was originally assigned the lead role in attempting to find Mrs. Murphy."

"You also investigated potential witnesses, things of that nature?"

"At the initial part of the investigation, yes, sir."

"Were you present during the interview with a Simona Callahan?"

"Yes, sir."

"Do you recall Miss Callahan giving you a description of someone that was walking away from Mr. Lucky's?"

"I did."

"Now, did she tell you that was a female, approximately five foot two to five foot four, weight one hundred and sixty to one hundred and seventy pounds? And did she further tell you that this person was wearing a yellow T-shirt and some kind of faded blue jeans; some kind of pants?"

"She said it was a polo shirt, and the rest is correct."

Mr. Beauvais's face shifted, reddened, he suddenly became adamant, and began speaking loudly. "You said, in your reporting this, you try to be accurate! Is that correct?"

"Yes, sir?"

"Can I show you a document that says 'Mundy Township Police Department' on it, and ask if that is a report that would have been generated by *you* yourself?" Mr. Beauvais pressed, shoving a paper at her.

"Yes it is."

"And *on that report, anywhere*, does it say…that the person was wearing a yellow *polo* shirt?" Mr. Beauvais demanded to know.

"No, sir, it doesn't. It says a T-shirt," Detective Diem said most apologetically, hanging her head.

"It in *fact* says, a yellow *T-shirt*…and you say you try to be accurate in this, would you not?"

"Yes, sir."

"Now you're not sure, but *something* in here is *wrong*. Because that's important, isn't it? The description of what the person was wearing?"

"Yes, sir, sometimes we make mistakes when we dictate."

"Your report says the suspect was wearing a yellow T-shirt, isn't that correct? And I suspect it was generated sometime close to when you interviewed the witness, is that correct? In fact, it doesn't say when you talked to her, does it?" he asked, all bug-eyed.

"Some of the reports I did over several days. This would have been when we did the canvass of the apartments over there. I believe, it was on the sixth…but if I can refresh my memory…?"

"Certainly!" Mr. Beauvais said sarcastically as he paraded around like a sanctified preacher.

"I'm sorry, that is a correction. It was on the seventh of July."

"And, how long would it have been to prepare that report?"

"This report was done on the eighth."

"So, you would have done this report the next day, the eighth of July?" His tone was demeaning.

"Yes, that is correct."

"And how do you prepare that report?"

"I dictate them."

"And someone else types them. Is that correct?"

"No. I take notes and do my transcriptions from them. No one else could read my chicken scratches. I dictate my notes and do my own transcriptions."

"And once this has been prepared, before you destroy your notes, you proof-read it, don't you?"

"Yes, sir."

"Again, your report, that you prepared and read, says that the female was wearing a yellow T-shirt, does it not?"

The prosecutor handed her a sheet of paper, and said, "Please identify this page, if you will."

"This is the composite sketch that was made up at the Flint Police Department, with Simona Callahan as the witness."

"Were you there?"

"Yes I was."

"Your Honor, I object. That is certainly hearsay," Mr. Beauvais shot back.

"Sustained," the judge said flatly.

Prosecutor Hanson continued. "Detective, when you do your report, is it possible that you made a mistake?"

"Yes, ma'am."

"Is it, in fact, that it was a *polo* shirt, instead of a T-shirt?"

"Yes, ma'am. It was a shirt with a collar."

"Nothing further."

⋅→⊨◉ ◉⊨⋜⋅

Detective Diem exited and the next witness was shown in and sworn in. "Please say and spell your name for the record," Prosecutor Hanson said.

"Sergeant G, E, N, E, D, U, B, U, C."

"And, what is your occupation?"

"I am a detective with the Flint Township Police Department. I've been a police officer for twenty-five years, and a detective for three."

"Were you working on September 26, 2003, Detective?"

"Yes I was."

"Were you called to River Oak, in Flint Township?"

"Yes I was. I went out there and spoke with Richard Gehrig, a Consumers Power employee. A Patrol Officer Beal pointed me to an area…that was east of River Forest and north of River Oak, where a there was a faint trail. Taking that trail a short distance into the woods, we found skeletal remains.

"I then called detectives from the Detective Bureau. I made several calls, one to the medical examiner, one to you (he motioned toward Mrs. Hanson), and one to the Michigan State Police crime lab. They did their scene examination and investigation."

Prosecutor Hanson handed the detective a photograph. "Please identify this."

"That is a scene sketch of the area surrounding the remains, showing the cul-de-sac, the wooded areas, and the balloons marking the location of the skeletal remains."

"May the photograph be entered as people's exhibit number sixty-one. Were you there?"

"At first Detective Schmitzer and myself inspected the area, took pictures of the area, documented all evidence, and only then was others allowed in. Yes indeed, I was an eyewitness there. River Oak, where the remains were found, and River Forest, the apartment complex where the defendant once lived, are very close in proximity. If I would estimate, the two locations are approximately a half mile apart. And I, myself, put those balloons out for the aerial photographs, marking the location of the remains.

"The skull was missing from the remains. But the remains still had a watch on the left wrist, and a necklace still around the neck. There was a row of teeth present on the lower jaw, which was still intact and connected with the skeleton."

A photograph of the lower teeth was entered into evidence as people's exhibit sixty-two.

"Forensic anthropologist Dr. Fenton was called to the scene next. We both were present at the autopsy the following day, at Hurley Medical Center.

"The right foot's shoe was located some distance from those remains, and very close to the road. The left shoe was still with the skeletal remains.

"Dr. Gary Johnson, from the Medical Examiner's Office, arrived at the scene next. He exhumed the remains and transported them to Hurley Medical Center, and that is where the autopsy was completed.

"I was still bothered by the missing skull, so the following day myself and thirty volunteer fire-fighters conducted a coordinated search of the entire area, looking for the missing skull. It was never found."

⋅►▬◉ ◉▬◄⋅

Mrs. Hanson stepped down. Defense attorney Mr. Beauvais stood to question Detective DuBuc.

"Who was the first person first upon the scene?"

"I was the lead supervisor of the scene. Myself and Detective Schmitzer were first. We personally inspected the scene. I was there until dark the first day, and I went back to the scene several other times, because not finding the skull still bothered me."

"Thank you. Nothing further, Your Honor."

Barbie Speaks

THE TRIAL WAS moving along briskly, and it was already becoming apparent that the prosecutor was setting a direct course for her target, Kimberly Morgan's conviction. With each new witness, she more clearly showed the defend-ant's connection to the case and more clearly proved her methodology.

The judge spoke to the assembly. "Court is adjourned for lunch until two fifteen."

We were more than ready for the lunch break because it would give us a long-overdue chance to use the restroom, and time to visit the Masonic Temple for lunch. I was way too keyed up to eat, so I had the Marlboro Lights, and Linda and I stoked up outside, while the others finished off their roast beef and pota-toes with brown gravy.

At two fifteen exactly, the trial resumed. The judge ran a very efficient courtroom. Kimberly was brought back and seated, and the bailiff brought the jury in and seated them. The first witness was called.

A buzz percolated through the courtroom as she slowly ambled in, and then the buzz turned into a chuckle as she sauntered past. She was a very voluptuous woman in her early thirties, and the way she was built and moved reminded me of Mae West. Her more than an ample rear end had the words *BABY GIRL* emblazoned upon it in large, shiny Rhine-stone letters, making it into a blinged out big-butt billboard.

Her long spare-hair extensions were blond and curly, her makeup heavy. From her ears hung extra large, door knocker-size golden hoop earrings that shone brightly against her ebony skin. A canary yellow oversize T-shirt was rak-ishly tied to one side of her shapely Rubenesque hips.

"Please say and spell your name for the record."

"Barbie Michelle Garrison. G, A, double R, I, SON," she softly said in a singsong manner. Her tiny girly voice did not synchronize with her ample stature.

Prosecutor Hanson began, "And Barbie, do you know a Kimberly Morgan?"

"Yes," she said very softly, practically inaudibly.

"And how do you know her?"

"Socially, through a mutual friend, Savannah Lie-dell."

"And, do you see her in the courtroom? Can you see where she is sitting?"

Barbie nodded in the direction of the defendant without looking.

"May the record reflect the witness had identified the defendant in this matter."

"So noted," the judge responded.

"How long have you known the defendant?"

"Since 2002, through Savannah, socially."

"Barbie, at some point in time, did you become friends with the defendant?"

"Yes."

"Did the defendant ever come to stay with you?"

"Sometime, for a couple a days, July, a year ago."

"Did you know the defendant moved to Tennessee?"

"No, she had called when she had moved there."

"When she moved to Tennessee, did you have much contact with her?"

"Not at first." Then she offered, "We started talkin' more in May."

"Oh?"

"Mmm-hmm," Barbie hummed.

"What did you talk to the defendant about?"

"About Savannah, mostly. She axed me if I seen her, how she doin', stuff like that. I tell her I din' see Savannah."

"Did she talk about an Alan Johnson?"

"No."

"Going back to July 2003. Did you talk to the defendant during that period?"

"I talk to her. She axed me how I was doin', stuff like that. But I really don't talk to her much till the end of July. That's when she come visit me."

"Now, you said she'd ask you what's been going on in Flint, is that correct? Was that unusual?"

"No."

"Did she ask you that before July 2003?"

"No…it was after."

"And during the month of July, did the defendant ask you to do anything for her? Did she ask anything specific about what was happening in Flint?"

"No, it was always about Savannah."

"Did she ever ask you to watch the news?"

"Yes," she finally offered after some hesitation.

"What did she say when she asked you to watch the news?"

"She axed me about a old lady, an' about a sketch of a person, an' did it look like her."

"A sketch of a person involved with an old lady? Did you see that sketch?"

"Yes I did."

Mrs. Hanson handed the witness a piece of paper. "Is this the sketch you saw?"

"Yes," Barbie said. "But it was a little lighter. I tole her, I was gonna watch the six o'clock news. She tole me she would call me back."

"You saw the sketch on the news? When Kim called you back, what did you say?"

"I saw it, but for a minute. I tole her, no, it don't look like you…but it could be."

"Could be *Kim*?" Mrs. Hanson said, her interest piqued.

"I forget…I don't talk to her. She tole me, if the po-lease had come here, don't tell 'em anything. That was the lass time I talk to her."

"Do you remember her asking about a burning car, or a man being shot?"

"No…nah-thin' like that."

"Nothing further."

Mr. Beauvais stood and started his questioning before even making it to the stand. "Miss Garrison, back in 2003, you were friends with Kimberly Morgan and Savannah Liddel, is that correct?"

"Mmm-hmm," Barbie hummed.

"You'll have to speak up for the record, *yes* or *no*," Mr. Beauvais said sternly.

"Mmm-hmm," she hummed just a teensy bit louder.

"As friends, would you ever call them up and ask them how they were doing?"

"Mmm-hmm. Kim would call me, not Savannah."

"And would Savannah call you?"

"No."

"She never called you?"

She shook her head from side to side without speaking.

"Now, you talked to Kimberly Morgan a number of times in July of 2003, is that correct?"

"Mmm-hmm."

"You have testified that she called you a number of times and you talked about usual things, is that right? How you doin'? How is Savannah? That right?"

"Mmm-hmm."

"Now, the prosecutor asked you about Kimberly Morgan asking you to watch the news. At any time did you see Kimberly Morgan face-to-face in July 2003?"

"Yes, in July the twenty-seventh or twenty-eighth. Somewhere in there."

"Thank you."

<hr>

Prosecuting Attorney Hanson rose once more to speak.

"Barbie, now, when the defendant asked you to watch the news, what did the defendant ask you?"

"She axed me if it look like her."

"And you told her?"

"No...it don't look like you, it was only on the TV but a minute. I glanced at it."

"Thank you," the prosecutor said in closing.

Dr. Todd Fenton Testimony

The next witness walked into the courtroom without an escort and confidently assumed the witness stand. He appeared to be about forty and wore a nice conservative gray suit and coordinating silk tie. Smiling easily, he appeared eager to testify.

"Please state and spell your name for the record," Prosecutor Hanson began.

"My name is Todd Fenton, T, O, DD, FEN-TON."

"And what is your occupation?"

"I am a forensic anthropologist and a professor at Michigan State University."

"Are you currently employed at your occupation?"

"Yes. I teach courses in the subject as well, and I have a lab at Michigan State. There are various duties that I perform there throughout the year. Basically we analyze unidentified human remains.

We have two different goals. First is to positively identify remains, and by remains I mean anything that might be skeletonized, decomposing, or even a fresh body. The second main goal that I have is as a forensic anthropologist, and that goal is to understand the circumstances of the death.

"Oftentimes it entails the analysis of the skeletal items, the bones, to see if the bones can tell a story about how that person might have died. So...those are the kind of cases that I get on a weekly basis."

"OK. And, approximately how many people have you been able to identify based on their remains?"

"Ah...over the fifteen years, hundreds I'm sure."

"And, have you ever testified as an expert witness for the court?"

"Yes I have, in Phoenix, Arizona, and in several different counties in Michigan. I have a PhD from the University of Arizona."

"Your Honor, I ask that the court accept Dr. Fenton as an expert witness."

"I object, Your Honor!" Mr. Beauvais jumped to his feet and yelled. "Doctor, you received a PhD at the University of Arizona, that correct? Was that for forensic anthropology?"

The doctor smiled and patiently clarified. "It was broadly in anthropology. The way anthropology works is like this. You have your degree, a PhD, in anthropology, and you would specialize, as doctors do. You have a medical degree then you specialize."

Attorney Beauvais pressed on. "Did you ever have to do any clinical work with your area when you received you PhD?"

"Absolutely! The lab I came from did the most cases in the history of science. In my years as a graduate student we had over a thousand cases go through the lab."

"What's the difference between forensic anthropology and just regular old anthropology?"

"It's a long story, but briefly there are four main fields of anthropology. They are archaeology, anthropology, cultural linguistics, and physical. My subspecialty is in physical anthropology, which is different, kind of a human variation. At this time, I specialize in the human skeleton."

"Judge, I have no further objections."

The judge accepted Dr. Fenton as an expert witness, and the prosecutor continued.

"Now, Doctor, were you present on September 27, 2003, when the autopsy was performed on the remains that are now known to be Dorothy Murphy?"

"Yes I was."

"Now, Doctor, with the body being that badly decomposed, how did you determine that those remains were Dorothy Murphy?"

"I brought the remains back to the lab at Michigan State University. The first part of my analysis was to do a dental radiography analysis, and do a complete dental comparison. We have a complete lab where we could do a complete set of X-rays. I took the X-rays and compared them to those sent by Mrs. Murphy's own dentist."

"Doctor, I'm handing you what is proposed as people's exhibit number sixty-four and asking if you recognize that."

The doctor examined the page and replied, "This is a photograph of the mandible, the lower jaw bone, and a shirt of Dorothy Murphy's, taken at the autopsy."

"Now, Doctor, you went to the scene, didn't you?"

"Yes I did. I also went to the morgue at Hurley, being present during Dr. Blight's autopsy. While still in Flint, I and my two graduate student assistants, assisted with the organized search of the recovery scene. We were specifically looking for the cranium of the remains. The skull was without its jawbone. Many hours were spent setting up a grid and doing a systematic search, but we did not find the cranium.

"With the existing lower teeth, there were several points in the dental exam that were specific to that person. It was a positive identification to Mrs. Murphy. Subsequent to that investigation, myself and one assistant cleaned the bones and spent many hours both macroscopically and microscopic-ally to see if there was any sign of trauma, blunt force, etc. It is a very tedious but important analysis."

"What did you find when you did the analysis of Dorothy Murphy?"

"There was only one thing that was unexplained. That was the fracture of the right tenth rib. It had a fracture that I couldn't explain, because it was an unusual place to have a fracture, especially of only one rib. This is an area of the rib cage that is very close to the spine, and the ribs are packed very close to each other in the back, where they join the spine. The tenth rib was fractured. What was odd about that was that the ninth and eleventh ribs, adjacent to it, were all right."

"Doctor, could you tell if the fracture was before or after death?"

"There was no healing, so the fracture did not occur while the person was alive. It was perimortem in nature, so certainly at, or around, the time of her death. It was unusual, because it takes a lot of blunt force to break a bone. If this were blunt force you would expect more than one bone to be fractured."

"Doctor, in your opinion, what would cause that kind of fracture?"

"As I said in my report, I could not explain it."

"Would it be consistent with a projectile going through the area?"

"It would be consistent with a projectile going through the area."

"Doctor, the skull was never found. When you looked at your notes of analysis, did you note any animal activity on those bones?"

"There was no marked animal activity. It doesn't always happen. What you sometimes see is that an animal has hauled away parts. So in our searching I felt that there was a possibility that a dog, or coyote, might have taken the cranium a short distance away; that is where we'd find it."

"Hence the search?"

"Yes."

"Nothing further, Your Honor."

⋅→➡️ ⬅️←⋅

Attorney Beauvais started right in. "You were present during the autopsy?"

"Yes I was."

"And after Dr. Blight got through with whatever her job was, did she turn the rest over to you?"

"Yes she did; I received all the skeletal remains."

"And when you took them back to Lansing, what did you do with them?"

"It was late in the day, and our protocol was to put them in a bag and refrigerate them."

"OK. At some point you brought them out, because you want to examine them."

"The next day we cleaned and x-rayed them."

"When you clean the remains, what do you do with them?"

"It's a technique in which you put the remains in a stainless steel pot, and using a cooking method, we take off the flesh and decomposition to do a skeletal analysis."

"In this case, was there any of the protein left?"

"There was a lot of odoriferous body fluid and greasy tissue that had to be removed. If we don't do that, we can't see the bones' surface."

"At some point you looked at the teeth? The thirteen teeth that are in the mandible, did you determine where the other two teeth came from?"

"Yes."

"So can you tell me, or don't you remember? Unless you need to check your report. Well, if that will refresh your memory, you can certainly check you report."

The doctor read his report. "Teeth numbers four and seven were recovered."

"Are those from the upper mandible?"

"That's called the maxilla," the doctor said, smiling smugly.

"Ah, I thought I'd know something…but I don't. What did you do with the teeth? You clean 'em?"

"After they were cleaned and x-rayed, they were placed in the files, and later we compared them with her dentist's X-rays."

"You had the two X-rays, and you compared them. What was it that led you to your conclusion?"

"There are many points of agreement. For instance, there were two crowns with porcelain fused to metal, and one gold crown; they were a perfect match. In addition to those the other teeth present matched the morphology of—the shape and size of—the tooth, roots, and crowns. This is my analysis that takes a lot of time. There were no inconsistencies."

"Other than the ID, was there anything else?"

"The other goal was to look at all the bony surfaces and check for trauma."

"Was there any way to pinpoint the time of death?"

"That is out of my realm."

"Other than the skull missing, was anything else missing?"

"There were two arm bones missing. I noted that in my report."

"Now, I'm not sure about this fractured tenth rib. Not sure where it is."

"That takes a bit of an anatomy lesson," the doctor said, smiling. "Would it help if I ran you through that?"

"Go right ahead."

"We have five lumbar vertebra, those are the lower ones. We also have twelve thoracic vertebra and seven cervical. You start at the skull and you count down. The right tenth rib is on the lower thoracic vertebra. It comes around to connect with the sternum."

"Where was this fracture?"

"It was very close to the spinal column."

"Thank you. Judge, I have nothing further."

⋆⇥◉ ◉⇤⋆

The prosecutor rose to direct one more question. "Any doubt in your mind that this was Dorothy Murphy?"

"Absolutely none."

"And the tenth rib, that consistent with a gunshot?"

"Yes it was."

"Thank you, Doctor. Nothing further, Your Honor."

⋆⇥◉ ◉⇤⋆

"Court adjourned," the judge decreed. "Bailiff, please escort the jury out."

And that was the end of day two's testimony.

Dr. Cathy Blight Testimony

THE TRIAL WAS moving along at a very brisk pace. For the third day, we once again assembled on the gracious limestone steps flanking the courthouse, soaking up the last summer sunshine while catching up on the events of the trial to date. Linda, Uncle Gerald, and I were desperately smoking a last few cigarettes before being x-rayed and scanned and taking the elevator to the second-floor courtroom.

Already, this early in the trial, it was evident that the prosecutor knew her business and she was aiming right at the center of her target, Kimberly Morgan. We could feel the momentum building with each witness's testimony. Step by step the prosecutor was methodically proving how Kimberly Morgan went about committing her crime spree.

The first witness was already seated. She was a pretty, mature woman with her hair "done up." Wearing a silky three-piece, unstructured ensemble in Pepto-Bismol pink, she would have been impossible to miss in any crowd. Around her neck was an even splashier silk scarf that was pinned to her jacket by a big broach with sparkling gemstones. Smiling pleasantly, she appeared extremely poised and ladylike.

·>═◉ ◉═<·

"Good morning!" the prosecutor said cheerfully. "Would you please say and state your name for the record."

"Dr. Cathy Blight."

"Please state your occupation."

"I am a physician, presently employed in the practice of pathology."

"And, where are you currently employed?"

"I am at Hurley Hospital Medical Center, here in Flint, Michigan."

"On July 27, 2003, were you working as a medical examiner?"

"Yes I was."

"Are you licensed in the field of pathology?"

"I am licensed by the state of Michigan and certified in analytic and clinical pathology. I have been for twenty-three years."

"OK. What are the duties of a medical examiner?"

"Well, the medical examiner is empowered, by our legislation and the courts, to investigate any suspicious deaths, homicide, suicide, accidental death, and deaths that might impact public health and safety."

"What kind of training do you have in the field of pathology?"

"Pathology is a part of what some medical examiners do. That is to do autopsies to determine the course and manner of death, and to come to a conclusion and testify in those. It was part of my basic training, and I took various continuing education courses to further my knowledge."

"Doctor, have you ever testified as an expert witness in the field of pathology?"

"Yes, ma'am, I am recognized in several courts in Michigan, in 67th District and 68th District courts, in this circuit court, and a couple others."

"At this time I ask the court that Dr. Blight be recognized as an expert witness in the field of pathology, Your Honor."

Mr. Beauvais said, "I have cross-examined the doctor twenty to thirty times. I have no objection to her being an expert witness."

"Accepted," said the judge.

"Now, Doctor, on September 27, 2003, did you perform an autopsy on what we now know as Dorothy Murphy? And where was it that it took place?"

"Yes, I did, and that was at Hurley hospital, in the autopsy suite."

"OK, Doctor. The body was quite badly decomposed, so how did you do it?"

"At the time that the remains came to us, we were not certain that they were Dorothy Murphy's remains. However, during examination there were items of clothing, jewelry, and other personal effects that people had reported her wearing, or were talked about. We made a tentative confirmation."

"Dr. Fenton, who testified yesterday, did the positive identification, correct?"

"That is correct."

"During your autopsy, did you do an external exam-ination? And what did that determine?"

"The remains were very skeletonized, there was very little tissue still left. With the remains there was a pair of tan slacks with an elastic waistband, one tan shoe, a discolored yellow-and-red-flowered shirt, a wristwatch with the name Acqua on its face, and there was a gold necklace around the neck. The lower jaw, bones of the abdomen, chest, arms, and legs were there, but there was no cranium—or skull—with the remains."

"Was there any signs of trauma with the remains?"

"The only thing that could have been thought to be significant, in my opinion, was there was a hole in the shirt about a half inch in diameter."

The prosecutor handed the doctor a picture and asked, "Doctor, do you recognize that picture?"

"Sort of, yes? That's a photograph of the shirt and some of the other material. There was a lot of dirt and other things brought in with her. Right there is the hole. It was in the front of the blouse," she said as she was pointing at it.

"Could that be consistent with a gunshot wound, Doctor?"

"Yes, ma'am."

"Doctor, did you determine a cause of death in this case?"

"No."

"And why not?"

"There were no internal organs to examine, and with the bones that were there, there was no obvious sign of trauma or knife marks. I could not come to the conclusion as to the cause of death."

"And, did you determine the manner of death, what that was?"

"Yes, ma'am. Homicide."

"And how did you determine that?"

"It was taking the entirety of the report at the time. This was an older lady. She was found in a field not close to where she lived, or where she was reported to be going. There was nothing else around; no bicycle, her car wasn't there.

"So, it came down to a body being found in a place where it shouldn't be, far away from home, and lacking any reasonable explanation as to how it could have gotten there. If this were a natural death, she probably wouldn't be out in the middle of the field. There was no other evidence showing how she got where she did, which would leave indeterminate, or homicide. Without the skull, it was my opinion that this *was* a homicide."

"You mention without the skull. The skull was not found, is that correct?"

"I never saw the skull."

"Doctor, I'm handing you what is proposed as people's exhibit number sixty-eight and asking you if you recognize that."

"Yes, this is a copy of my autopsy report that I, myself, prepared."

"Doctor, looking at that picture, where that hole is located, is that consistent with a gunshot to the chest?"

"Yes."

"I have nothing further," the prosecutor said, returning to her seat.

⇥⟞⊙ ⊙⟝⇤

Mr. Beauvais took the podium. "Dr. Blight, you are no longer a medical examiner at Hurley hospital. Is that because the Prosecutor's Office determined that the medical examiners at Hurley hospital are not qualified? Isn't that correct?" he said angrily, and ambushing her.

Mrs. Hanson's face immediately turned red. Jumping up, she shouted, "I object, Your Honor!"

The attorneys marched to the bench and began a heated discussion with the judge. After talking for some time, Mr. Beauvais returned to the podium and resumed most respectfully. "I remove my objection, Judge. The court determined it's not relevant at this point."

"It is not relevant at this point," the judge said in confirmation, looking over his half spectacles directly at him.

Mr. Beauvais continued. "Doctor, how did you determine the identity of the skeletal remains?"

After a lengthy and deliberate hesitation and sounding a bit perturbed, she answered. "As I stated in my report, first there was some evidence because of the clothing that she was wearing, and the personal effects that were listed in the missing persons report on file with the local police. The skeletonized remains were taken from the morgue to Michigan State University, and Dr. Fenton was able to compare the dental records."

"Based on *that* you determined that those skeletal remains were that of Dorothy Murphy, correct?"

"Yes."

"And, when you do an autopsy of skeletal remains, what do you do?"

"The pathologist's role is primarily to look for major trauma to the body or the skeletal remains; the important work is done with the forensic anthropologist. We do some broad work, but Dr. Fenton was asked to assist in the autopsy, because a pathologist would have more experience in the more 'subtle' details."

"Now, you yourself did not find any cause of death, is that correct?"

"Yes. That is correct."

"Now, there is a difference between cause of death and manner of death. What is that difference?"

"The cause of death is the event which leads to the person's death. The manner of death is sort of *how* they died. There are five. There is homicide, that is death at the hand of another; suicide, death at one's own hand; accidental; natural, heart attack, stroke, etc.; and where there is not enough evidence, indeterminate."

"And, with the partial remains there wasn't a toxicology report, was there?"

"No. I don't think we did any."

"There was no blood there, nothing other than the skeleton and a little tissue for you to make any determination. Is that correct?"

"That's correct."

"Now, you say that you found a hole on the blouse, correct? And that hole was approximately how big?"

"Correct, about a half-inch hole."

"Is there any way to tell when that hole occurred?"

"No."

"Was there anything around that hole to determine if that was an old hole or a new hole? Was there some blood or anything like that?"

"I did not make note of that. No."

"Now, given the fact that this blouse had been out in the woods for a period of time, if there would have been blood, would it still be there?"

"In my opinion, it would be. It would be in the inner part of the fabric."

"Now, you stated the cranial bulk was not present. What was that?"

"It's the upper part of the head, minus the mandible."

"It's this part of the head." He said, while placing his hands upon both sides of his head and motioning upward. "So, if I would have walked by, could I have simply walked by and taken it away?"

"Yes."

"Thank you, Doctor," Mr. Beauvais said.

⋆⇛ ⇚⋆

Prosecutor Hanson rose to ask a few more questions. "Doctor, you're aware of Dr. Fenton's report, is that correct? Is that hole in the shirt consistent with gunshot?"

"Yes."

"So the manner of death was homicide. And, it's your expert opinion that the hole is from a gunshot?"

"It is consistent with a gunshot wound, yes."

"Doctor, Dr. Fenton determined that the rib wound was near or at the time of death. He indicated there was no time for that wound to heal. Could you explain that?"

"There are a number of things you look for. As the body is injured it goes through a regular sequence. Bone differs from soft tissue, but there are still things that you look for. So if something happens at or near the time of death, the body doesn't have time to repair itself. There is a window."

"Dr. Fenton's report says that there is no conclusive evidence to explain that personal trauma had been inflicted to any of the skeletal remains."

"At the time the lady died, there was no sign of trauma. In addition, he put in his report that there is a fracture in the right tenth rib, which cannot be explained. Is that consistent with your report?"

"I did not make note of that. I did not spend a tremendous amount of time on that. I would defer to Dr. Fenton's expertise in that area."

"Now, you stated that this hole in the shirt would be consistent with a bullet, is that correct?"

"Yes."

Mr. Beauvais stood and belted out, "It could also be consistent with other things, isn't *that* correct?"

"Yes."

"There is nothing conclusive, as to what caused hole?"

"From what I could see, nothing was conclusive."

Mr. Beauvais took his chair and the prosecutor rose. "Dr. Fenton testified that the tenth rib was fractured, and in his expertise that injury happened perimortem."

"In the report I have from him, it says that no perimortem trauma was inflicted, but...it *was* noted...that the tenth rib was fractured. He made no note of the time of the fracture."

"Nothing further."

Detective Ron Ainsley, Detective Ronald Crichton Testimony

THE NEXT WITNESS was sworn in and seated. Sporting a military cut, he had the posture to match. The man was perhaps forty and wore a white shirt, dark narrow tie, dark sport coat and olive dress slacks.

⊷⊷⊜ ⊜⊶⊷

"Detective Sergeant RON, A, I, N, S, L, E, Y."

"And Detective, what is your occupation?"

"I'm an explosive, firearms, and tool mark specialist for the Michigan State Police, in Bridgeport."

"What kind of education do you have in this field?"

"I have a bachelor of science, with extensive training in firearms. I underwent an intensive seventeen-week training academy in explosives and firearms, and had a two-year train-ing period in Grand Rapids in firearms subunit, with the FBI. I have extensive training and expertise in the field."

"Sergeant, what are the duties of a firearms expert?"

"To examine fired cartridges, cases, bullets, and to inspect suspect firearms."

"Your Honor, I requested that Detective Sergeant Ron Ainsley be accepted as an expert witness.."

"So noted."

"Please identify what is in this envelope, Detective."

"This is a manila envelope that was given to me by the Flint Police Department. The Mundy Township Police asked me to identify it. It is number F-1, a fired cartridge case and fired bullet."

"I am handing you what is proposed as people's exhibit number sixty-nine and asking if you will identify that."

"This is another manila envelope which was turned over to me. It contains a fired .380 cartridge case, numbered F-2. This particular cartridge case has been through a vehicle fire. It was taken out of the victim's vehicle."

Mr. Beauvais shot to his feet and objected. "He doesn't know that that was taken from that vehicle." The objection was sustained.

The prosecutor resumed. "Detective, and what were they examined for?"

"These cartridge cases were examined to see if they came from the same firearm."

"In fact, what was the result of that examination?"

"Through microscopic examination, I was able to determine that both items F-1 and F-2, the two fired .380 cartridges that I compared, were fired from the same firearm."

"Detective, please examine people's exhibit number seventy and identify it."

"It is my own ballistic report."

"Your Honor, I submit this report. Thank you for your testimony."

--⊷◉ ◉⊷--

Mr. Beauvais rose and fired more questions at the expert for over fifteen minutes, going on and on in laborious minutia about how he did his job. I will spare you from having to listen to all of them. The bottom line is, you cannot argue with science.

--⊷◉ ◉⊷--

The next witness was shown to the stand and sworn in. Like me, the detective was showing advanced signs of male pattern balding, and his gray hair was cut very short. Gold wire-rimmed glasses made him appear older than he probably was. He looked knowledgeable and composed, dressed in a nice blue-gray suit with a coordinating tie.

→≡◎ ◎≡←

"Sergeant Crichton, what is your occupation?"

"I am with the Michigan State Police Bridgeport crime lab. I am a firearms and tool arm examiner. The primary responsibilities of my job is the examination of firearms and bullet casings."

"Detective, have you ever been qualified as an expert witness by the court?"

"Yes. The courts in Iosco, Clare, Gladwin, Lapeer, Saginaw, and Genesee county recognize me."

With no objections being expressed, he was accepted as an expert witness.

"Did you respond to a scene where remains were found on September 26, 2003?"

"Yes I did. I went there as part of the crime scene crew, to collect evidence. No firearm evidence was found at the scene at that time."

"I'm handing you what was proposed as people's exhibit number seventy-one and asking if you recognize this."

"Yes I do, it's a sealed paper bag with a related lab number, and my initials."

"Detective, please open this bag."

"This is a pair of Solar Shield glasses, missing the right earpiece. There is also a hole in the right lens. They were located at the scene where the remains were recovered."

"Will you hold those up for the jury to see?"

The detective obliged and held them up. From my seat, twenty feet away, I could clearly see the hole in the glasses. They were quite large, shaded, wrap-around "Terminator" style glasses.

"Now, why did you examine those sunglasses?"

"After first being examined by scientist Watkins, they were handed to me for testing to the lenses, to determine if the hole was caused by a bullet wound."

"Did you make that determination?"

"Yes, three different ways. A chemical investigation was conducted by scientist Watkins, to see if it was positive for bodily fluids, DNA, fingerprints, and particles of lead. It was positive for lead. Then the detective involved with the case submitted to us three pairs of the same sunglasses for testing, to see if the damage would be consistent with rifling imparted onto the plastic from a bullet being fired. The testing was done at the lab by firing a bullet through the lenses, to see if they resemble the pair of damaged lenses coming from the victim, to see if the damage was consistent. It *was* consistent."

"Detective, I'm handing you a package and asking if you recognize that."

"Yes I do. It's a container with the three lenses. We used them to do the testing. To see if the rifling was the same, we mounted the lenses to a piece of cardboard, and then we took .38 and .380 guns to see what type of characteristic damage was made, if it's the same."

"What did you find out?"

"One, the microscopic examination was consistent with a bullet; two, that the chemical analysis experiment was the same, consistent with a bullet; and three, that the damage to the lens, which I was able to duplicate in the lab, was very, very similar to what was seen on these glasses."

"Did you do a report bases on those findings?"

"Yes I did. This is in my report and the results of my examination. It states that the damage to the lens is *consistent* with firearms damage."

The report was entered as evidence. Mrs. Hanson thanked him for his testimony and left the podium to Mr. Beauvais.

⋅⊷⊜ ⊜⊶⋅

"Now, Detective, you went to the scene with a team when the remains were recovered. Is that your duty as a member of the Michigan State Police crime lab?"

"Yes."

"While you were out there, you didn't find any firearms evidence at that time, isn't that right?"

"Yes."

"Your role was to go out to the scene to look for bullets, shell casings, things of that nature."

"Correct. Or damage that may have been caused by bullets, or lead me to a gun."

"And you say you recovered the sunglasses from Tawny Watkins. What is her purpose?"

"Serology, the collection of bodily fluids and things of that nature, which lead to DNA.; also, any trace evidence. Particularly in this case, if there is anything with fingerprints. That collected evidence goes first to Tawny Watkins for her testing, and then comes to me. So I don't contaminate it." The courtroom chuckled.

"So, she'd look for fluids, things of that nature, or anything that might have been on those glasses? And when you got it, your job was to look at the *hole* in those glasses? Specifically, what did *you* do?"

"A microscopic examination. I was able to determine that the projectile was coming in at an angle, thereby making consistent markings. The plastic material will stretch when a bullet passes through it. During this part the stretched portions became rifled, and we found those characteristic riflings to be similar in all three of the lenses we tested, and the other lenses gathered from the crime scene."

He went on, at some length, about how he accomplished his work. Meanwhile, there was a small but heated conversation going on at the table of the prosecutor. I became distracted while watching it.

Mr. Beauvais resumed. "Could you tell how long that hole had been there, and could you tell the angle of projection?"

"No I could not tell you how long that hole had been there, but the hole in the lens was made from the right side, entering at a downward angle."

That appeared to be enough, and Mr. Beauvais returned to his seat.

Randall Johnson Witness * Daniel Murphy Speaks

THE SMALL BUT heated discussion going on at the prosecutor's table spilled over. Then the prosecutor's assistant left the table and walked over to the front row to speak with me. "Can you join me outside in the hall for a moment please, Dan?"

Obliging, I followed him into the hall. "Do you think that you could take the stand and answer a few questions for us, like who Dorothy was, and what your mom was like growing up? We want to give the jury some concept of this woman and her life. We need to give the jury a feeling of her personality. That, and stall for time until the DNA expert arrives."

"Absolutely. Anything I can do to help."

⇀▮⊙ ⊙▮↼

The next witness was shown in, sworn in, and seated in the witness chair. He was a sturdy dark-skinned man in his late twenties. His hair was close-cut, nearly shaved. A large T-shirt hung loosely atop his oversize blue jeans. His street attire was inappropriate for court.

⇀▮⊙ ⊙▮↼

"Please state and spell your name for the record."

"R, A, N, D, A, L, L, J, O, H, N, S, O, N."

"Now, Mr. Johnson, do you know a Savannah Liddel?"

"Yes…she is like, my god-sister. I have known her for twelve years."

"And, do you know a Kimberly Morgan?"

"Yes I do," Mr. Johnson said softly.

"Can you point her out in the courtroom?"

Turning toward Ms. Morgan, he nodded in her direction without looking.

"May the record reflect the witness has identified the defendant in this matter."

"Yes," the judge flatly said as he continued to read.

"Do you recall the last time you saw the defendant?"

"Last time I *physically* saw her was when I helped her move her stuff out from Savannah's house."

"And, did you ever see her after that?"

"I *thought* I seen her…at Walgreens parking lot, in her car."

"Would that be July 2, 2003?"

"Yes."

"I'm handing you a photograph and asking if you recognize that."

"It looks like Kim's car. I met with a detective, we went over there, and I told him I saw a black Probe at the Walgreens. I saw what looked like Kim's car backing up between two cars."

"When you say you saw the car, was someone actually in the vehicle?"

"Yes. Someone was maneuvering the car around, pulling forward and backing up. From my position, on Atherton Road, I couldn't tell who it was."

"Do you recall what you told Detective Reaves?"

"I told him I *thought* it was Kim."

"Thank you. Nothing further, Your Honor."

--><==@ @==><--

Mr. Beauvais stood and pressed the witness. "Course, the reason you thought it was Kimberly Morgan was because she drives a black Probe, correct?"

"Basically, I was familiar with the car from knowing her. I was thinking it was her car."

"But you didn't actually *see* the person in the car to identify them, correct?"

"No, I wasn't," the witness said softly. "I was coming to make the turn onto Atherton off a Dort."

"You were headed south on Dort, and you were making a left-hand turn, which would take you east on Atherton, correct?"

"Yes. I was waiting for traffic to stop, so I could make my turn. And when it did, I turn-t into Walgreens, and the Probe was gone by then."

"To get into Walgreens is a left, and then another left? I mean, its right there, right on the corner, right?"

"Yes," the witness said, looking most confused.

"Nothing further, Your Honor."

⋆⟫⬤ ⬤⟪⋆

The assistant to the assistant prosecutor ushered the next person to give testimony into the court, and seated him in the witness chair. He was short, nearly fifty, aging, graying, and balding, and I was the witness. I had on a short-sleeved yellow seersucker shirt, tan chinos, and brown loafers.

⋆⟫⬤ ⬤⟪⋆

"Do you swear to tell the truth, and nothing but the truth?" the judge asked me.

"I do," I replied.

"Will all three of the lawyers please approach the bench?" The judge asked. Once assembled, they started a very frank and animated discussion that lasted for several minutes. My guess was that it involved questioning parameters.

The assistant to the assistant prosecutor resumed the podium and began his questioning. "Could you please say and spell your name for the record?"

"Daniel M, U, R, P, H, Y."

"And you are part of a larger family?"

"Yes, I am."

"And you lost your mom?"

"Yes."

"I'm sorry for your loss. Your mom's name was Dorothy Lee Murphy? What was her birth date?"

"March 2, 1921. Oh, I'm sorry; my dad was born in 1921. Mother was born on March 2, 1923."

"And she would have been eighty years old?"

"Correct."

"Now, your mom had some physical limitations, right?"

"My mother had a couple different forms of arthritis, osteoarthritis and rheumatoid. She also had an arthritic lower-back condition, which limited her mobility. A few years ago she had a hip replacement."

"Did this limit her mobility to walk?"

"Correct."

"Specifically, to walk long distances, or at all—how would you describe that?"

"Walking a long distance would be difficult. She usually only walked short distances. She drove almost everywhere and took full advantage of handicapped spaces. She didn't do a whole lot of walking."

"And how do you know that she took advantage of handicap spaces?"

"My mother was belligerent about it, actually. She had a handicapped license plate and a little plastic thing that you hang on…"

"I object, Your Honor," attorney Beauvais said, strongly protesting, and looking most irritated.

"Regardless of the handicap plate, how do you know?"

"I rode along with my mother in her vehicle; she parked in them."

"Did she have hip replacement surgery?"

"Yes, she did."

"And did you actually see the device they implanted in her? Or, do you know what kind it was?"

"Yes, I was at the hospital when she had the surgery; I assisted in her recovery."

"Basically it was a replacement ball and socket on her hip, so it could rotate?"

"Yes, sir."

Mr. Beauvais again stood and strongly objected. "I am going to object, because I don't see how this is relevant."

The prosecutor responded, "It is relevant because of where the victim was carjacked and abducted from."

The judge stared directly at the assistant prosecutor over his glasses. "You have a careful area that I want you to stay away from."

"Yes."

"What was it; in respect to the belligerence about your mother's attitude, about the handicap parking that you observed?"

"It was her *right*, and privilege to have a handicapped space."

"So if anyone parked in that space that didn't have a sticker, she'd be adamantly against that?"

"Yes."

The attorney then handed me a photograph, and asked, "Are you familiar with the Walgreens on that corner? Now, without any regard to anything about the car, do you see a handicapped space there?"

"I can see there is a blue line painted to the far right of the photo, which usually indicates a space for handicapped parking."

"Now, handicap spaces are typically up close to the door. Correct?"

"Yes."

"Now, Walgreens, at that corner, is a relatively new store, isn't it?"

"Yes."

"You're familiar where it is? Corner of Dort and Atherton?"

"Correct."

"What stores are adjacent to that, that you know your mother frequented?"

"My mother was a bit of a discount shopper. She shopped Big Lots…"

"She was thrifty as well?"

"Yes, she shopped Big Lots, Mazel's, the Dollar Store…"

"Mazel's? M, A, Z, E, L, S?"

"Judge! Now I'm going to object… May we approach?" Mr. Beauvais protested.

"Yes."

The two attorneys approached the bench and had a very frank discussion.

"Now, I know this is difficult to talk about, but let's talk about your mom. Did she go by Dorothy, Dorothy Lee? You called her Mom, didn't you?"

"We referred to her as Dort, actually."

"Really? OK," the attorney said, smiling and acting surprised. Then he tilted his head to one side and asked, "Was that at her request?"

"Excuse my terminology, but it sort of started as a smart-assed nickname. Short Dort."

"OK. Did she accept that after a time?"

"Yes, it became a term of endearment."

"OK. How long had she been called Dort?"

"Probably thirty years or better."

"Your mom had a colorful personality?"

"Feisty."

"Feisty, at eighty years old?"

"Yes. You didn't mess with Mrs. Murphy." The courtroom chuckled.

"Now, you're one of four siblings, and you're the second?"

"Yes, the second."

"Only to ask you…about what your mother was fond of saying, are you familiar with certain phrases your mom was fond of saying?"

"Yes," I replied, not certain where he was heading.

"In respect to what your mom said, was your mom a religious person?"

"Judge, approach!" Mr. Beauvais shouted, jumping to his feet.

"I understand the objection. I didn't until Mr. Beauvais objected."

"I think he knows *exactly* what he is doing, Judge!"

"That's not the issue we talked about at the bench, Your Honor."

Mr. Beauvais gave the assistant prosecutor the stink-eye and responded, "I don't think I need to talk about every single issue at the bench, Your Honor. He *knows* what he is doing is improper."

"Move on to the next area, Counselor," Judge Neithercut said flatly.

"Did you have occasion to see your mother interacting with other people before her death? Specifically strangers, did you see her interact?"

"I'm not sure what you are asking me."

"You said you were with her at times in the car. Were there times when she interacted with store clerks, or other strangers?"

"Certainly," I said, still not sure where he was going.

"How would you describe her social interaction with other people?"

"Our mother was very social, she was quite gregarious."

"In what way?"

"She played cards regularly, went on trips with a group, was in the Ladies of the Altar Guild, and volunteered at the church. She had a very active social life."

"You mentioned the hip replacement surgery, and that she had trouble walking long distances. Did your mom have problems with her eyes?"

"She had cataract surgery in one eye a year before her death, and the other one in May of 2003."

"Now, along those lines, had she been driving a long period of time or a short period of time before her death, in respect to her eyes?"

"There was a period of time when she didn't drive, but she resumed shortly before she died."

"Was her driving, in respect to her eyes, anything of concern to you?"

"No, my mother was very sharp."

"Then you wouldn't tell your mom what to do."

"No, you didn't mess with Mrs. Murphy."

"Do you know where your mom liked to shop at?"

"She lived across the street from the Meijer's Thrifty Acres Store; it was the closest to where she lived. She did the majority of her food shopping there. But she was also thrifty and shopped the sale papers, and if there was ten cents off on toilet paper somewhere across town she would go there for it."

"She would go there for just ten cents?"

"Yes."

"And where did she get her prescriptions filled?"

"Across the street from her..."

The attorney cut me off in midsentence. "How close is the Meijer's store from the Walgreens?"

"They are on opposite sides of town."

"And there are a number of stores near the Walgreens, correct?"

"Yes, practically that entire area is discount shopping."

"Thank you, Daniel. Again, I am sorry for your loss."

⋯⟫⊙ ⊙⟪⋯

Attorney Beauvais stood and sarcastically said, "I have no questions for this witness, Your Honor."

Judge Neithercut smiled at me warmly and said, "You may step down."

⋯⟫⊙ ⊙⟪⋯

We all watched as the bailiff led the jury out for their lunch break. Kimberly Morgan was, once again, handcuffed by a court officer and taken away for her meal.

The judge turned to address those of us sitting in the front bench. "To the Murphy family, I am really sorry that you have to look at those bad pictures. That's a terrible thing to have to go through. I get a little squeamish myself when I watch that, and I am sorry that you have to.

"Court is dismissed. Court will resume at one thirty, sharp."

⋯⟫⊙ ⊙⟪⋯

As a group we meandered across the street to the Masonic Temple for lunch, anticipating that we would have plenty to discuss.

Dr. Nibedita Mahanti Testimony

COURT WAS CALLED to order and the trial resumed at one thirty on the dot.

⊷⊶

"At this time the people call Dr. Nibedita Mahanti to the stand," the prosecutor proudly announced.

A tiny dark-skinned woman gingerly walked into the courtroom and took the witness chair. She was as small as a child, East Indian I would guess. She had dark-chocolate skin, and her heavy dark shiny hair was parted in the middle and pulled back behind tiny ears. Her heavily accented speech was delivered in a nasally, high-pitched, almost childlike singsong tone. It was difficult to hear, let alone understand, her.

⊷⊶

"Please say and spell your name for the record."

"My name is Nibedita Mahanti," she softly stated.

"And what is your occupation?"

"I am a forensic scientist with the Michigan State Police, in the DNA Unit. I have been there for about nine and a half years."

"What are your duties?"

"I analyze forensic evidence, using DNA and serology methods."

"What type of education did you get to do your job?"

"I received a bachelor and master's degree from India where I specialized in genetics. Then I came to Michigan State University and received a PhD degree in microbiology, mostly dealing with DNA methods. Then I did a postdoctoral degree in MSU for three years, working in serology and code DNA methods. And after that, I went with the Michigan State Police crime lab, since January of 1995."

"OK. And, have you participated in research in your area of expertise?"

"Yes I have."

"Doctor, have you ever testified for the courts as an expert witness in DNA analysis?"

"Yes I have in several courts, Ingham County, Macomb County, Flint, and Saginaw."

"Your Honor, at this time the people move to have Dr. Mahanti qualified as an expert witness for the courts."

"She's qualified," Judge Neithercut said without ever looking up.

"Thank you, Judge. Now, Doctor, could you explain briefly for the jury what DNA is."

"DNA is an abbreviation for deoxynucleic acid; it is a substance that is present in every cell of our body. DNA is unique to an individual, excepting for identical twins. That is why we test DNA as a tool for forensic evidence."

"So, is there ever the same DNA in two people?"

"Except for identical twins, no."

"Can exposure to environmental conditions, like moisture, heat, and sunlight, change DNA?"

"No. It cannot."

"Now, just briefly, can you explain to the jury what DNA profiling procedure you use."

"PCR, or polymerase chain reaction, is the method we use. We look at thirteen different areas of DNA plus the anlagen, which shows the gender of the person. When these fourteen different areas are amplified, using different chemic-als, the product is separated by jell electrolysis, which separates it by the size of the DNA fragments.

"After being separated, these fragments are labeled with a dye, so we can then visualize them as peaks, or types. This is done with all the different samples that are submitted to us, to see if it is a match, or, to see if it's excluded."

"OK. Do you recognize this photo here, Doctor?" Prosecutor Hanson said as she flashed a photograph of the lotion bottle upon the projection screen.

"This is evidence that was sent to me; a burnt bottle of lotion, which was then swabbed for DNA."

"Did you conduct DNA analysis, as you just said a minute ago, on this bottle?"

"Yes, I did."

"And, did you come to any conclusions, based on your analysis?"

"Yes. I got DNA from the swabbing sample I took from the lotion bottle. I was also given a sample, allegedly from Miss Morgan, and I compared the types. I was *not* able to exclude Miss Morgan as a donor to the sample."

"Doctor, once that DNA profile is obtained, from those matches, you determine the frequency of the DNA profile. Is that correct?"

"Yes I do."

"Did you do that in this case, and what was that frequency result?"

"For the sample that we got, we wanted to show how *rare* that DNA type was in the human population. I was given a small sample from the lotion bottle, and we base the estimate on three different ethnic backgrounds: one, Caucasian; two, African-American; and three, Hispanic.

"This particular DNA combination occurs only once in three hundred and seventy-two billion inside the Caucasian population, once in one hundred and six point two billion in the African-American population, and in the Hispanic, only once in ten point seven trillion. That is how *rare* these DNA types are in the human population."

"I am handing you people's exhibit number seventy-eight and asking if you recognize this."

"Yes I do. It is the DNA report that I provided after my testing was done."

"Doctor, is this report, up on the screen, is this what you were just talking about?"

"Yes."

"Now, explain for the jury, so they can see what it is that you are talking about."

"OK. If you select an individual from the random population that could have contributed this DNA type that I obtained from the lotion bottle, then statistically you would find only *one person* having that combination of gene types in one hundred and six point two billion people."

"So, if you sample one hundred and six point two *billion* people, statistically, you would find only one person having that DNA. Is that what you're saying?"

"That's correct; statistically that's what we will see."

"How many people are there in the world?"

"There are six billion people in the world."

"I have nothing further," the prosecutor said. "Thank you, Your Honor."

⋅▸▦◉ ◉▦◂⋅

Mr. Beauvais took the podium, arranged his papers, made notes, and then spoke. "Doctor, so, DNA testing is based upon a *theory* that no two people, other than identical twins, have the same DNA. Is that correct?"

"That's correct."

"Now, we haven't had a chance to go out and test everybody to see if there are any repeats out there, isn't that right?"

"We haven't tested all of them, no, but the research that has taken place says no two people have the same exact DNA, except for identical twins."

"Based on the tests done *so far*, is that correct?"

"Yes."

"Now, where did you locate this bit of DNA you found on the lotion bottle?"

"The sample that I took - from the lotion bottle, it was from a charred lotion bottle. I opened the cap, and when we normally put lotion on, we would make contact where the lotion comes out of the tube. I swabbed that area, where it was not charred."

"And, when you obtained the DNA you tested it using a known DNA type and you try to locate its thirteen locis?"

"Yes. Thirteen loci," the doctor said, smiling while correcting him.

"And the truth is, we're all made up of probably thousands of DNA locis, are we not?"

"Loci. Yes we are."

"A lot of those are the same, like two eyes, legs, arms, things of that nature."

"Correct."

"Based on what's been done, in terms of testing, there are thirteen that are thought to be different in every person, correct?"

"Going back to what you said. Over ninety-nine percent of the DNA, in most individuals, is similar. But we are only looking at less than one percent of the DNA we have totally. There is a lot of 'junk' DNA. We base our research on those specific thirteen loci."

"What you did was, you obtained this DNA from this lotion container, and you look at the thirteen loci, correct?"

"It's all done in a test tube. Yes."

"And, on some of the loci you are at least going to find *some* genetic marker, but there was something else there and you were not able to determine what the genetic matter was. Is that correct?"

"That's right, some of the genetic markers I did not have."

"In fact, some of them you had put down that you found something, but you were unable to determine any of the genetic markers in relation to that one loci."

"That's correct."

"And, on some of the loci you were able to find one genetic marker, but there was something else there, and you weren't able to determine what that genetic marker was. Is that correct?"

"Um…yes. This was a tiny sample; the size was very small considering where it came from. Therefore there are some markers that did not give any activity, or any result, and that is what happens when you get peaks of that type. After doing the markers that threshold has to be between a hundred and fifty and forty-five hundred peak heights. If it's below one hundred and fifty, we will call it inactive. If it's over forty-five hundred we will disregard it, and not record it. The statistics that I gave you was recorded on the types that I *could* call."

"Which meant that there were types that you *couldn't* call at all, correct?"

"That's correct. I did not use the word *matches*. I said I could not exclude her as a donor. There were four markers that matched completely, and four markers that were partial. That is why I say, 'I cannot exclude her.' The sample was so small, and when you are dealing with a small amount of DNA there's a phenomenon that occurs. There are two types at that locust, one is from the father, and one is from the mother; out of those two it preferentially amplifies the one, and not the other. All of the types I tested could not exclude her."

Mr. Beauvais pressed on. "But, in fact, again, out of the thirteen you found you had a match for only four, is that correct?"

"Correct."

"And again, how many people are in the world?"

"Over six billion."

"I have nothing further, Judge," Mr. Beauvais said, returning to his chair.

⋯⊷⊶⋯

The prosecutor rose once again. "Now, because it was such a small sample that you were testing, you weren't able to determine all the thirteen points, isn't that correct?"

"Yes."

"If you had a larger sample you may have been able to determine all thirteen points, and that would make your number be higher?"

"Yes, that's right."

"OK. But as you say, you were not able to *exclude* Kimberly Morgan from this sample. Is that correct?"

"That is correct."

"And you would find that combination once in one hundred and six point two billion samples statistically?"

"In one hundred and six point two billion people, statistically, only *one* person would have that particular combination of types."

"OK. Nothing further."

Mr. Beauvais, needing to have the last word, stood once more and added, "And that calculation was based on eight or nine of the loci, not all of the thirteen, correct?"

"Yes, that is correct."

Carolyn Kennedy Testimony

THE NEXT WITNESS was sworn in, and seated. She was a soft and motherly-looking woman with crepe-like skin. Well-dressed in a navy blue collarless suit and white knit top, she wore gold wire-rimmed glasses and conservative earrings.

⋅➤⊜ ⊜⊰⋅

"Please say and spell your name for the record."

"Carolyn Kennedy."

"And where do you work at?"

"I work at the Mundy Township Police Department."

"And what are your duties there?"

"My primary duties are to maintain the evidence room and any properties or evidentiary materials that are turned in to the police department. I receive it and secure it into a locked evidence room, where it is kept until it is either sent out for further evaluation, used as evidence for court, or it is given back to the owners; or what-have-you."

"Were you present when Detective Kathy Taylor, the fire expert, came to your facility?"

"Yes, I was."

"And what did she bring?"

"She had brought in some items that she recovered from a vehicle that she had just processed."

"I'm showing you what's proposed as people's exhibit number sixty-nine. You recognize that?"

"It is a plastic bottle and a spent shell casing."

"Do you know where that shell casing came from?"

"Yes, I do. It is one of the items that Sergeant Taylor brought in. It was found in a burnt purse. As she was looking at it, this spent shell casing fell out of the folds of the purse."

"OK. And, what did you do with that spent casing?"

"It went to the lab. The property log shows that it was checked out to Detective Diem, on July 9, at 8:50 a.m., to be transported to the Michigan State crime lab in Bridgeport."

"Your Honor, I move to have the envelope and the log that accompanies it entered as evidence."

"Items sixty-nine and seventy-nine are admitted."

"Did you receive it back from the lab at some time?"

"Yes I did. According to the property log, Detective Diem transported it back from the crime lab and delivered it back to me on December 12, 2003."

"Nothing further, Your Honor."

⊷≡◉ ◉≡⊷

The judge turned toward the jury and leaned way back in his big leather chair and spoke. "We're done for the day, so relax. Go home and have a nice and relaxing weekend. Please be back here on Tuesday morning at 9:30 a.m.. There is a possibility that you may begin to deliberate on Tuesday, but you should plan on being here the rest of the week anyway; hopefully, you'll start on Tuesday.

"You will avoid Beecher Road between Ballenger and I-75, Walgreens on Dort and Atherton, and Mr. Lucky's on Lapeer Road. You will not call your friends up, or people you know, to ask for information. You will not conduct any experiments; you will go home and enjoy the long weekend."

The third day of testimony and trial was concluded.

My Fiftieth Birthday

·→═◉ ◉═←·

As you've just read, attending Mother's murder trial over the past few days had been intense. So a chance to get away from abduction, murder, arson, and death for a while, and to celebrate fifty years of life, would be a good thing.

For well over a year I'd planned on throwing myself a fiftieth birthday party. I had already asked all the people I wanted to attend long ago, way before all this shit happened, and I still fully intended to see it through. However, there were a few stipulations. My cottage was small, so if you planned on attending you'd better be very flexible about your sleeping arrangements, and there was only one small bathroom.

A couple of tents were being pitched down by the lake's shore, and a trailer or two would be parking in the piney woods. But with four acres of woodlands and ample lakefront, there was plenty of room to spread out. Plus there was the big old barn and studio for shelter, if the weather decided to turn bad. All were welcome if they just remembered there was only one toilet.

Michigan's weather is often quite unpredictable, and in late August, on my birthday weekend, it decided to turn unseasonably cold and quite shitty, with a constant dampening drizzle. Murphy's Law was in practice. Many of my guests arrived wearing their winter coats. Some even had on woolen hats and gloves, and everyone was hanging very, very close to the campfire.

·→═◉ ◉═←·

But my previously preplanned personal party was preempted by my devious sister, Mary Ann. She and my two brothers managed to arrange a surprise fiftieth birthday party for me at Tim and Patty's place the week before my own party. Somehow Mary managed to reach most of my old friends in the Flint area, and she even invited a few relatives, too. I truly was surprised.

But in the process I was also lied to, deceived, and hoodwinked by my own family, because I was told I was invited to a birthday party for my nephew Patrick, since his birthday was right before mine. But it was a lovely surprise, nonetheless, and a great evening was spent with my family and friends.

⋅⊷⊷⊛ ⊛⊷⊷⋅

My big-old birthday bash at the cottage was a week-end-long event, complete with the eternally flaming campfire and nonstop eating. Spirits were dampened only slightly by the inclement weather, and the party went on as planned. It wasn't a noisy, drunken, youthful affair; it was a pleasant get-together with long-time friends and family.

Of course I managed to receive the obligatory stupid gag gifts that one gets at age fifty. Denture cream, hemorrhoid cream, Metamucil, adult diapers, ha, ha, ha. I would save these items, as Mary would be the next to turn fifty in just a few more years. Paybacks are hell, aren't they, Mary?

My friend Mike Putnam was not included, and that still bothers me to this day. He was sober at the time, and I did not wish to jeopardize that or have to worry about him on this weekend. And when I explained my thinking on this subject to him, he seemed to be all right with it.

The weekend turned out to be a welcome relief for everyone, and we returned to the trial chilled, smoky, rested, renewed, and just a wee bit older.

August 31, Fourth Day of Trial

AT EXACTLY 10:02 on August 31, 2004, the fourth day of Mother's trial began. Today Ms. Morgan looked different, because she was wearing a big and bulky loose-knit brown sweater with an oversize cowl neck. Somehow this made her look smaller and larger at the same time.

Her Attorney, Philip H. Beauvais III, appeared to be a changed man, too. While addressing the courtroom today his demeanor was much more conciliatory, uncharacteristically polite, humble and congenial.

⋅⋗▬◉ ◉▬⋖⋅

"Are there things to say before we bring the jury in?" the judge said, scanning the courtroom.

Mr. Beauvais rose to his feet and politely began.

"Judge, there is. There's a couple of things we need to do, in terms of the defendant. I believe that the prosecutor will be resting after Sergeant Schmitzer testifies today?" he said, while looking toward the prosecutor for an answer.

"That is correct, Your Honor," she responded.

Mr. Beauvais resumed. "The balance of endorsed witnesses, we will waive their presence. We do not require the prosecutor to produce those witnesses. And, I would ask the court to advise my client - as to her right to testify, or not testify.

"Also, there is the issue of her prior conviction; I believe it is for bank robbery. I'm not sure if the prosecutor will try to impeach my client with that or not, but it will be my position that will be inappropriate. However, we can deal with that however the court decides.

"Now, the defendant has on a leg brace, and that is going to make it impossible for her to get to the witness chair without the jury being very much aware she is wearing them. Perhaps what we can do is, when the prosecutor rests, we can, ah, send the jury out, or take a break, to do this outside the presence of the jury. We can get Ms. Morgan, if she deems it appropriate to testify, into the witness chair before the jury gets back. And we will bring them back out after she testifies."

"We will take care of that when, and if, the time comes," the judge replied.

"Thank you, Judge," Mr. Beauvais said in a most uncharacteristically heartfelt manner.

The judge then inquired, "Anything else?"

There were no other points expressed.

"Then Mr. Newland, will bring the jury in."

⋯⊱⊱⊰⊰⋯

Today the prosecutor looked well rested; she wore a well-tailored dove-gray suit and a simple white cotton button-down blouse. Confidently rising, she pushed her unruly, white-blond hair behind her unadorned ears and announced, "At this time, the people call Detective Mark Schmitzer to the stand."

Detective Schmitzer entered wearing an unbuttoned dark navy blue suit that hung loosely about him, making him look as if he'd just lost a great deal of weight. Even though he was here for most of the trial assisting with the case, you hardly noticed him. He was not a man who stood out. He was past middle age and a tad overweight, well-dressed but somehow always appearing disheveled.

⋯⊱⊱⊰⊰⋯

"Would you please say and spell your name for the record."

"Detective Mark S, C, H, M, I, T, Z, E, R."

"And what is your occupation?"

"I am a detective with the Flint Township Police Department. "I've been in law enforcement for twenty-five years. In investigation for ten years, and for the last four years I've been in the Detective Bureau."

"Detective Schmitzer, you became the officer in charge on September 26 of 2003; that correct?"

"Yes, I did."

"And, can you tell the court how that happened?"

"I was dispatched to the River Oak, and River Valley area, after a call came in that they had found a body."

"OK. And at some point, did you find out whose body that was?"

"Subsequent to the investigation, it was identified as being Dorothy Murphy."

"Now, things had happened prior to finding the body, and you kind of had to…I don't want to put it this way, but, get caught up to speed. To find out what this case was all about. Correct?"

"Correct. I'd been involved with a couple earlier searches, at the request of the Mundy Township Police, and had completed those. But yes, I did have to come up to speed more fully, after the twenty-sixth."

"OK…and did you go to all the scenes involved with this case? Did you go to Walgreens, did you go to Grand Traverse and Third, and Fourth, in the city of Flint? Did you speak with an Alan Johnson?"

"Yes I did."

"Did you also go to Mr. Lucky's on, oh I forget, on Lapeer Road in Flint?"

"Yes, I did," he said, showing a faint smile.

"Why did you go to all these places?"

"I wanted to familiarize myself with the case. I also wanted to drive any possible routes from Grand Traverse and Third, to Mr. Lucky's."

"Did you do that, and what did you find?"

"I was with Detective Sergeant Mark Reaves, as he has previously testified, and depending on the route you take, it's between two point four and two point seven miles, depending on the traffic. It takes between five and ten minutes to get there."

"OK. At some point in time you find that the defendant had received a speeding ticket in Indiana?"

"Yes."

"Do you recall what time that stop occurred?"

"There is an hour's difference. It was about eight o'clock our time, and nine o'clock their time. The exact time, with minutes, I don't recall. They do not use daylight savings time."

"So they are on a different time schedule. So, did you, in fact, get all the lab reports as they came in, the casings, the DNA, the sunglasses, things of that nature?"

"Yes, all those reports were submitted to myself."

"Did you, at any point, have occasion to sit down and talk to the defendant?"

"Yes I did."

"And do you recall when that took place?"

"There were three different occasions."

"When did the first one occur?"

"On December 22."

"December 22, 2003? And where'd this take place?"

"December 22, 2003, at the Michigan State Police Post, at Linden and Corunna Roads."

"OK, was the defendant read her rights?"

"Yes, she was."

"And did the defendant waive her rights?"

"Yes."

"Did she appear to be competent?"

"Yes."

"What, if anything, did the defendant tell you about the events of this investigation?"

A noticeable hush fell over the already silenced room.

"She admitted to me, on that day, that she had been the one that approached Dorothy Murphy at Walgreens, to take her car. That she had been in town earlier that day. She met up with an unknown male in a rusty brown truck. She hired him to shoot Alan Johnson, and that *he* was the one that met her and Mrs. Murphy on the cul-de-sac off River Road and that he had been the one to shoot Mrs. Murphy."

"Did she talk, at all, about Alan Johnson being shot?"

"Yes. After the 'unknown male accomplice' shot Mrs. Murphy, they went back into the city of Flint, and did some-thing with the vehicles as far as positioning them to go back to. She then went over and watched this unknown gentleman shoot Alan Johnson. They went back to Arbor Village; he left, and she took the car back across the street to Mr. Lucky's on Lapeer Road and burned the car."

"Did you ever talk to the defendant again? And when did that take place?"

"I next met with the defendant on the fourth of January, 2003."

"Do you mean the fourth of January, 2004?" Mrs. Hanson said, clarifying.

"Correct."

"OK, how did you happen to talk to her again?"

"She requested that we talk."

"OK, where did this interview take place?"

"At the Michigan State Police Post in Flint Township, at Linden and Corunna Roads."

"OK, was she again read her rights?"

"Yes."

"What, if anything, did she talk to you about at this time?"

"This time, when confronted with her truthfulness about the original statement she told me, she said she would tell me the truth this time. That she was the only one that was involved with all the incidents that day: the killing of Dorothy Murphy, the shooting of Alan Johnson, the burning of the car, and possession of a firearm."

"Did she tell you why she did those things?"

"It was the result of her past love relationship with Savannah Liddel."

"OK...did she indicate to you where and when she got the gun?"

"She claimed she got it in Tennessee, from an unknown individual."

"OK, what did she say to you about Mrs. Murphy?"

A deeper hush fell over the courtroom.

Detective Schmitzer had been speaking in a fast manner in the beginning, but now he slowed way down, spoke each sentence deliberately, took pause between each point, and then moved on. I am not sure if it was to recall correctly, or because the nature of the subject was so weighty.

"In her original statement, on the fourth, she said she'd driven to Flint and she wanted to talk to Savannah, but that wasn't possible. That was her original statement on the fourth. That she saw Mrs. Murphy, inside Mrs. Murphy's car, parked at Walgreens. She approached Mrs. Murphy, had Mrs. Murphy get into the backseat of the car. They drove around for a while before she went over to the cul-de-sac area between River Forest and River Valley; as she basically knew the area, because she'd lived there with her father. She knew about the cul-de-sac, she said it was a good place to 'hide things.'"

"That she brought Dorothy Murphy from the car, and walked her back to the wooded area. They had a conversation, a short one."

"And did she say what that conversation was about?"

"That Kim did not seem like she was a bad person, and she would pray for Kim."

"OK," Mrs. Hanson said. "Go on."

"That the gun 'went off' two or three times, striking Mrs. Murphy in the face, and in the chest."

"OK…did she say how the gun 'went off'?"

"Again, in the interview, she said, 'It just went off.' She didn't know how."

"OK. Did she say what happened after she'd shot Mrs. Murphy?"

"She then left the area, took her car—correction—took Mrs. Murphy's car, went over to Arbor Village, parked it, and got back into it, after putting some things into it. She then drove it over to Grand Traverse, between Third and Fourth, and waited for Alan Johnson."

"Detective Schmitzer, in doing your investigation, did you find if it was possible to walk from Arbor Village to Walgreens?"

"It was within easy walking distance."

"It was… OK…so…she indicated she went over to where Alan Johnson was shot, is that correct?"

"She pulled up in front of him; she was the only one in the car. She shot him. She knew she'd hit him because he screamed. She knew it. She continued to chase him and shoot at him. She knew she'd hit him again, because he went down. After he'd run off, and she was not able to get to him, she drove off."

"OK…did she say anything about the burning of the vehicle?"

"After leaving the Grand Traverse and Third and Fourth areas, she went over to Lapeer Road. She took the car behind Mr. Lucky's. She had some gasoline with her. She lit the gasoline off with her lighter. She then carried a bag from the burning car with her, across Lapeer Road, went back to her own vehicle, and then left Flint."

"OK, did you ask any questions about the phone calls that were made between July 2 and July twenty-seventh?"

"Yes I did. Phone calls were made to the area hospitals, to see what condition Mr. Johnson was in, and if he would have been admitted. She also called the Ennis Center to gain information on him. She also called Mr. Lucky's, Arbor Village Apartments, and the South Side Party Store to see if anybody could give her any information on the car fire. She knew she'd been seen by people when she was leaving there."

"Did you ask her, and did she tell you, why she took Mrs. Murphy's car?"

"She needed a vehicle that wasn't her own, so that she could use it to shoot Alan Johnson, so that it would not be able to be traced back to her."

"Did she say anything about whether Mrs. Murphy had any involvement with any of this?"

It was so quiet in the courtroom that I could hear my own heart beating.

"She said that Mrs. Murphy did not give her any problems, and she did not fight with her."

"Did she talk about being stopped in Indiana?"

"Yes, she did. She said she had the gun, and it was in the car at that time; she was very surprised that the trooper didn't search the car. After that traffic stop she got scared, and threw the gun out before she entered the state of Kentucky."

"Did she say why she burned Mrs. Murphy's car?"

"To destroy her fingerprints."

"Was that interview taped, Detective?"

"Yes it was."

"And do you have the entire tape?"

"Yes."

"And do you also have an edited version?"

"Yes."

"And, why is that tape edited?"

"By the court's mandated rules, and the state law guidelines. This is an edited version of the taped interview with Kimberly Morgan on January 4, 2004."

"Your Honor, the people will move to have this tape admitted."

"It is admitted," the judge flatly said.

The prosecutor plugged in the videotape and displayed it upon the screen for the courtroom and jury to see. There wasn't much action happening, Kimberly sat quietly composed while eating potato chips and sipping bottled water. She chatted quite comfortably with Detective Schmitzer, who was sitting across the table from her with his arms casually folded over his broad chest, leaning back in his chair.

The courtroom was beyond hushed, straining to hear the audio portion. Kimberly was well spoken, her speech slow and deliberate, articulate yet matter-of-factly detached, and expressing little emotion. She paused and thought before speaking each new sentence as she explained how each step was accomplished. The detective appeared to be relaxed. He would pose a question from time to time, but she did most of the speaking, directing the conversation.

All the while the videotape played, the judge continued to go through paperwork, seemingly not paying attention to what was going on but never missing a thing. When the tape finished playing, the prosecutor continued.

"Detective, during that interview, do you recall when Dorothy Murphy came out of Walgreens, do you recall if the defendant said she had a gun at that point?"

"I do. And she said she did not have a gun out at that time, but that the gun was with her."

"The gun was with her? How'd she get Dorothy Murphy into the back of her car?"

"She told her to get in the back. And she said that probably Dorothy could see by the look on her face that she was serious, and that she complied."

"Did she indicate whether Mrs. Murphy seemed afraid?"

"She did not."

"OK…now, did you talk to the defendant again?"

"Yes, on January 5, 2004, the very next day."

"How did that happen?"

"She called Detective Reaves and myself, collect, to come downtown to talk to her at the jail."

"And was she once again read her rights?"

"Yes she was."

"And did she waive those rights?"

"Yes she did."

"And what, if anything, did she tell you at that time?"

"She said that she had told us part of the truth the previous day, and that, at this time, she wanted to tell the whole truth. It would be the right thing to do."

"Did she tell you the truth, as you believe it to be?"

"Yes."

"What did she tell you?"

"She again reiterated that she had acted alone. But at this time she told me, on the morning of July 2, 2003, that she had met with Savannah Liddel. They had a conversation about getting back together. They also had a conversation about Alan Johnson. And that Savannah had told her that the only way to get back together was if Alan was out of the picture.

"I pressed her in questioning. As far as Savannah, did she tell Ms. Morgan to shoot Alan? And she said *no*. Just that, 'It would be better if he weren't in the picture.' Kim then said she asked Savannah if she wanted Alan just scared, or killed. Again, she said, Savannah said he needed to be 'out of the picture.' Then Kim, later on, formulated a plan to shoot him."

"Did she tell you if, in fact, she did go to the Walgreens at Dort and Atherton on that day?"

"She said that she rode around for quite a while, looking for a vehicle. And that she went back up to the Mazel's area - where Savannah worked, that she then came into contact with Dorothy Murphy at Walgreens, at Dort and Atherton. Savannah was just across the corner at Mazel's."

"Did she tell you *when* she came in contact with Dorothy Murphy? What happened?"

"That as Dorothy exited the store, she stopped her. She told her to get into the car. She put her into the backseat of the car...they rode around for a while, they ended up going over to the cul-de-sac off River Forest and River Valley. Then she took Dorothy Murphy out of her car...then she walked her back into the woods...where Dorothy ends up being shot.

"Again, she said, 'The gun just went off a couple of times.' Actually three times. It went off a couple times, and the third time, she pulled the trigger."

You could have heard a feather drop in the court.

"She say why she pulled the trigger the third time?"

"She knew she had to finish her."

"So she wanted to make sure she was dead?"

"Yes."

"OK." The prosecutor said, exhaled audibly, and continued. "Did she say what she did after that?"

"She said she took ten dollars from Mrs. Murphy's purse, because she needed money for food. She went back to Arbor Village and parked Dorothy's car, walked to Walgreens, got her car, and brought it back. She then went to Grand Traverse and Third, where she confronted Alan Johnson and shot him. She told me it was her intent to kill him at that time.

"From there she went back to Lapeer Road, put Mrs. Murphy's car behind Mr. Lucky's, and burned it with some gasoline that she had with her, to cover up her fingerprints. She then left the state of Michigan.

"She got stopped in Indiana for speeding on her way back to Tennessee. She got rid of the gun, which she had gotten in Tennessee some weeks prior; she said she threw it out into a trash Dumpster before entering Kentucky.

"I confronted her, in that interview, about the shell casings found inside of Mrs. Murphy's car and the ones from Alan Johnson's shooting site matching; she said they would."

"And did she say anything about talking to her friend Barbie Garrison?"

"Later, after that shooting, she spoke to Barbie Garrison. She wanted her to watch the news to compare her to the composite."

"Did she indicate why Mrs. Murphy was killed?"

"No, other than the gun 'went off' and she knew she had to 'finish her off.' Her sole purpose was to have the car."

"Did she say anything about whether Dorothy deserved that?"

"She said that Dorothy didn't deserve to be in any of this."

"Detective, I'm handing you people's exhibit number seventy-nine, and asking if you recognize that," she said while walking a large white poster board with several photographs glued upon it over to the detective.

"Yes, that's the board that was compiled to show all of the different locations in this case."

"And why is that important?"

"To show the relationship of the crime scenes, as they were committed."

"Detective, using this pointer, could you please explain the different sequence of the events as they happened, so the jury has a clear understanding of these events."

"Here is the Walgreens, at the corner of Dort and Atherton. We know that at some time, between eight and noon, Dorothy Murphy was confronted by Kim Morgan at the Walgreens and her car was taken. Randall Johnson says that is where he saw the car."

Mr. Beauvais jumped to his feet, shouting, "I object, Your Honor. That's hearsay."

"Please limit it to what you know," the judge said.

"Dorothy Murphy was abducted from Walgreens between nine and twelve o'clock on July 2, 2003. She was then taken to the cul-de-sac off River Valley and River Oak, where she was killed. And it was there that her remains were found, at that location, on September 26, 2003.

"After that, at 5:08 approximately, in the afternoon, Alan Johnson was shot at Fourth and Grand Traverse. At approximately 5:22, the car was found being burning behind Mr. Lucky's on Lapeer Road. That is the Walgreens where Mrs. Murphy's car was taken from, and then subsequently found behind Mr. Lucky's."

"OK. Thank you, Detective. By the way, did the defendant say whether or not she went back to the scene where Dorothy Murphy's body was found?"

"Yes she did, in late July."

"Did she say why?"

"She said she just wanted to go back to see if the body had been found."

"Did she tell you if it was still there?"

"Yes it was."

"I have nothing further at this time, Your Honor."

Attorney Beauvais Crosses Detective Schmitzer

DEFENSE ATTORNEY BEAUVAIS took his notes and carefully placed them upon the podium, and took his sweet time doing it. "Detective Schmitzer, you are the officer in charge of this investigation, that correct?"

"That is correct."

"What, exactly, are the duties of the officer in charge?"

"My duty is to oversee the investigation. In this case, it involved working with several different agencies and compiling their separate cases into one."

"Did you have any role in this investigation prior to September 26, 2003?"

"Yes. I had been contacted by the Mundy Township Police Department to conduct two different searches on the north side of the Flint River, on tips that they received."

"Other than that, you weren't involved. As of September 26, 2003, you became involved, and you were assigned officer in charge, correct?"

"That is correct."

"And the reason it occurred on September 26, 2003, is that is when Dorothy Murphy's remains were located correct?"

"Correct."

"And they were located within your jurisdiction."

"That's correct."

"Now...you had an opportunity to talk with Kimberly Morgan at least three times, that right?"

"Yes."

"Now…did you ever talk to her other than those occasions?"

"I did not."

"Did anyone else, at your request, talk to Kimberly Morgan?"

"They talked to her, but prior to my involvement with the case."

"Once you became involved, the only times you talked to Kimberly Morgan would have been on December 22, 2003, January 4, 2004, and January 5, 2004, correct?"

"Correct."

"Now, when you talked to Kimberly Morgan, did she tell you she lived in the state of Tennessee?"

"Yes."

"Did she tell you when she returned to the state of Michigan from the state of Tennessee, around July 2, 2003?"

"She originally said early morning. First she said on the first, then she said on the second."

"So sometime between July 1 and 2, she returned from Tennessee to Michigan, correct?"

"Correct."

"Now, when executing a search warrant in the state of Tennessee, some of the police officers located a license plate, is that correct?"

"Correct."

"And that license plate has been entered as evidence, is that correct?"

"Correct."

"And that license plate was at some point reported as stolen, is that correct?"

"That is correct."

"And when would that have been?"

"I do not recall. It came off a Corsica, that's all I recall."

"Now, it would have been prior to July 1, 2003, correct?"

"Yes."

"Now, you said that everything that was located in this case is sent off to the lab for various purposes, correct? Look for trace evidence, fingerprints?"

"That's correct."

"Any incriminating fingerprints found in this case?"

"No."

"Originally, you talked to Kimberly Morgan on December 22, 2003. During that first portion of that interview she denied any involvement with this case. Did she not?"

"That is correct."

"At some point in your discussing the matter with her, you bring up the fact that you could have her charged federally, and she could get the death penalty."

"I did."

"And still she told you, 'I didn't have anything to do with it.'"

"Correct; words to that effect."

"Then, at some point you say to her that because she's not cooperating, you're gonna have to go to a judge and say this person deserves to die; or words to that effect."

"Words to that effect."

"And it was only *after that* that you get what *you want*, your testimony here today. Correct?"

"Correct."

"Now, originally, on December 22, 2003, when you were giving Miss Morgan her Miranda rights, she originally requested that an attorney be present. Is that correct?"

"Correct."

"And you to tried locate an attorney, did you not?"

"That's correct."

"You then came back and told Ms. Morgan that it would take a while before an attorney would be present. Is that right?"

"That's right."

"Is it, at *that* point, that she waives the presence of an attorney?"

"Yes, she did."

"Now, again, this videotape that we've seen, that was taken on the fourth of January, that correct?"

"Yes."

"Did you ever determine how far it was from Arbor Village to Walgreens?"

"No, I did not."

"Now, Arbor Village would be located on Lapeer Road in the city of Flint."

"Lapeer, just west of Dort, yes."

"And the Walgreens is located on Dort and Atherton, is that correct?"

"That's correct."

"The other interviews that weren't videotaped, were they audiotaped?"

"The interviews were audiotaped, yes."

"Any of the other ones videotaped?"

"Ah…yes."

"Which ones?"

"It would have been the one on the twenty-second of December."

"Just so we know, on that video we see the back of someone. That's you, correct?"

"Yes."

"Did Kimberly Morgan ever tell you what type of weapon she had?"

"I believe it was an automatic, either a .38 or a .380."

"Did she tell you it was a pistol?"

"She said it was a handgun."

"And, in terms of the ten dollars that she told you she took from Mrs. Murphy's purse, when did she say she did that?"

"In the first interview, the robbery took place before Mrs. Murphy was shot. In the second interview, it was taken after she was shot."

"And, did she ever discuss that in the third interview?"

"Not in the third interview."

"Thank you."

Attorney Beauvais took his seat at the defense table.

Prosecutor Hanson arose once more. Seeming to be irritated, she glanced at Mr. Beauvais and spoke directly to him. "Detective Schmitzer, were you making up the part about sending the case over to the Feds?"

"No."

"In fact, you were aware that Federal Prosecutor U.S. Attorney Bob Havelind of the Department of Justice was interested in this case."

"Yes."

"Did you lie to the defendant?"

"No."

"In this video-tape we saw your demeanor, and the defendant's did you use this demeanor all three times?"

"All three times."

"Did you ever threaten to hurt or harm her?"

"No."

"Anything like that?"

"No."

"Did she look under duress in that interview?"

"No!"

"How could you tell?"

"She was pretty calm throughout most of it; she was eating potato chips and drinking bottled water through the entire interview."

"OK, did you force her to tell you what she told you?"

"No."

"If I might just ask, when Dorothy Murphy came out of Walgreens, during the second interview, did the defendant talk about whether or not she had a gun?"

"The gun was there, but there were different versions from the first interview."

"What did she say about that?"

"In the first interview, she said she took the car at knifepoint. On the twenty-second, and on the fourth and fifth, she said that she confronted Dorothy Murphy and verbally told her to get into the car. She said she had a gun with her, but it was not out."

"OK. Did she say why Dorothy got in the car?"

"She said because she could tell she was serious by the look on her face."

"All right, nothing further."

Kimberly Morgan Testifies

THE TWO ATTORNEYS had an extended and heated conversation going on that was barely audible. They both approached the bench and conferred, at some length, with the judge. After finishing their negotiations and returning to their seats, Mrs. Hanson rose and spoke.

"Your Honor, it is my understanding that the defendant will stipulate the fact that she has a prior felony. At this time the people rest."

The judge, turning his big chair toward the jury, smiled and said, "At this time, I'd like you all to step out for a few minutes while I take care of a few matters."

The bailiff then escorted the jury out of the courtroom.

⊷⊷⊶ ⊙⊶⊶

When they were gone, Judge Neithercut turned toward Kimberly Morgan. "Please stand and raise your right hand. Do you solemnly swear to tell the truth in this matter, so help you God?"

"Yes I do," replied Ms. Morgan, while blinking profusely.

"What I want to talk to you about is whether or not you choose to testify. Now, let's talk about your rights, your constitutional rights. The constitutions of our country and our state guarantee you the right to testify in your trial, if you choose to. Do you understand that?"

"Yes I do."

"The constitution also turns it around - on the other side, and it guarantees you the right to *not* testify, to not say anything. No one can make you testify, or ask you to testify. No one can even suggest that you testify. You just have the right to be silent. Do you understand that?"

"Yes I do."

"And if you choose to remain silent, the constitution says that they cannot comment on that. They cannot use your silence against you. They can't say, 'Well, if this woman is so innocent, well then, why is she afraid to testify?' They can't say, 'If she's not testifying she must be hiding something,' because you have the right to not let them use your silence against you. Do you understand?"

"Yes I do."

"Now we're at a point where you can decide to testify, or not to testify. The choice is yours alone. Do you understand?"

"Yes I do."

"Now, if you decide to testify there's a catch, there's a kicker. The catch is this: you can come up to this witness stand, and you could be sworn to tell the truth, and you can testify and say whatever it is that you choose to say. So then that opens the door to allow the prosecutor to ask you all kinds of questions, and some which could be damaging. Because if you offer your own testimony you give up your right to be protected by the right of silence, and be protected by the constitution, against self-incrimination.

"And if the prosecutor starts asking you questions - that you know are incriminating, you will not be able to refuse to answer them. I'll have to make you answer them. Do you understand how that works?"

"Yes I do," she said, blinking profusely.

"So...I want you to consult with Mr. Beauvais and decide whether or not you choose to testify. Either way, we will honor that. Do you understand?"

"All right."

There was a hushed huddle happening at the defendant's table. Both Kimberly Morgan and Mr. Beauvais were hunched down, face-to-face, nearly ducked underneath the table and engaged in a secret exchange. This conference went on for several minutes. When heads popped up and it was obvious that they were finished, the judge resumed.

"How shall you proceed, Mr. Beauvais?"

"Your Honor, the defendant has informed me she wishes to testify on her behalf."

"Will you be calling other witnesses also?"

"I will not, Your Honor."

The judge once again turned to Ms. Morgan and addressed her directly. "Miss Morgan, you are saying, that you are giving up your right to be protected by the Fifth Amendment and the right against self-incrimination. Do you understand? Yes or no?"

"Yes I do."

"OK. Are you ready to proceed Mr. Beauvais?"

"Judge, the only thing is, Ms. Morgan has a prior felony conviction. I believe that it is for bank robbery. Given that the court will rule regarding whether, or not, that will be used against her, there's some element of theft involved with that. My argument will simply be that the element of truth and voracity that is involved in that conviction is extremely small, and given the fact that she's been charged with not only armed robbery and carjacking, which, in fact, are similar offenses to bank robbery, that the prosecutor should be prohibited from bringing up the fact that she's been convicted prior for bank robbery."

"It's already out in front of the jury that she's been convicted of a felony; we just haven't named that felony."

Mrs. Hanson, looking irritated, stood and said, "Your Honor, if she gets on the stand and the issue comes up, we should be able to address it."

Judge Neithercut responded, "Well, are you saying if he does not bring the issue up, you will not address it?"

"No. I'm not saying that. The fact is, the defendant might bring it up."

Mr. Beauvais responded, "Obviously, Judge, if I open the door or my client opens up the door regarding that, then I do believe she would have that ability to cross-examine based upon that. But I don't intend on doing that."

The prosecutor replied, "Your Honor, the conviction is within tenure. Bank robbery is a theft."

"It qualifies for impeachment purposes. Mr. Beauvais, your request is denied. Theft involves an element of dishonesty. Bank robbery is theft. Therefore it qualifies."

"Judge, I'm not going to argue with the court. Court has made its ruling, but it's not an absolute; it's still the up to the discretion of the court. Now, if it had been something such as the perjury or a crime that involved truth or voracity, then it would be an absolute. Only when it…it's an element of theft, then it becomes up to the discretion of the court. And I will understand that the court has made its ruling."

"So be it," said the judge.

Another round of huddling went on, with both parties at both tables. When they finished, the judge spoke up once more. "Are you ready, Mr. Beauvais?"

"Yes, Your Honor."

"Deputy, remove the chains. Bring the jury back in, Bailiff."

Kimberly Morgan on the Stand

KIMBERLY'S ARM RESTRAINTS were removed first, then the leg bracess, so she could walk to the witness stand unencumbered. The judge turned his chair to look squarely at her and addressed her. "After the jury is brought in I will swear you in again. Take the chair, please."

"OK."

While the jury was being brought back in, Kimberly prepared herself by unzipping the collar of her bulky sweater, turning the oversize turtleneck into a broad shawl collar, and pressing her short hair into place. She appeared to be composed, with her hands neatly folded together and resting upon her lap.

·›▬◉ ◉▬‹·

The judge turned to Kimberly Morgan once again, and said, "Now, I'd like you to stand and face me. Do you swear to tell the truth and nothing but the truth in this case, so help you God?"

"Yes I do," she said; blinking profusely.

"You may now sit down."

Defense attorney Philip Beauvais III stood and spoke next. "Your Honor, for the record, we will call as our witness Kimberly Morgan."

"Thank you."

·›▬◉ ◉▬‹·

"Please state your name for the record," Mr. Beauvais said to his client.

"Kimberly M, O, R, G, A, N." She was articulate, speaking in a controlled and measured manner.

"And Kimberly, you've been convicted of a felony before, is that correct?"

"Yes, I have," she said, exhaling audibly afterward.

"What felony was that?"

"Robbery."

"How long ago was that?"

"November '94," she said softly.

"I want to take you back to July 1, 2003, last year. Where were you on July 1 of 2003?"

"During the day... I was in Tennessee. I left Tennessee later that night."

"Did you reside in Tennessee at that time?"

"Yes I did."

"OK. Whereabouts?"

"Nashville."

"Had you lived in Flint before?"

"Yes I did."

"And how long had you lived in Tennessee?"

"Roughly, about six months."

"And prior to that you lived, where?"

"In Flint."

"On July 1, 2003, you said that you got in the car to return to Flint, is that right?"

"Right."

"About what time would that have been?"

"I'd say, approximately ten o'clock."

"At night?"

"Yes."

"How far is that from Nashville to Flint?"

"Mileage-wise, I don't know, but it takes me about nine, sometime ten hours."

"You were in an automobile, correct? What kind of car was it?"

"It was a '94 black Probe."

"What was your purpose in coming to Flint?"

"I spoke with Savannah, my ex-lover, about getting back together."

"What is Savannah's last name?"

"Savannah Liddel."

"Has she testified in this trial?"

"Yes she has. We had spoke through the months about getting back together, and she told me she was having problems with um, her child's father, which was Alan."

"Alan who?"

"Alan Johnson."

"And he has testified in this trial?"

"Yes."

"And you're coming to Flint to see Savannah?"

"Yes I was."

"What was your and Savannah's relationship?"

"We had a very serious"—she inhaled deeply—"lesbian relationship," she said then exhaled.

"When did you first meet her?"

"In July of 2001."

"How long did it take before the two of you got together as a couple?"

"It didn't take any time at all, maybe a month or so."

"Did you ever move in with Savannah?"

"Yes I did."

"And when would that have been?"

"I'd say maybe, end of September of 2001."

"How long did you stay together?"

"Off and on, a year." Kimberly started to blink.

"And after the two of you broke up, did the two of you keep in contact?"

"All of the time."

"And how did you talk to her?"

"Sometime, depending on how serious the breakup was, through phone. I'd meet her, she'd meet me, but mostly through cell phone conversation."

"Were you in love with Savannah?"

"Yes I was." For the first time Kimberly's composure slipped, and she began to tear up. But the tears did not spill.

"And, in July 2003, were you still in love with Savannah?"

"Yes, I still was." Shaken, now she was weeping. The tears that had welled up in her large brown eyes spilled onto her round cheeks and trickled down her face.

"When would you arrive in the Flint area, back in July 2003?"

"I would say, seven or eight in the morning," she said, trying to regain composure.

"And where did you go in the morning?"

"I went to her house." Kimberly was blinking again.

"Did you talk to her?"

"Yes I did."

"Did she know you were coming?"

"Yes she did. She knew I was coming sometime in July. She just didn't know the exact date." Kimberly had completely regained her composure, her posture stiffening.

"Now, you stated that the two of you had discussed getting back together, is that right?"

"Yes."

"Were there any impediments to you getting back together again?"

Kimberly exhaled loudly, inhaled, and then spoke. "At first, no, when we first spoke in January and February, no. Then, in late February maybe, but by March she'd gotten back with her child's father, which is Alan. He was in the way."

"Again, that's Alan Johnson?"

"Yes."

"And you went over to Savannah's, at seven, eight in the morning; would that have been July 2, 2003?"

"Yes."

"And what took place?"

Kimberly inhaled deeply. "We talked, um…she told me she was on her way to work…so we didn't have a lot of time to talk, maybe about twenty or thirty minutes. And, um…she said, 'Kim, I love you, I always loved you.' She said, 'Alan wants to get married, but I don't want to get married.' And she said, 'I want to get back with you.' And I said but that was not possible, because I know he didn't care for me, because of things that she had told him about me."

"Had you ever met Alan Johnson before?"

"Yes, I did, that one time in the library."

"Like he testified to in court?"

"Yes."

"To your knowledge, had he ever seen your Probe?"

"No, not to my knowledge."

"So, after you had talked to Savannah that morning, what did you do?"

Kimberly exhaled deeply. "As far as, what?" She quickly angered, making her eyes into menacing little slits, shooting an enraged face directly at her lawyer.

Exasperated, Mr. Beauvais rephrased the question. "What did you do? I mean, did you get in your car? Go to sleep? Did you leave? Go back to Nashville?"

"No…no, no. She had told me that…um…she wanted to get Alan out of the picture. She said that in order for us to be together, he would have to be out of the picture. I say, what do you mean? Do you want to scare 'em? What you want us to do? She said, 'He'd be better off dead.'"

"So, what are you thinking at this point?"

"That was *not* what I had intended to do." Kimberly regained her composure completely; she was defiant in her tone, angry. "That is not what I came up for that day."

"What *did* you come up for that day?"

"Try to talk to her, to reconcile."

"After you heard this, what did you do?"

"She said she needed to go to work. I said we need to talk more, because nothing was concrete. Um…I was not prepared for that type of thing to happen. So I told her we'd have to talk about that later, maybe on her break. On her lunch break, after she went to work."

"And where did she work?"

"Mazel's."

"And where is Mazel's located?"

"Corner of Dort, I believe, and Atherton."

"That's in the city of Flint?"

"Yes, it is."

"So, do you do anything while she is at work? Did you ever meet her again that day?"

"She came to the back door, where she works, and told me not to stay at her job, because the people at her job knew my car. She told me to meet her over to Walgreens."

"And where is Walgreens located?"

"On the opposite corner, Dort and Atherton."

"And did you go over to Walgreens to meet her?"

"Yes I did."

"Approximately what time would that have been?"

"It took awhile, because she didn't show up like I thought she would. It took maybe a couple hours, it was may-be eleven, or twelve."

"She give you a particular time to go to Walgreens?"

"She just said she would be getting a break between ten and twelve."

"So, you go over to Walgreens starting when? Ten o'clock?"

"Yeah." She coolly nodded in affirmation. "I'd say it was about two hours later."

"And when she appeared, what did you do?"

"She woke me up, 'cause I had fell asleep 'cause I had waited so long. She asked me to get in the car, and I ask her where'd the car come from? Was a blue car. So I went over to the passenger side and I saw Ms. Murphy in the car. I ask her what she was doing. And she said we needed a car. And I said, for what? And she said, 'Just follow me and we'll go from there.'

"So I got into my Probe, and we had thought about going over to River Valley, but she didn't have that much time off from work, so we went to a vacant house."

"Where is this vacant house located?" Mr. Beauvais asked, interrupting her.

"It was near where Alan stayed."

"All right. And you went to a vacant house. How'd you get there? Did you ride in the car with…?"

"No," Kimberly said, interrupting him. "No. I was gonna ride with her but I took my car. I took my car and she drove the blue car."

"OK. The blue car, that was driven, there was somebody else in the car besides her, correct?"

"Miss. Murphy."

"You get over there, at this vacant house, and then what happens?"

Kimberly exhaled deeply and glanced up as if to recall. "I parked in the back, and Savannah parked in the driveway. Um, we walk Ms. Murphy into the house, and she was a little feisty then, she say, 'Whaddya doin'? Where you takin' me?' And I told her everything's going to be OK, and she knew I really didn't mean her no harm. And that's when she said, 'I'll pray for you.' I think she felt a little scared."

The room was absolutely silent. You could hear Kimberly breathing into the recorder.

"Did you have a gun?"

She looked up, as if trying to remember. "Um…at that time, I didn't see a gun."

"How long were you in this house?"

"I'd say twenty minutes, maybe thirty."

"While you're at this vacant house, what do you do?"

She again exhaled deeply, audibly, paused, and began speaking slowly. "I'm taking a look around, to make sure no one else is in this house; it's a pretty big house, so I check the outside, upstairs, the kitchen, and the back of the house. And I waited by the back door. Then I went to the front door, 'cause I thought I had heard a noise."

"Did you ever leave that house?"

"You mean, as far as at that particular time? Not at that time, no. I'm still at that house."

"When do you leave the house?"

She exhaled, looked up as if to remember, and said, "Savannah took Ms. Murphy into the basement... I heard a shot go off. So I's going to the basement to meet Savannah, to find out what had happened, but she meet me upstairs instead. So I say, what'd you do? She say the gun accidentally went off. I say, did you hurt her? She said, no. Then we left."

"When you left, how did you leave?"

"I left in my car, and she left in Ms. Murphy's."

"Where was Mrs. Murphy?"

"Still in the basement."

"Did you go down to check and see if she was OK?"

"N-n-n-n-n-o-o."

"Did Savannah say that she'd tied her up or secured her in any form?"

"When I went in the house, I believe"—she looked up again—"Savannah had, I believe it was like, a telephone wire, like a coil wire."

"All right. When you left, you left in your car, and Savannah left in Mrs. Murphy's. Is that right? Somebody's supposed to follow somebody?"

"I follow her back to work."

"OK. So you went back to work, at Mazel's?"

"Her work, right."

"OK. What'd you do at that point?" Mr. Beauvais asked, as if he wanted to know himself.

Kimberly let her air out all at once, in one big hissing blast, which was picked up by the recorder. Reflecting up and to the left, she thought before answering. "I left my car parked on the side of Mazel's. I dropped her off, and I took Ms. Murphy's car and took it to Arbor Village."

"And what did you do at Arbor Village?"

"Basically, I didn't have a lot of time. I left the car there."

"You say you didn't have a lot of time. Why didn't you have a lot of time?"

"I wanted to get my car out of Mazel's parking lot, for one, and then it was just getting late."

"Did you think about maybe just calling the police, because some poor old lady was in a house, or something?"

She took a long time before answering.

"At that time, no. Savannah had pretty much took control of the situation. I pretty much followed her lead."

"So, what did you do after you took Mrs. Murphy's car over to Arbor Village?"

"I left her car there, and I went back to Mazel's and picked up my car."

"What did you do with your car then?"

"I drove my car over to Arbor Village, um…" She shook her head left to right as if saying no while answering. "I believe somewhere around that time I probably fell asleep, ate, ran a few errands, and called a few people."

"What happened to Mrs. Murphy's car?"

"I left that in Arbor Village parking lot."

"Did you ever see it again?"

"Later that evening, yes."

"When would that have been?"

"After five o'clock."

"And, where did you see it?"

"It was not parked where I had left it. I had parked her car on the side of Arbor Village. When I had come back, it was parked in the back of Arbor Village."

"Who, if anyone, had access to that car?"

"The only person who knew where I was gonna park the car there was Savannah. And I had left the keys under the seat."

"Did she know where the keys were?"

"Yes, she did."

"When you saw the car again, you said it was around five."

"Yes I did."

"Where was it again?"

"It was in the parking lot at Arbor Village."

"What, if anything, did you do?"

"You mean, before five?"

"Yeah, whaddya do between when you left that car and picked up your car?"

"I watched Alan, his route, to see if what she had told me, so far as where he'd be at, when, as far as his work, whether he'd walk home, or if he caught the bus. Where he'd be at when he got off the bus, stuff like that."

"OK," Mr. Beauvais said, as if he was believing it. "And when you have this discussion, again, you said *she* told you. Who is she?"

"Savannah."

"When did you have this discussion?"

"That was in the morning."

"Did she tell you *why* you were watching Alan?"

"Just to see his methods of, his route."

"So, you were in your Probe, and you went where?"

"I went to his job."

"Approximately what time?"

"It was about five."

"And did you see him?"

"No."

"How long did you stay?"

"It wasn't very long. I'd say maybe, about, close to ten minutes."

"Then where did you go?"

"I drove around to the bus station, I drove around to the alley, then I drove over to where she told me he'd be getting off the bus."

"And where was that?"

"Third or Fourth Street, I mean Avenue."

"And when you got over there, what did you see?"

Her face grew tight and angry as she hunkered down into the witness chair. "It was crazy. Was lots of people. A lot of cops, a lot of people out of cars, and there was a ambulance. An' I ask this lady what happened. She say, she don't know. She say some guy just got stabbed or shot."

"So, what are you thinking when you see that?"

"I'm thinking"—she exhaled deeply—"I need to get *out* of the area, because I'm not sure *what's* going on."

"Did you think maybe something had happened to Alan Johnson?"

"At that time, yes."

"So you get in your car, and where do you go?"

"I drive to Arbor Village, and I see the car has been moved. I'm trying to figure out where the car is at. So I go out back, and it was behind the Dumpster. The car was in disarray, papers inside tossed like somebody had just scrambled through the car. Had ramshackled the car."

"So, what do you do?"

"I take the car and I"—she looked up and left again, thinking—"I didn't want my fingerprints inside that car, 'cause I had been inside that car. So I took the car across the street, and I burned it. I didn't know the name of the club at the time, but I found out later it was Mr. Lucky's."

"So, after you burned it where did you go?"

Ms. Morgan exhaled deeply. "I went across the street to my car an' I high-tailed it back to Tennessee."

"And that's when you got the ticket?"

"Yes."

"At this point do you know what's going on?"

"Not really…um, I felt that… ah… somebody needed to do some explaining, but I didn't know how to get that info-rmation. So, I'm just driving back to Tennessee with a whole lot of thoughts as to what had happened."

"So do you do anything to try to find out what happened?"

"Yeah, I did. It was a long trip, 'cause I had had a lot of car trouble. I returned to Tennessee about seven in the morning. And um, I called, I don't know in what sequence, but I called the different locations."

"You made a lot of phone calls?"

"Yes I did."

"And you made those phone calls to find out what was going on, is that right?"

"When I made the calls my first thing was to find out what happened. I had made eye contact with a couple of people when I walked away from the car fire, but I wasn't sure if they actually saw me. So I called the different locations in that area to see if there was any description, that maybe they saw me."

"Did you get on the phone right away to call up Savannah and find out what was going on?"

"We had made an agreement not to call each other."

"Now, how are you supposed to get information to and from your lover?"

"Indirectly. I would have Barbie, Barb Garrison call her and try to find out what happened."

"At some point later did you talk to her?"

"Barbie Garrison?"

"No. Savannah Liddel."

"Not that I can recall, that day."

"Later on in the month of July, did you talk to her?"

"Yes I did."

"And how did you talk to her?"

"Um…" She reflected up, moving her eyes to the left as if to recall. "My mother called me to tell me that a Mundy Township police officer wanted to question me. I didn't under -stand why the Mundy police went to my mother's house. So I get home later that day and I talk to a Officer Diem. She tells me she needs to question me about a shooting that had taken place on July 2. She wanted to know my itinerary.

"Um…she calls me back, maybe a couple days later. Throughout that time she's constantly asking, do you know about a shooting? She never did mention anything about an elderly lady at all. She just asked me about the shooting of Alan Johnson. She told me I needed to go to the Tennessee Department of Police, to talk to the detective there."

"So when *do* you talk to Savannah?"

Kimberly exhaled deeply again, completely letting all her air out this time. "I called Savannah maybe, late July."

"And did you ever see her in person?"

"Not then. I came up the twenty-fifth or twenty-sixth. At that time we just talked on the phone."

"When did you learn that Mrs. Murphy was dead?"

"I learned she was missing when I went in for questioning in Tennessee. I wanna say, maybe August."

"When did you learn that she was dead?"

"I didn't realize that until I came back to Flint." Kimberly was blinking profusely now. There was a long pause, and then Mr. Beauvais resumed.

"Now, you talked to Detective Schmitzer on three different occasions; that right?"

"That's right."

"And at some point, as you've seen here today, you tell Detective Schmitzer that it was you that committed these crimes."

"Yes I did."

"Why would you do that?"

"For one, I was still in love with Savannah. I didn't want her involved."

"Why wouldn't you want Savannah involved?"

"Um…she's not as strong as me, I guess you'd say. Um…I had previously been in trouble; I had done a little time before, and I considered her children; the fact that she had children, and I don't."

"Is that the only reason, because of Savannah?"

"I'm feeling, if this could happen to this lady, and I didn't know anything about this, and I knew that Savannah knew where my parents stayed. In a sense I feared for my family's life, because she told me that *I* messed up the plan, 'cause *I* was seen walking away from that fire, and nothing would have been seen or done had *I* not been seen walking away from that fire."

"Did Savannah, at some point, tell you that *she* was the one that committed these crimes?"

Kimberly exhaled a really big one this time. "She didn't come right out and tell me that, no. She just told me that when we were at the house, when the gun went off, that it…accidentally hit Ms. Murphy."

"Now, in these statements that you made, you give a lot of details. Don't you?"

"Yes I do."

"How is it that you know all these details?"

"A lot of it…I kinda…Savannah told me some details. I went out to the scene later on that month to see if that body was still there, out where I used to live at. And I guess I gathered information from being questioned over and over again, and also through Savannah, like I had said."

"What you're telling us today is that you did not murder Mrs. Murphy. Did you?"

"No I did not."

"You didn't shoot Alan Johnson, did you?"

"No I did not."

"You didn't steal Mrs. Murphy's car?"

"I took it from Mazel's, but I didn't take it from her."

"You *are* telling us that you did burn the car, correct?"

"Yes I did."

"Did you ever have a gun in your possession?"

"No. 'Cause I can't have a gun."

"Did you ever see Savannah with a gun that day?"

"Not till after the gun went off in the basement."

"The answer is yes? You did see her with a gun?"

"Yes." She said exhaling loudly.

"Thank you, Judge. I have nothing further."

Prosecutor Hanson Crosses Kimberly Morgan

"Quite a story! Miss Morgan, you are aware that there was a PPO against you, isn't that right?" Prosecutor Hanson said, smiling wryly.

"Somewhat, yes." Now she had copped an attitude.

"You knew that Savannah had a PPO against you."

"Not before, but after I was questioned, yes, I knew." She was steely, her body rigid.

"So, you do remember telling Detective Schmitzer that Savannah had a PPO against you?"

"I believe I did."

"What plates did you have on your car when you left Tennessee?"

"Ah, oh I wanna say, maybe, my Corsica plates."

"Your Corsica plates?"

"But I had two cars."

"And it was your plate on that car when you left Tennessee?"

"No it was not," she replied in an angry, defiant tone.

"Whose plate was it?"

"That, I'm not sure."

"Where'd you get it?"

"I got the plate"—she paused and looked up and left again, as if to recall—"I wanna say from Savannah."

"OK. Do you recall talking to Detective Schmitzer about your mom always telling you to tell the truth?"

"That is right."

"Do you recall talking to a Tanya Robertson in the jail, and telling her that if you go down, you're gonna take Savannah down with you?"

"No I don't," Ms. Morgan said, even more defiantly.

"You don't remember that?"

"No, I did not say it."

"OK, let's just go through the day. You get up here from Tennessee; what time?"

"I'd say seven thirty…eight."

"And you go to Savannah's house?"

"That's right."

"Where you meet Savannah?"

"I went to her house, and she said she had to go to work, said let's meet up on the corner by Oak Street, which is close to her house."

"And when you met Savannah on this morning, you went through the whole plan of how to get rid of Alan? Savannah said, go kill Alan?"

Kimberly was shaking her head side to side as if to say no. "*No!* Nothing was concrete that day. She just told me she was havin' problems, and she said she was still in love with me. She wanted to be with me. She said she didn't want to marry Alan. She wanted him to be out of the picture, and us to be together."

"Who was she living with at that time?"

"At that time, only her children."

"Did you go in the house?"

"No I did not."

"OK…so what'd you do after you talk to Savannah?"

"I told her we need to go ahead and plan this out. Whatever we do, we need to plan it." She was looking up and left again. "So she went to work, and I told her that I'd stay outside her job till she went on break. And she told me to park over by Walgreens, and that's where she met me, over at Walgreens."

"So you both talk about killing Alan?"

"Not at that time. No. We didn't ever talk about that."

"OK. Do you recall telling Detective Schmitzer that you got a gun in Tennessee, and that you were upset because Savannah didn't love you, and that you were gonna kill your-self? Instead, you decide to come up here. Do you recall that?"

"I believe so."

"OK...yeah...do you recall telling Detective Schmitzer that you, in fact, brought that gun here?"

"Yes I did."

"So you talk to Savannah, and suddenly Savannah says, 'We gotta get rid of Alan'? So you go sit at Walgreens to wait for Savannah, is that correct?"

"We wanted to make the plans a little more concrete." She was looking up again. "That's when I come up to Flint."

"Why'd you bring the gun?"

"I did not have a gun!"

"You did not have a gun? Oh, OK. So you're sitting at the Walgreens, and then what happens?"

"Savannah pulls up in the car."

"What car?" Mrs. Hanson asks, sounding surprised.

"The blue car."

"Who was in the car?"

"Ms. Murphy was in the backseat."

"What did you do?"

"I was shocked. I asked her what she was doing. She said that we need to get a car. I said, what we going to do with this lady? She said, 'Just follow me.'"

"Do you recall telling Detective Schmitzer that you saw Mrs. Murphy coming out of Walgreens, and that you, in fact, approached Mrs. Murphy and made her get into the backseat of her car? Do you recall that?"

"Yes I did. "

"Twice telling, three times telling Detective Schmitzer that. So...suddenly, now it's Savannah who got the car?"

"I have to tell you what happened."

"OK. So *tell* me what happened!"

"Savannah pulls up in the blue car. We had no intentions of getting the car, no discussion about a car. So she pulled up at Walgreens and I was gonna ride with her. She said we're gonna go to River Valley, but I decide to follow her to a vacant house, like downtown."

"Where at?"

She was looking up again. "I know, it was on Grand Traverse, and maybe Third, or Fourth Street."

"Where Alan got shot? You have Mrs. Murphy in this house where you shoot Alan later that day?"

"Right."

"Where is the house?" The prosecutor seems to be amazed, she's making a surprised face.

"The house was in that area."

"What's the address? What color is it?"

"It was white."

"Whaddya do when you got there?"

"I park the car in the back. Savannah parked in the driveway. We walked Ms. Murphy in the house. Savannah walks her in the basement. I check to make sure there is no one in that house."

"Then what did you do?"

"Um…I went to the front door, 'cause I thought I had heard a noise. Then I heard a shot go off. As I come around to the steps, Savannah comes upstairs, I ask her what happened, and she said the gun accidentally went off. I said, 'You hurt Miss. Murphy?' She said no."

"Just so you know, the detectives have checked, and Savannah was working that day. So you're telling me that Savannah was gone for two to three hours that morning?"

"I'd say, maybe, I'd say about an hour."

"Oh! OK. Do you recall telling Detective Schmitzer that *you* knew an area where your dad used to live and *you* drove Mrs. Murphy out there, *you* got her out of the backseat of that car, *you* walked her into those woods, and *you* shot her?"

"I took the rap and fell for everything. Yes I did."

Mrs. Hanson was now defiant, reddened. "Isn't it *amazing* that you knew *exactly* where Mrs. Murphy was shot? She was shot in the face twice; she was shot in the chest. Now, is that something you could have ever known, had you not done it?"

"I had talked to Savannah, to find out what was going on."

"I thought you said Savannah wouldn't talk to you."

"She talk to me when I found out a lady was missing."

"OK! So, what happened while you're at this house, and you have Mrs. Murphy in the basement?"

"Like I said, I'm running around. Savannah went to the basement; the gun went off, and then she meets me up-stairs. She said, 'I gotta get back to work.' So I get in my car, she gets in Ms. Murphy's car, we drive back to Mazel's, and I take the blue car and park it at Arbor Village."

"Why would you do that? That makes absolutely no sense. Why would you even think about taking a car and parking it there, if you already got rid of Mrs. Murphy?"

Kim squinted making an angry, menacing face, and defiantly said, "We did not, get rid of her."

"Uh…OK, where was she?"

"She is in the basement."

"And you know this because…?"

"I was there."

"OK. So, then what happens then?"

Kimberly looks up again, as if to remember. "I left my car, so I walk back to Mazel's to retrieve my car. And from there, I just killed a lot of time until five o'clock."

"Do you recall telling Detective Schmitzer that after you shot Dorothy Murphy, three times, that you took that car and you went back to Arbor Village where you left it? You walked back and got your car, brought it back, and then you took that car over to shoot Alan Johnson?"

"I remember all that, yes."

"Do you recall telling Detective Schmitzer that you were upset because Savannah didn't want *you*, Kimberly Morgan! Savannah *did not want you*!"

"That is not correct, I do not recall saying that," Kimberly said, angrily glaring, making her eyes into barely opened darkened angry slits.

"Oh! OK…you heard Savannah testify?"

"Yes I have."

"OK…so what happened after you take this car back over to Arbor Village?"

"Like I said, I killed a lot a time, maybe a couple hours. And then I went to watch Alan's route, to see exactly where he would be at certain times and locations."

"And that makes no sense to me, because Savannah would already know Alan's route. Savannah knew Alan. Why would *you*, if you were Savannah, have to go watch Alan's route to know where he was gonna be?"

"I was gonna make sure this was what his route was."

"Savannah didn't want to give you that little bit of information? She wants you to kill him, but she didn't want to tell you that?"

"She already told me where he worked at. She just told me he would be getting off about five."

"So what do you do after that?"

"I watched, and he never came out of the building."

"Then what do you do?"

"I drove around where the bus station was. I didn't see anybody. I drove down the alley. I didn't see him. So I drove where I thought he might be. I thought he took the bus, or maybe was walking home."

"And…?" Prosecutor Hanson pressed.

"I saw that it was a lot of cop cars, and the ambulance. I pull-t up and I asked a lady. I said, 'What's going on?' She said somebody was either shot or stabbed. I asked her did she know who it was? She said no. And that's when I left."

"You know, Alan testified that his eyesight is bad. And he really didn't see the person in that vehicle that shot him, but it looked like a young black male. Now, if I am looking at you in a car, or looking at Savannah in a car, who do you think looks more like a young black male?"

"By my short haircut, I'd say I would," she said, beaming proudly and smiling smugly.

"So…you go back over to Arbor Village and there's the car just sitting there?"

"It wasn't in the same spot where I left it."

"OK, and then you decide to burn it because...?"

"I knew I had been in that car."

"Do you recall telling Detective Schmitzer that in fact *you* waited and *you* wanted to kill Alan Johnson? You knew all those details. You drove up just as he was approach-ing the curb. *You* pulled up, *you* lean over, and *you* shoot him out the passenger side window. You even knew he screamed when he got hit. You even talked about your chasing him all around the city streets. *You knew all those facts.*"

"Yes I did."

"*You* also knew where Mrs. Murphy was shot and fell. That picture shows you exactly how Mrs. Murphy fell." She pointed to the board, still standing on the easel, showing Mother's decomposed remains. "She got shot in the face twice. She got shot in the chest. And that is where she fell!"

Prosecutor Hanson was defiantly pointing at the pictures. "She didn't die in a basement. She didn't die anywhere but where *you knew* she was!"

"That's not true," Ms. Morgan shot back, her lips pressed tightly together, eyes glaring, hate filled.

"That's an incredible story! One minute, please." Mrs. Hanson went to the prosecution table and conferred with her assistant and Detective Schmitzer for a few moments. "I have nothing further, Your Honor." She returned to her seat at the table, red-faced and winded.

⋯⊶⊙ ⊙⊷⋯

Mr. Beauvais rose. "We would also rest at this time."

"Is there a rebuttal at this time?" the judge asked, peering over his spectacles. There was none. The jury was led out of the courtroom by Bailiff Newland.

Judge Neithercut turned to Kimberly Morgan and said, "Would you go back to your seat please."

Prosecutor Hanson, Closing Statements

THE BAILIFF BROUGHT the jurors back in and escorted them to their benches. Judge Neithercut placed his glasses upon his head and turned his big black leather chair toward them. "Ladies and gentlemen of the jury, you have heard all the evidence that you're going to hear. Now the lawyers will summarize their cases, from their points of view. I'll talk to you when they are done. Mrs. Hanson will speak to you first."

The prosecutor rose, adjusted her trim tailored suit, placed her notes upon the podium, pushed her curly unruly hair behind her ears, and put on her reading glasses.

⊷═◎ ◎═⊶

"Ladies and gentlemen of the jury, we have proved our case to you without a reasonable doubt. And I think you'll agree with the defendant when she said, Dorothy Murphy didn't deserve to be in this.

"This case comes down to one thing, and one thing only." Mrs. Hanson pointed to Kimberly. "The defendant wanted her own way…and she was willing to kill to get it. You've heard over the past few days a number of witnesses, and I will just briefly go through and talk about some of the things you've heard.

"Ladies and gentlemen, we heard from Mary Deering, Dorothy's own daughter, who came in and told us a little bit about her mom. Told us, Dorothy was on her way to the doctor's on July 2, 2003. Of course, Dorothy never made it to the doctor's that day.

"Mary also told us that her mom was a religious person, and that it would be characteristic for her to say something like, 'I'll pray for you.'

"We heard testimony from David Filmon, Dorothy's neighbor, who also stated that on July 2, 2003, he looked out the window and saw Dorothy Murphy leaving her house, as she had done a hundred times before. In her same blue car, all by herself.

"We heard testimony from Randall Johnson, how he was driving by Dort and Atherton in the city of Flint, and he saw the defendant's car parked at that Walgreens. He said he was familiar with the defendant and Savannah Liddel, and he was familiar with her car.

"Detective Schmitzer said the defendant admitted seeing Dorothy Murphy that morning, at the Walgreens. She watched Dorothy walk out, forced Dorothy into the backseat of her car. She said, 'I already had a gun, but I didn't need to use it. I told Ms. Murphy to get in the backseat of the car. I guess she saw the look on my face, and she was scared.'

"We heard how she knew about the secluded location, out by where she used to live in Flint Township, and how she drove out to that location. She said, 'If you ever want to hide something, this would be the spot to do it.'

"We listened as Detective Schmitzer told us that in her confession, she spoke about getting Dorothy out of the backseat of the car. She said she had the gun. Then she walked Dorothy back to the woods, and she shot Dorothy. She shot her three times. Two times in the face, and once in the chest, but not before Dorothy said, 'I'll pray for you.'

"And if you noticed, in her confession, the defendant pointed at her eyes when she was talking about shooting Dorothy.

"She told Detective Schmitzer she left Dorothy there. She didn't go back till the end of the month, to see if Dorothy was still there. She told us through her confessions that she had committed armed robbery, because she took money from Dorothy's purse to buy lunch. She said, 'I took money from Dorothy's purse, maybe ten dollars from the purse.'

"You heard Alan Johnson come in and tell you, that he was getting off the bus that day at approximately five o'clock, and he walked from Grand Traverse and Third toward Grand Traverse and Fourth, and he noticed a blue vehicle parked on the corner of Grand Traverse. He told you he didn't think a whole lot about that, but as he approached the curb the car pulled up with the passenger side facing him. And the driver of that car leaned over and shot him in the stomach. He actually stood up there and showed you where he'd been shot.

"He told you he had bad eyesight, and he couldn't really see the driver of the car, but the driver resembled a young black male. He went through all the steps and showed you how he ran when he was chased through the streets of the city, being chased by this blue car, with this person in it. And, that again, he was shot in the shoulder when he was trying to hide in a brush-filled lot, on Grand Traverse and Fourth.

"He told you he hid behind a tree on Mason while trying to get away from the driver, as this driver was chasing him around the city and shooting at him.

"The defendant admitted, 'I was in a rage, and I guess I meant to kill him.' And Officer Terry Lewis came in and told us how he found a .380-caliber shell casing at the shooting scene, where Alan was shot, at Grand Traverse and Fourth; and what he did with that casing. He also told us, at 5:22 on July 2, 2003, a call came in that a car was burning be-hind Mr. Lucky's. And how he went to that scene and saw that car burning. And that car was then taken to Complete Towing.

"We had Ron Nelson come in and tell us that he identifies vehicles, that his primary job at GAIN is to check on stolen vehicles. He told you he positively identified that vehicle as being Dorothy Murphy's.

"Sergeant Kathy Taylor, the fire investigator, came in and told you what she does to investigate a fire. She told you she found a burned purse inside that car, a purse that we now have as evidence, and it contained a partially burned credit card with the name 'Murphy' on it.

"She told you she was turning that purse in to Mundy Township Police for evidence, when a spent .380 shell casing fell out of it. She got some debris out of that car, and it was tested for accelerants. She said the report came back positive for gasoline. And the defendant's own statement was, 'I torched the car with gasoline to cover up my fingerprints.'

"The fingerprint expert said that fingerprints are easily destroyed, and in fact, the fire would destroy any fingerprints.

"Detective Schmitzer told you all the pieces were starting to fit together, and how his investigation led him. You heard testimony from an Indiana state trooper that he had stopped the defendant in Indiana for speeding. The car had the wrong plates and wasn't registered to the defendant. He'd given her a ticket, which was in Indiana at 8:30, in our time that would have been 9:30.

"Simona Callahan told us she was on Lapeer Road across from Mr. Lucky's when she saw smoke coming from behind the building. She saw someone walking from behind the building. She described her as a female, black, midthirties, dark hair, short style, wearing dark glasses. She told you that person was carrying a bag, and it held a screwdriver and license plate. She helped complete the composite sketch.

"Barbie Garrison came in and told you that she had talked to the defendant numerous times on the phone, and that the defendant had asked her to watch the news, and to tell her if there was anything about a missing old lady, a car fire, or a guy getting shot. And when Barbie, in fact, told her she'd seen the composite on the news, the defendant asked, 'Does it look like me?'

"Detective Schmitzer told you he started getting reports back. The .380 casings found at Fourth and Grand Traverse, where Alan was shot, and inside Dorothy's purse were a match. Ron Ainsley came in and told you they were fired from the same gun.

"We also heard from Detective Reaves. He came in and said that he went back and sifted through the ashes looking for anything, and he found a lotion bottle. He sent it off for DNA testing.

"Dr. Mahanti came in, and she told us that she was able to get a tiny bit of DNA from the threads of the bottle. From that, she said, she could not exclude Kimberly Morgan. She told us that DNA type she extracted is so rare, that statistically there will be only *one* match out of one hundred and six point two billion people. She said there were only six billion people in the world.

"Sergeant Gene DuBuc came in, and he told us about finding the body on September 26, 2003. And he described the scene for us; he spoke to us about some of the things he found out there, such as Dorothy's watch and shoes. He also told us about a pair of sunglasses that were found out there; glasses that had a hole in the right lens. They sent those off to the lab for testing.

"Detective Diem came in and told us about how she got three identical pair of the glasses and took them to be test-ed. Detective Ronald Crichton told us, after doing testing on those glasses, that the hole in those glasses was consistent with a firearm projectile. Ladies and gentlemen, a gunshot wound.

"We had Dr. Fenton come in and identify Dorothy by the teeth in her lower jaw. He also talked about an unexplained fracture in one of her ribs, T-10. He found it unusual, because T-9 and T-11 that were adjacent to it were not injured at all; that the only explanation for that fracture would be a projectile, a gunshot wound.

"Dr. Cathy Blight came in and talked to us about the bullet hole in the clothing that was on the body. She said that the hole was consistent with a gunshot hole, and that would be in the chest area of the body.

"She also told us that she ruled the death as a homicide, and she told us why. The fact that Dorothy was in a location that was unfamiliar to her, there was no car around. The hole in the shirt, and the skull was missing. All these things led her to rule in her expert opinion that in fact it was a homicide.

"Sergeant Russ Fries told us about phone calls that were made, and about getting a search warrant, about compiling the records and making it into a chart for us to be able to read. And he noted the difference after July 2 through July 27, when numerous calls were made to the local hospitals, Mr. Lucky's, South Side Party Store, and Arbor Village.

"When the defendant was asked about those calls, she said, 'I knew there were people that saw me, I just wondered if they reported it.' She also asked about the hospital calls. She said, 'I wanted to know if he was admitted, and what kind of condition he was in.'

"We talked a little bit before about intent. You will agree with me when I say, that people don't walk around stating their intent. We infer intent through actions and the circumstances surrounding those actions. I'm going to ask you to do that, to use your logic that you bring with you. You'll be able to infer the defendant's intent.

"We also talked about reasonable doubt. I told you that you bring that with you, your logic and your reasoning. Collectively you decide cases based on that logic and reason.

"You also agreed not to hold me to a higher standard than beyond a reasonable doubt. That does not mean beyond a shadow of a doubt, or beyond a mathematical uncertainty, but beyond a reasonable doubt.

"We talked a little bit about evidence. In the beginning, I told you, you would be seeing direct evidence. I told you that if it's raining outside you can look out the window and see it's raining out there.

"We also talked about circumstantial evidence. I gave you the example, that if someone walks into the courtroom and they're dripping wet and holding an umbrella, you can infer that it's raining outside.

"I'll ask you to use that same logic and reasoning when looking at the evidence we've shown to you, as both types are equally important. The defendant was charged in this case with ten counts. I am just briefly going through those and show you how we've proven our case.

"The first count is first-degree premeditated murder. It reads, in short, that the defendant did, deliberately, with intent to kill and with premeditation, kill and murder Dorothy Lee Murphy.

"Ladies and gentlemen, we know that Dorothy was murdered. The casing that came from Dorothy's purse was matched to the casing that shot Alan. We have the hole in the glasses that Ron Crichton said was in fact a bullet hole. And those glasses were found with Dorothy's body.

"We've got premeditation. The defendant knew the location. The defendant thought about taking Dorothy out to that location. The defendant said, 'I was driving around, my mind was going crazy, I didn't know what I was going to do, if I was gonna let her out of the car, or what.'

"It's about choices, ladies and gentlemen. The defendant had hers. She decided to kill Mrs. Murphy when she got her out of that car. She said, 'If you ever want to hide something, this would be the place to do it.' She thought about it. She knew she was going to kill Dorothy Murphy.

"This was a deliberate act. Again, you got the bullet hole in the glasses showing she was shot directly in the face. The defendant said she shot her in the face. She shot her in the chest, and then she shot her the third time because she wanted to make sure that Dorothy Murphy was dead. That's a deliberate act, ladies and gentlemen.

"Felony murder reads, the defendant did, while in the perpetration of, or attempted perpetration of, a carjacking, and kidnapping, and/or robbery, murder one Dorothy Murphy. We've proven that she shot Dorothy Murphy. That she murdered her.

"We've shown the carjacking. Carjacking reads, the defendant, by threat and force of violence, did put in fear and rob, steal, or take a 1998 Blue four-door Buick motor vehicle, from one Dorothy Murphy. This happened at the Walgreens at Dort and Atherton, and that the defendant said, 'I had a gun, I didn't need to use it. I told Mrs. Murphy to get in the back of her car. I guess she saw the look on my face and was scared

"Kidnapping is the next charge, ladies and gentle-men, and it reads, did forcefully imprison her against her will, and move her from one place to another, which movement was not incidental to that carjacking. When the defendant got Dorothy out of the backseat of that car, forced her to walk back into that wooded area, and shot her three times; she said, 'I had the gun with me, I walked her back into the woods.'

"Armed robbery is the next count, ladies and gentlemen. It reads, the defendant assaulted Dorothy Murphy while being armed with a gun. That then and there, did in a felonious manner, rob, steal, and take from the person Dorothy Murphy, or while in her presence, the purse and the contents therein, including currency. The defendant admitted taking money out of Dorothy's purse for lunch.

"The next charge is assault with intent to murder. And it reads, the defendant did make an assault upon Alan Johnson, with the intent to commit the crime of murder. Alan Johnson came in and showed you where he got shot. He talked about running around the city of Flint, trying to get away from this blue car. You have the defendant's statement, 'Yeah I was enraged, and yeah, I guess I meant to kill him.'

"The next count is arson of a vehicle costing one thousand dollars or more but less than twenty thousand, and it reads, the defendant did willfully and maliciously burn certain personal property, a 1998 blue Buick, and that the value of the vehicle was more than one thousand dollars but less than twenty thousand dollars.

"You heard the testimony about the car burning behind Mr. Lucky's, testimony that gasoline was the accelerant used in burning that car, and you have the defendant's statement, 'I torched the car with gasoline and burned it, to cover up my fingerprints.'

"Carrying a concealed weapon is the next charge, ladies and gentlemen, and it reads, the defendant did carry a concealed weapon, a handgun, concealed on or about her person, and it was in a vehicle operated by the defendant.

"You have Alan Johnson saying that the person driving that car shot him. You have the defendant saying, 'I pulled up to the curb and I shot at him.'

"The next count is felony possession. In this count the defendant stipulated that, in fact, she was a felon and not supposed to be in possession of a firearm.

"The final count, ladies and gentlemen, is felony firearm. It reads that the defendant did carry, or have in her possession, a firearm at the time she committed a felony. Any one of these felonies will work; the first-degree murder, or felony murder, or carjacking, or kidnapping, or armed robbery, or assault with intent to murder, or arson of a vehicle, or felon in possession of a firearm.

"Ladies and gentlemen, Detective Schmitzer talked to you about the defendant's statements, how she made numerous statements, and what she said. I asked him, 'Did you force her to make any of these statements; did you threaten her in any way?' His answer was, 'No, she was eating potato chips and drinking water as she was confessing.'

"You heard statements from the defendant, testifying about this incredible story. But if you look at the facts you'll see that the detectives did a very good job on this case, putting all the pieces together.

"And you'll see that all those pieces fitted together, and in fact, the defendant confessed to every one of these crimes that she is charged with. We have proven our case without a reasonable doubt. After considering all the facts in this case, I'm confident that you'll find the defendant guilty.

"Guilty of first-degree murder.

"Guilty on the charge of felony murder.

"Guilty on the charge of carjacking.

"Guilty on the charge of robbery of Dorothy Murphy.

"Guilty on the charge of intent to kill Alan Johnson.

"Guilty of the arson of Dorothy Murphy's vehicle.

"Guilty of the carrying of a weapon.

"Guilty of being a felon in possession of a firearm.

"If I might just take a minute here, because I don't want you to be confused. Now, there are two counts of murder here; you can find the defendant guilty of both. The first one is premeditated murder. We believe she *knew* she was going to kill Dorothy, and she did kill Dorothy.

"There is also felony murder, which is, if you kill somebody in the course of committing another felony.

"Ladies and gentlemen, we will leave it to you.

"Thank you."

Attorney Beauvais Closing

Defense attorney Beauvais rose and confidently stood before the jury, not the podium, to speak. He pushed back the glasses on his regal French nose, adjusted his gray suit, and launched into his summation. Hands and arms were instrument -al to his presentation as he waved them about while pacing back and forth in front of the jury and making his points.

"Ladies and gentlemen, first I want to thank you for the time. I know the county pays you a small amount of money. And a couple of times, they've even taken you out to lunch. And I know this is woefully inadequate for the service that you have done for us today.

"First thing I want to say is, there is one thing that we can all agree upon. That is Dorothy Murphy did not deserve to die. That's a given. Everyone in this courtroom agrees to that. And I want to remind you again, this is the last time you get to hear from me. You are probably thinking, *'Thank God* I don't have to hear that man's voice again.' But this is the last time I get to say anything.

"Now, the prosecutor gets to talk again in what's called rebuttal. I've always had a problem with that, 'cause there's nothing I can say. But I always want to jump up and down to say, 'That's not the way it is.' But I don't get to do that. So if you would, when she is talking in rebuttal, just imagine me jumping up and down shouting.

"First and foremost, something I talked about in my opening. The judge talked about this a number of different times. There are three very important concepts you have to keep uppermost in your mind. And I'm going to remind you of them once again. The reason for that is those three things make our system the best criminal justice system on the face of the earth.

"Number one is the presumption of innocence. Even if today, right now, after you've heard everything"—he walked over and put his hand on Kimberly's shoulder in a reassuring, fatherly way, and she smiled warmly in return—"this woman, sitting right here, is presumed to be innocent. The burden of proof lies with the prosecutor. They bring the charges. They have to show whether or not, beyond a reasonable doubt, if Kimberly Morgan is guilty of anything.

"Kimberly Morgan does not have to do anything; she does not have to show anything, does not have to produce anything. That's not her burden. Now, the prosecutor had to do that, to prove guilt beyond a reasonable doubt. And again, that is something I talked about in my opening, and I'll talk about it now, because it's not a thing we do all the time.

"It's not as easy as it sounds, because all the time we are doing things, even when we have reasonable doubt, I can't do that here. Reasonable doubt leads to one conclusion, and that is a not guilty verdict. That's all you can do. You promised to do that, and we're gonna hold you to that promise.

"Each one of the crimes that Kimberly Morgan has been charged with are made up of what is called elements. Now, the judge is going to instruct you as to what the elements are of each and everyone of those charges.

"In order for you to come back with a guilty verdict, you have to find each and everyone of those elements, without reasonable doubt. Not just four or five, or three out of four, but each and every element has to be proven beyond a reasonable doubt in order for you to come back with a verdict of guilty. If there is reasonable doubt, if there are only four out of five, one conclusion, one verdict, and that is *not* guilty.

"Now, what sort of things are reasonable doubt? I don't have a computer to show you all this stuff, because my 'computer expert' is off at college, along with most of my money. But I'm gonna tell you what it is. I'm gonna tell you what some of these things are that would lead you to reasonable doubt in this case.

"First and foremost, you have to think about why would this woman need an automobile different from her own in order to shoot Alan Johnson? Alan Johnson never saw her car. Alan Johnson doesn't know what kind of car she drives. So why would she need a different kind of car if she was going to shoot Alan Johnson? She wouldn't.

"How is it that she knows the exact route that Alan Johnson is going to take on his way home? How does she know that? How does she know where Alan Johnson lives? She's only met him one time. He doesn't live with Savannah Liddel. How would she know that Alan Johnson was going to leave work before five, when his shift was up, to head home?

"How would she know that, having walked to work, he was taking the bus home? Alan Johnson, when the police get to him, right after he's shot, says, 'I'm walking to the corner, the car comes up, and I think they might want directions. The window comes down, I look in, it's a young man around nineteen years of age, and I got shot.'

"It's only *after* he's coming in here to testify against Kimberly Morgan that he discovers, 'Oh, I need glasses. My eyes aren't so good. I didn't necessarily see what was there.'

"That's not what he told police right after he got shot. He told the police it was a *man*. Why is it that the automobile is taken from the corner of Dort and Atherton? Who is it that has a connection to that area of town? Who works right over there? Not Kimberly Morgan, *she* doesn't work there.

He began to sound, and pace again, like a born-again preacher.

"We've heard from several 'expert witnesses' in this case, experts who use the term *'consistent* with.' Now, we don't want you to confuse 'consistent with' with 'beyond a reasonable doubt.' Consistent with does not mean that's what they've said. Because things can be consistent with a number of different items. Just remember, consistent with doesn't mean that it is true beyond a reasonable doubt.

"We heard from some of the witnesses. We heard about DNA. We heard about this big huge number, one in one hundred and eight billion. If the odds are that if you're only gonna find someone one time in one hundred and eight billion when there are only six billion people on the face of earth, then the odds are that you're not going to find them at all! Those numbers are hocus-pocus!

"But you do have to understand what they did say about the DNA. They said we have to match up thirteen different areas. And how many areas were they able to match up? Thirteen? Nope. Ten? Nope. *Four.* Yes, four. And they cannot exclude somebody based upon four. Not upon thirteen, upon four. All they had to do was find *one* and that would have excluded Kimberly Morgan. They weren't able to match up on nine, so we don't know where those other nine are.

He is red-faced now, animated and agitated. "We've seen some of the evidence that has been brought in, and *boyyyy*, there's been a lot of it! You didn't see me object to the vast majority of it. In fact, I may not have objected to any of it, because a whole lot of it doesn't mean much. The one thing they want to tell us is that Kimberly Morgan showed up in Flint area somewhere around July the first, or second, 2003.

"They bring in a license plate that has been stolen sometime before that date. How is it that she gets a hold of a stolen license plate before that day, if that's when she arrives in Flint? That's what they want you to believe. How does that happen? Those are the sort of things that are reasonable doubt. Those are the sort of things that you have to think about, come up with some answers for, 'cause you are the ones that have to do that. That's your job.

"Prosecutor has done her job, police officers have done their job, I've done mine, I hope. Now it's up to you. Now it's your job. You determine who is credible, who is not credible, based upon the evidence that you have heard.

"All of the things, the pluses, and the minuses…you have to decide what is the truth in this case, beyond a reason-able doubt.

"Kimberly Morgan came in here and testified. She didn't have to, but she did. And she talked to you. *You* have to decide if she was credible. *You.* Not me. And once you have listened, taken a look at the evidence and looked at it from all sides, we're confident that you'll come in with a fair and impartial verdict, one of *not* guilty as to all of the charges.

"Thank you."

Prosecuting Attorney Hanson, having the final word, rose and assumed the podium for her rebuttal. So imagine Mr. Beauvais jumping up and down at this time, if you will.

⋅⊷▆◉ ◉▆⊷⋅

"Defense counsel said a lot of things, but if you concentrate on the evidence, ladies and gentlemen, I'm confident you're going to find the defendant guilty, because all of the evidence points directly to the defendant.

"The DNA, the doctor said it was a small sample. She did the best she could with what she had. She told you if she had a larger sample the number would have been bigger.

"Alan Johnson didn't say he could positively see the person. He said the person, from what he could see, looked like a young black male. If you saw the defendant in a car, at a distance, you could have easily mistaken her for a young black male.

"Savannah Liddel got a PPO against the defendant, to keep the defendant from going over to Mazel's. But if she loved Savannah, the way she said she loved Savannah; she would be parked across the street just to see Savannah.

"While every single question can't be explained, I ask that you use your common sense, your logic, and your reasoning, and if you do that, and you look at all the evidence and all the testimony you've heard, I'm confident that you'll find the defendant guilty on every single count, guilty of every count that the defendant *herself* has confessed to.

"Thank you, ladies and gentlemen."

⋅⊷▆◉ ◉▆⊷⋅

Judge Geoffrey Neithercut leaned forward in his chair, looked over his glasses at the jury, and addressed them in a very cordial manner. Speaking in a very personable way, he even introduced some humor into the otherwise somber proceedings.

"You heard all the evidence, you've seen the evidence. You heard the witnesses, and you heard the lawyers. Now it's *my* turn to speak. I'm going to start talking to you about *the law.*"

And for the better part of an hour, he spoke to them about the ten counts brought against Ms. Morgan and the elements of the law.

Those elements are:

1. Ex-post-facto laws (with retroactive effect or force) are written, and certain acts become illegal after those laws have been violated.
2. There is no crime without a criminal act being committed.
3. There is no crime without intent.
4. There is no crime without concurrence, meaning that the crime and intent are occurring at the same time.

He spoke about the evidence that was presented, the statements made, the expert witness testimony given, and the many intricacies of the legal system. He spoke in very plain language. His instructions to the jury were to the point.

Six men and six women were going to deliberate the case. Bailiff Newland raised his right hand, was given an oath to oversee the jury, and swore that he would uphold that sacred trust. Then he led them back to their sequestered jury room to begin their secret deliberation.

Kimberly Angenette Morgan was once again placed in leg restraints and handcuffs and taken out of the courtroom by the armed deputy. She seemed somber and retreating, as she had been during most of the trial.

The judge popped up out of his chair and quickly retreated to his chambers, his black silk robe trailing in his wind wake, and the rest of the courtroom was then excused. Many of us would be going outside to hold vigil in the shady, park-like north-side yard of the courthouse, for what we hoped would be a "slam dunk" verdict. We expected a quick and unanimous verdict of guilty on all ten counts.

Waiting for a Verdict

THE TRIAL WAS finished, but the verdict was yet to be determined. The technical experts had stated their scientific facts, the witnesses had given their sworn testimony, and many different policing agencies had spelled out how, when, where, and why this crime was committed. We believed they had clearly proved their case and hopefully had convinced the jury of Kimberly Morgan's guilt on all ten counts.

The prosecutor clearly showed how she methodically, and with premeditation, kidnapped and murdered Dorothy Lee Murphy, our mother. In two different videotaped confessions, Ms. Morgan admitted committing these ten crimes, saying, "This is what I did, and this is how I did it." Clearly there was enough evidence to prove her guilt.

But quite unbelievably, when taking the witness stand, she attempted to re-write the entire crime spree and incriminate her ex-lover, Savannah, instead and thereby exonerate herself in the process. Maybe she wanted her company in the "big house."

The members of the jury would now decide her fate. Brown, white, young and old, normal and radical, these men and women represented a true cross-section of our community. And we had placed our trust in these good people and their ability to sort the truth from the lies.

This trial had been intense, many facts previously unknown to us were revealed, and we were exposed to graphic and disturbing photographs and testimony. This was very difficult material to see and hear, especially when it involved your own mother. Just like these jurors, we were trying to absorb the testimony and assess the truth.

The trial ended in the early afternoon, so we chose to stay on until the verdict was announced. While outside waiting on the park-like courthouse lawn it would be possible to smoke profusely, pace, and pass the excruciatingly slow time with my family and friends, so for a couple of hours, we rehashed the details of the trial and the events of the past year. Everyone was marveling at the fantastic whopper of a story Ms. Morgan concocted while on the witness stand.

Unbelievable!

Cigarette after cigarette was inhaled as the afternoon dragged on. Tim purchased the largest tub of soda I'd ever seen. I didn't know how he managed to carry the giant thing, because it looked more like a powder room wastepaper basket than beverage container. Throughout the afternoon he was slurping on the sweetened caffeinated cola, pacing, wearing a groove into the cement, and repeatedly remarking that he was not worried, not worried at all.

As the afternoon slowly dragged on, we all started feeling anxious, and we became more worried with each passing minute. Long shadows were now being cast upon the front of the old courthouse as the sun moved closer to the horizon, and we welcomed the shade, because it turned out to be a very warm afternoon. Now we could smoke, pace, and worry in the shade.

The massive cast-iron courthouse doors opened and two of the alternate jurors walked out. We recognized them right off, because we saw them every day of the trial. One was the middle-aged man with extremely thick eyeglasses from the back row, and the other was the pretty motherly woman who sat in the front row. They walked over and took a seat at a park bench in the shade, probably waiting to hear the verdict announced, too.

During the trial the jurors were prohibited from reading the newspaper, watching television, or even speaking about the case with anyone, but they were able to talk now, so Mary and I decided to go over and speak with them. Before long, Mike, Patty, and Tim joined us to hear what they had to say, and they were more than willing to share.

While there was nothing new to add about the evidence or the testimony that we had all heard, there was some news. They told us that it was entirely possible that one of the jurors, or even more, might not be convinced beyond a shadow of a doubt of Ms. Morgan's guilt. What? How could that possibly be? She confessed on videotape, twice, and explained in detail how she went about committing her crime spree. How could anyone dispute her own testimony? "Yes I did it. This is how I did it."

Now we became worried. Could this jury possibly become deadlocked? Because if one juror of the twelve dissented, then a verdict could not be reached. What would we do if she was found innocent and released? What if she got away with murder? That sobering realization rattled us, made us more anxious.

The evening Angelus rang out from Saint Paul's Episcopal Church's bells and went reverberating down the brown brick pavers of Saginaw Street. Shortly thereafter a uniformed officer of the court came out to make an announcement.

"The jury has not been able to arrive at a verdict today. They will resume their deliberations in the morning. Thank you."

We were most deflated at that announcement and not yet ready to give up our vigil, so we decided to move the group down the street to The Verdict Lounge, where we could hang out at a bar, with members of the Genesee County Bar, and spend a few more hours together commiserating over dinner and a drink before going home to what would surely be another restless night.

The following morning we were once again assembled in the shady yard of the courthouse. I brought along two extra packs of cigarettes, sunglasses, and sun block, too. Patty and Patrick arrived with Tim, and another giant vat of cola. Mike, Mary, Uncle Gerald, Aunt Shirley, Aunt Jean, Uncle Elin, Cousins Angie and Nelson, Linda, and a few other close friends came along to keep us company. The only time we left our vigil was to go to the restroom, with Tim leaving at least three times.

When noon finally arrived, we moved across the street to the Masonic Temple's basement dining room for lunch. This was a local favorite, with their tables nicely set with white linens, real china dishes, silverware, and good home-cooked food. You couldn't find a better or more economically priced meal in downtown Flint.

"The Temple" quite often fed the jurors from the trials taking place across the street, as it was up to the discretion of the bailiff where the jurors dined, but today they would be eating elsewhere. I was much too wound up to eat anyway, so Linda and I picked at a salad and left early to resume smoking.

After lunch we all returned to continue our vigil, and the time really dragged on. Shortly after two thirty, a uniformed officer came out to summon everyone back to the courtroom. They had arrived at a verdict, at last. Although it seemed like an eternity had passed, in reality it was twenty-four hours. Twenty-four long hours.

Making our way through the X-ray machines, security checkpoint, and into the elevator, we rode to the second floor. When the doors parted, we viewed a hallway swarming with people. Reporters, law enforcement officers, Detective J Diem, Chief Guigear, and several officers involved with the investigation were present to hear the verdict read. They were our allies now. Family and friends filed in, taking the remaining seats. It was standing room only, with the back wall and side aisles filled, too.

The room was buzzing with low-frequency chatter as everyone anxiously awaited Judge Neithercut's reappearance. Saying a silent prayer, I tried to brace myself for whatever verdict they would be announcing and reminded myself at the same time to breathe.

Sitting off to one side were Kimberly's proper parents. They silently sat there every day of the trial, and it surely must have been excruciating for them to hear the terrible things that their child was accused of doing. They seemed like nice, respectable people. We felt no animosity toward them.

But I wanted their daughter to pay for the harm she inflicted upon our mother, family, and our entire community. She should pay for the countless hours of time spent searching and the vast sums of money spent to investigate and prosecute this case. She could have alleviated so much suffering at any time by just disclosing the location of Mother's body.

⋅⊱⊱⊙ ⊙⊰⊰⋅

The Verdict is Read

Bailiff Newland rose, and the overflow crowd immediately hushed to silence. "All rise for the Honorable Judge Geoffrey Neithercut," he loudly announced.

The people of the courtroom rose in unison, creating a wind-making whoosh. Then the judge breezed in, sat down, pulled his spectacles down from the top of his head, peered over the top of them, and really scanned the packed room well.

"All be seated!"

· ·▷══◎ ◎══◁· ·

"OK. We are back on Kimberly Angenette Morgan's case, number 04-013968. The jury, after having several questions and over a day of deliberation, is ready to bring in their verdict. So, Mr. Newland, bring the jury in here."

The husky bailiff escorted the sober jury from the sequestered jury room and seated them. The judge continued, "Now the clerk of the court will take your verdict, and the proceedings will begin."

"Will the jury please rise," the court clerk command-ed. When all were standing, she continued. "Members of the jury, have you arrived at a verdict? If so, who speaks for you?"

"I will," responded a petite young woman dressed in pink and seated in the first row.

"What is your verdict?" the clerk asked.

"Go ahead and read it," the judge directed, peering over his glasses. Then he added, "Read it from the top, and go all the way down."

I held my breath.

"We the jury find the defendant, on the count of homicide, murder, and first-degree premeditated murder...guilty."

Taking a moment, she breathed in and resumed.

"On count two, of felony homicide, murder, we find the defendant guilty.

"On count three, carjacking, we find the defendant guilty.

"On count four, kidnapping, we find the defendant guilty.

"On count five, armed robbery, we find the defendant guilty.

"On count six, assault with intent to murder, we find the defendant guilty.

"On count seven, arson of personal property of one thousand or more or less than twenty thousand dollars, we find the defendant guilty.

"On count eight, carrying a concealed weapon, we find the defendant guilty.

"On count nine, felony possession of firearm, we find the defendant guilty.

"On count ten, felony firearm, we find the defendant guilty."

All the people in the courtroom, including myself, were still holding their breath and watching as the process unfolded further.

"Members of the jury, if you agree with the verdict in this case, raise your right hand."

Every arm shot up.

"You, and each of you, do say upon your oath, that you find the defendant, Kimberly Angenette Morgan, guilty of all ten counts. So say you the jury?"

"Yes," the jury answered in resounding unison.

The judge continued, "Now I'd like to poll the jury individually, and ask if they agree. The clerk will read your number, and you will say if you agree or disagree." One by one, the clerk read each number, and one by one they all responded yes.

"It is unanimous. The court will accept the jury's verdict and find Kimberly Angenette Morgan guilty as charged on all ten counts. Sentencing is scheduled for October 6, 2004, at 8:30 a.m.," the judge said. Swinging his chair around and rising, he quickly disappeared into his chambers.

⋅⊶⊷⋅

Once the judge departed, the courtroom burst into a buzzing clatter. Finally I could breathe again, and I found myself exhaling, letting out what I'd been holding in for well over a year. People were shaking hands, hugging each other, and embracing. Tears were flowing down many cheeks, including my own, but we were smiling through our tears.

We caught Mrs. Hanson and properly thanked her for a job well done. It had been a hard-fought battle, and she had represented us well. This was a victory for our mother.

Justice.

⋅⟫▬◉ ◉▬⟪⋅

During this odyssey we learned that if we did not address the media they would make up their own version of the story that may or may not be accurate. So before leaving the courtroom and facing the media people in the hallway, we met in a small conference room to draft a statement for the press. What follows is the written text submitted to them.

⋅⟫▬◉ ◉▬⟪⋅

The family of Mrs. Dorothy Lee Murphy wishes to express our heartfelt thanks and gratitude for those assisting us with this case.

While this is not a victory, we do feel that justice has been served. In behalf of our mother, grandmother, and family matriarch, we wish to thank you.

The Murphy Family

Another Wake, After the Trial

THE TRIAL WAS over, the verdict read, but it was still only midafternoon. We were not ready to call it a day just yet, so Mike extended an invitation to everyone to join him at his home for a small get-together.

This truly was a time to let off some steam, because this trial had been intense. Certainly this hollow victory did not call for a celebration, but we decided to gather once more and have another wake, of sorts, to celebrate a life, a death, a vindication, and everything in between.

The afternoon was sunny and comfortably warm, with deep blue cloudless skies, just perfect for being outside, socializing, and grilling. The garage door was swung open and Mike's Tiki Bar was once again in business. Once again the grill was wheeled out, and the food began to miraculously appear, along with a wee bit of the drink, too.

The usual suspects started appearing, along with a few surprise guests. Detective J Diem arrived, dressed in her street clothes, and she fell right in with the crowd. Now she was part of the family, so we fixed her a plate and found her a drink.

We personally credited J, along with those in her department, as being the most instrumental in solving Mother's case. She personally knew our mother, and that made all of the difference. It was her connection to Mom, and her instincts pursuing the correct leads, that helped solve this case. She helped to bring this case to justice and had earned a place of honor among us.

J, as they called her at the office, was fairly short for a law enforcement officer, was very personable, somewhere in her early forties, proper, and had lots of curly black hair that she pulled back into a fat ponytail. Her cadence revealed telltale traits of being raised somewhere in the Southwest, and her carriage suggested a military background.

For well over a year now, she'd kept her professional decorum, but she could cut loose now. She had plenty to share with us, and we were eager to listen to everything that she could tell.

We all chuckled when Mom, at age seventy-five, took a citizens patrol, neighborhood watch, and personal safety class that Detective J held at the Mundy Police Department. Mom just loved this class because her instruction included riding along in a police car, using the police radio, and receiving tips on how to keep yourself, your home, and your property safe from muggers, buggers, and such.

Mother repeatedly told us this story, as children and old people can sometimes do. Basically it goes like this: J was new to the Mundy Township squad and new to the area. So, one afternoon she was on patrol when an APB bulletin went out describing a crime in progress. A vehicle description and suspect profile were radioed out, and the officers were dispatched to apprehend the criminal, who was reported to be heading west on Grand Blanc Road.

Not being very familiar with the area, J lit out heading due west in a big hurry. She was going the right way—down the wrong road. Well, it just happened to be the right road after all when she accidentally crossed paths with the escaping suspect and singlehandedly apprehended him. Little did we know that this legendary wrong-way police-woman would be instrumental in Mother's murder case.

⋅→▶● ●◀←⋅

"I couldn't tell you guys any of this stuff while the case was being investigated, but I can sure tell you now," J said with a crooked grin.

We all laughed at her lighthearted delivery.

"At first, I couldn't believe that *your* mother was involved with anything like this, because, as you know, I knew your mother and liked her very much. And I'm so sorry this happened to her, and to you-all."

We accepted her condolences, and then thanked her once again for all of her assistance. Her warm and steady presence was reassuring; her delivery was slow, well thought out, sincere, and respectful. She was a natural storyteller.

"You know, we we're pretty sure at the beginning that your mom's car was used in that drive-by shooting. And I knew that, that car was the way to follow this case. I knew it. But I had to prove that. Because the only connection we had to your mother was her car.

"When we first questioned the guy that was shot, Alan, he didn't even know what happened to him; he just knew that someone was trying to kill him. He didn't know why. He wasn't any part of this either; he was just another victim in this strange drama.

"Sure he was shot at, several times, and hit twice by what he *thought* was a young black man. But still, even with all that confusion, that, that car was the only connection we had to your mom, and that shooting connected Alan to that car. We had to follow that lead. We pretty quickly found your mom's car, but she had seemingly disappeared into thin air. We had to find her.

"But, who was driving her car? What was that shooting all about and how the heck was your mom involved with all of this?

"Thankfully Kim was a bad shot and only winged the guy who stood in her way. And thankfully he lived to tell us what happened, and even testify against her. But she mistakenly left those shell casings at the drive-by shooting, in your mom's car, and inside her purse, too. *Big* mistake. Break number one.

"Your mother's Buick had a full tank of gas and that sucker really blazed, but somehow those shell casings miraculously made it through that car fire intact. When the crime lab positively matched them with the ones recovered from the drive-by shooting, and connected the two events, that was break number two.

"It was also a miracle that the little hand lotion bottle that she left inside your mom's car, made of plastic no less, survived that blaze. But it only survived because a bit of the insulation from the ceiling had fallen over top of it and protected it from the fire. And it was also a miracle that that little bottle contained enough DNA to place her inside that car. Break number three.

"That speeding ticket in Indiana placed her in Flint on that day, at that time. When I figured in the time difference thing, between Michigan and Indiana that made it possible to construct a timeline positively connecting her to Flint, the vehicle, and the shooting. That was break number four.

"Did you guys know that Kim has an older brother? Uh-huh. As young children they were adopted by their parents. Her brother is currently serving time in prison for committing multiple murders; he's a really dangerous guy, and did some truly gruesome stuff. Kim was just a teenager when it happened, and we think she may have even witnessed it.

"You-all understand, we were following up on all kinds of leads in this case, but I just felt, in my bones, that *she* did it, and that this line of questioning was the right one. I took this case very personally."

We all knew that was true, and once again expressed our gratitude for her efforts and those of her entire squad. We explained that some of the reward money had been set aside for the Mundy Township Police Department to purchase some-thing it might need in our mother's name. Detective J shied away from the personal praise placed upon her, but graciously accepted the gift offered in acknowledgment of the entire department's efforts.

"Unless that money is earmarked for a special purpose it will have to go into the general fund, so how about if we plant a memorial garden up in front of the police station in your mom's name and that way everyone can enjoy it. And since I care for the gardens surrounding the building anyway, I will gladly take care of it, too."

We all heartily approved the motion.

"We never did recover the gun that she used, and believe me, that gun would've really helped us get her. And we still think that the girlfriend had to be involved with all of this, too. I mean, how else would Kimberly know what bus the boyfriend took on his way home from work, where to look for him, and what time he would be there? Or even, that he had walked to work that day and was taking the bus home? She had to be in on it, but to what extent, or in what capacity, we just can't prove.

"Heck, we needed to subpoena the girlfriend just to get her to testify, because she did *not* want to talk to us. She was held in jail on contempt of court charges until she agreed to speak. She probably didn't want to testify against Kim because I think she was really afraid of her. And believe you me; she had plenty good reason to be scared of her. She is one tough cookie.

"They probably figured if the boyfriend was out of the picture, they could collect the Social Security survivor benefits paid to his children. Maybe they thought they'd live on that. Who knows what they were thinking. And, may-be, this was all just Kimberly's twisted fantasy. We can't prove any of this, mind you, but I have a sneakin' suspicion that the girlfriend was involved way more than we'll ever know.

"Ms. Morgan is intelligent, but she wasn't nearly as clever as she thought. She was the manager of a store in the shopping mall in Nashville. I think she really believed she could talk her way out of anything, fancied herself as being smarter than most people, but she outsmarted herself this time.

"She sure talked a lot. While in jail she confided in her cell mates. She talked to me and Detective Schmitzer, too. She even seemed happy to come to Flint to be questioned, so she could talk some more. I think she actually thought she could talk herself out of her troubles.

"And can you-all believe that whopper of a story she made up on the witness stand, after all that evidence was already presented proving her guilty? Unbelievable!

"But we got her. We got her. Now, I suspected that they would convict her on all ten counts, and they did. And I fully expect that she will receive life in prison, without a chance of parole. We can't execute people in this state, because we don't have the death penalty...but boy, if ever..."

⋯⋰⋯

Friends continued arriving at the gathering, because many people were just now finishing work for the day. And in what had become a familiar ritual, we all moved inside to gather in front of the television and catch the six o'clock evening news.

⊷⊷⊷ ⊷⊷⊷

"Tonight I am standing outside of the Genesee County Courthouse, where the verdict was announced in the trial of Kimberly Angenette Morgan, she has been found guilty, on all ten counts, of kidnapping and murdering Dorothy Murphy.. Sentencing would be held at a later date."

⊷⊷⊷ ⊷⊷⊷

There was no cheering from any of us. And yet, somehow this was a vindication. One more large step was completed in this very long journey we had been on, and at last we were nearing home.

⊷⊷⊷ ⊷⊷⊷

Aimee's Wedding

Tim and Patty's eldest and only daughter, Aimee, had grown into a lovely young woman. She had the "Murphy good looks," with dark, thick, wavy hair, creamy skin, rosy cheeks, and clear blue sparkling eyes. Aimee was always a perfect child, and I don't believe she ever got dirty in her life. In fact, she seemed to have somehow practically raised herself, and she was now working on raising her parents properly.

She was always a self-directed and self-disciplined child who attended years of ballet and piano instruction and participated in cheerleading. She had grown into a beautiful, poised, and sweet young lady. Aimee had graduated from the University of Michigan the previous spring with her law degree, passed the state bar exam during the summer, and was planning a fall wedding. Everything was right on schedule.

As girls do, Aimee had been planning her wedding all her life, long before this trial happened. And in spite of some major scheduling conflicts, it was still happening, right between the ending of the trial and sentencing.

All Saints Church, on the far northwest side of Flint, was where Aimee chose to be married. Her maternal grand-parents were charter members of the small suburban church, which was built in the 1940s. This nonprogressive parish still had some of the Masses celebrated in Polish, by its well over eighty-year-old priest. For decades he had been the chief celebrant of this century-old parish, which was now inside hostile territory.

The day of her wedding turned out to be unusually warm for early September. In fact, it was downright hot. The church quickly filled with melting family and friends, who were fidgeting, fanning themselves, and trying their best to keep cool because the old church didn't have air-conditioning.

For her wedding, Aimee wore a billowing white strapless dress that showed off her lovely milky shoulders. A full billowing skirt flared out from her slim waist and floated on layers of rustling crinoline netting. Her intended, David, was dressed in a classic black tuxedo, and together they looked like the picture-perfect couple on the wedding cake, brimming with promise and beaming with love.

My dear friend Patty Hogan was my date for the evening because she had been adopted into the family. Tommy Taylor was also drafted to do the wedding party's hair, and was seated at our table for the reception. If you were seated with Tommy, you were certain to have entertainment for the entire evening. Rounding out our table were my good friends Lloyd Witt and Linda De Groat.

During the reception Tommy shared the story from earlier, when Aimee and Patty were in the salon to have their hair done. Aimee, who was usually a very sweet girl, had a small nuclear meltdown. Apparently the stress of the wedding had gotten the better of her, and when she saw her mother in Tommy's chair receiving her final dousing of hairspray before being discharged, she blew a gasket.

"You are not letting her out of here looking like the Flying Nun, are you?"

Apparently, Tommy had given her hair a flip of sorts, some volume with wings. So Tommy, who does *not* take criticism very well, took a deep breath and took it all in stride - this time. He swung the chair around, compressed the hairdo a bit to reduce the volume, sprayed it thoroughly one more time, and announced, "There you go, you can't improve upon perfection."

Luckily Aimee adored Tommy, and the love affair was mutual, because before every appointment she brought him something yummy from Zingerman's Deli in Ann Arbor, and that always scored real big points. And Tommy, taking the incident in stride, had already turned it into an amusing anecdote for retelling during the reception.

The meal was simple and lovely, the understated decorations and flowers flawless, all in white. The evening was warm and soft, and the dance floor full of well-dressed, smiling guests having a wonderful time.

It was a shame that Aimee's grandmother could not be there to see her first grandchild married. And I was certain that, at some point during the evening, we would all be think-ing of her. I imagined that she was watching, approving, and thrilled that another milestone was being accomplished in her thriving family.

Victim Impact Statements

O<small>N</small> W<small>EDNESDAY</small> O<small>CTOBER</small> 6, 2014, more than a month after the trial was ended, the day of sentencing arrived. Kimberly Angenette Morgan was once again ushered into the courtroom. This time she was dressed in an oversize orange jail jumpsuit, with the sleeves and pant cuffs rolled up, which somehow made her look even shorter and rounder.

The courtroom was packed to capacity, with mostly familiar faces. Many of the detectives investigating the case were here, as well as many family members. We had a lot of support. The abrasive reporter from *The Flint Journal*, whom we'd grown to tolerate, was also here. A large presence of media people were assembled in the hallway outside the courtroom, awaiting the sentencing announcement.

Judge Neithercut briskly entered the courtroom and immediately launched into speaking.

⊷⊶ ⊷⊶

"Today we begin the sentencing of Kimberly Angenette Morgan, case number 04-013968. Miss Morgan is to be sentenced today on many charges.

"Count one, homicide murder of the first degree, premeditated.

"Count two, felony homicide murder.

"Count three, carjacking.

"Count four, kidnapping.

"Count five, robbery, armed.

"Count six, assault with intent to commit murder.

"Count seven, arson of personal property.

"Count eight, carrying a concealed weapon.

"Count nine, being a felon in possession of a weapon.

"Count ten, felony firearm.

"Miss Morgan, they have written a report, and it describes *you*. Have you had a chance to read it yet?"

"Yes, I have," Kimberly respectfully responded.

"They use this report in the prison system, and that determines how they treat you, so if there is a mistake in it, you'd better correct it now. Did you see any mistakes?"

"No, not to my knowledge."

"Mr. Beauvais, do you have additions or corrections?"

"No, Your Honor."

"What about the people, Mrs. Hanson?"

"No, Your Honor."

"Before you have your opportunity to speak, Miss Morgan, I just want you to understand that Mrs. Murphy's family wishes to address the court. So, I want you to sit there. And listen." The judge pointed to a chair that was placed opposite the podium. Kimberly shuffled around to the folding chair, clanking as she went, and obediently sat down.

"Mrs. Hanson informs me that you all wish to speak. It is unusual, but all four of Mrs. Murphy's children wish to speak, and I have allowed it."

"Your Honor, that is correct," Mrs. Hanson affirmed.

"Walk right up here," Judge Neithercut said, motioning for us to step forward. Fixing his gaze upon us, he smiled warmly and said, "Why don't you all huddle up around the podium there a bit. It will give a little strength that way. This has been a long odyssey for you, an experience that has gone on for what, a year and a half; your lives being in limbo for that long."

He then motioned toward Mike and said, "Go ahead, sir. You will have to tell me your name first."

Mike, clearing his throat, looked the judge in the eye and responded, "My name is Michael Murphy, and I'm Dorothy's youngest." Mike then turned and fixed his gaze on Kimberly, who was sitting in the chair directly in front of him, and directly addressed her.

"Hi, Kim. When I first saw your name in the paper, I thought, what a pretty name. I'm sure when you were born your parents never imagined all this, not in their wildest dreams or their worse nightmares; what you would grow up to become, a spiritless killer, a bank robber, carjacker, arsonist, and kidnapper; not exactly what every parent dreams of for their kids.

"I'm sure that you have devastated your family in what you have done; I hope that you realize this. Seriously, you senselessly murdered an eighty-year-old woman, my mom, mother. She had many brothers and sisters that cared for her, and she was a deeply religious person. My father died when I was eleven. She was my mom, she was my dad. She put her family above everything in her life. She was the definition of love. Above all she put God, above even her family.

"It took a long time to write this down, because there are not enough words, not enough time, to say everything to you that needs saying. But her faith just kept growing stronger as she got older. She has been preparing for heaven all her life. You, Kim, sent her there. What you did to our mom was pure evil. No one deserves to be left out in a dump site, in a field by themselves, to rot.

"You have taken a beautiful spirit, a friend, a grandmother, away from us all. You frightened an entire community of senior citizens. We had people calling us that were afraid to go out after this happened. And I can't imagine what you made your own family go through.

"Words can't accurately describe this, but I hope you'll hear my mom's voice inside your head at night when you're in bed, for the rest of your life, telling you that she'll pray for you; because you need it.

"You will have the rest of your life to become a person who has a spirit, and gain a soul, because right now you're a soulless spirit. I have no doubt that you'll burn in hell for what you did to my mother, if you do not find God.

"We will continue to pray for your family, as we have done, to hope they can be strong and overcome this terrible thing you have done to them, because they will never be the same, as will our family never be the same, all because of your selfish and misguided idea of love.

"My family has also been united by this tragedy, and we are closer than we have ever been before. You did not take our mother's spirit. It goes on within us, and grows stronger. It will never die."

⤙⟶ ⟵⤚

Our sister Mary was the next to speak.

"We would like to first thank all the legal community and the policing departments that worked on all the searches for my mother, and the Prosecutor's Office, and the members of the jury. And the community that helped us search for our mother.

"The first part of my statement I wrote on July 13, 2003, and it says, 'Today we held a memorial service for my mother. She was a good mother and grandmother to all of us. We loved her deeply and miss her very much.' As my brother Mike said, 'We lost our mother, but we found her spirit.'

"Kimberly, you have deprived us of many things. Two weeks after she disappeared she missed the eightieth birthday party we had planned for her. The party will go on without her. The memorial service we had was the first one I ever attended where the deceased person was nowhere to be found. At eighty years of age, she had lived a good long life. But who gave *you* the right to end her life?

"We will no longer have our mother with us on her birthday, at Christmas, or on Mother's Day. In committing this evil act upon our mother, we in turn have found only love and support from others, her family, her brothers and sisters, our cousins, neighbors, and complete strangers; they have prayed for us, comforted us, fed us, and cried with us. This shows love triumphs over evil. In the end, love will overcome our pain and help us.

"I will not wish this pain, which we have felt, on anyone. In our hearts we know that divine justice will be ours. I have prayed for you, because you truly need it."

"You didn't get to know my mother, so I would like to tell you a little bit about her. This is part of her obituary. She was eighty years of age, she died in Flint. She was born in Marion, Michigan, the first daughter of Mark and Lena Lee. She married my father, Joseph, on June 21, 1952.

"She belonged to the Altar Society and Altar Guild. She belonged to many other organizations as well. She truly devoted her life to the service of others. She was also a secretary, wife, mother, and the oldest member of her family. She is survived by three sons, me, four grandchildren, her brothers, one sister, and many nieces and nephews.

"This is another obituary that I took out of the paper. The woman was also eighty years old, and it reads, 'She died peacefully at home, surrounded by her loving family.' The difference between those two obituaries is that our mother's death was not peaceful, and we, her family, were deprived of saying good-bye to her. She died without the benefit of her family's presence. And no one deserves to die this way.

"She would have willingly given you the car. My comfort is in the fact that she knew you were probably going to kill her, and that she said that she would pray for you. My mother was a deeply religious person and she believed in God, Jesus, and the saints in heaven, and also in hell. I know she is in heaven, and at peace.

"Kimberly, I pray for you, that someday you will have the peace and love of God, and have a relationship with Our Lord. The rest of this, I'm not going to read, but it is Psalm 94, and it talks about divine justice. The last paragraph says, 'They band together against the righteous, and condemned the innocent to death. But the Lord has become our fortress and our God, and our rock in whom I take refuge. He will repay them for their sins, and destroy them for their wicked ways.'

"My mother never hurt anyone intentionally in her life, maybe other than an unkind word. I just hope you realize the impact that you've had on our entire family."

⋆⟞◉ ◉⟝⋆

Brother Tim walked up to the podium, he looked squarely at Kimberly, and then the judge.

"Judge, it's as you said, our case was very different than most cases. There were not any eye-witnesses to testify as to what happened; only the confessions from the defendant as to what happened, and we had to take her word for everything. It's a shame that this family can't find out the whole truth about what happened in this case. And we will probably never know the whole truth, because she won't tell us.

"We had bits and pieces to go on, but nothing concrete. My younger brother and his friends searched down the Flint River in canoes looking for her. We held organized ground searches where we took square miles and searched for her, and had a couple hundred people out searching. My aunt slipped into a ditch and broke her leg.

"Everyone helped us put up missing posters. A memorial service was held at Holy Redeemer Church for our family and the church community in Flint. Our family put on a benefit to raise extra money for a reward fund. We raised over six thousand dollars from community, friends, family, neighbors, and concerned citizens.

"We were all in shock. We were only going through the motions. We felt guilty if we weren't out searching more, but we were exhausted from all the stress and frustration. And as the time went on, things only became worse. When they finally found my mom, I was personally glad that we could finally lay her to rest where she belonged and not just out lying in a field somewhere.

"When it was on the television and in the newspaper about how Kimberly shot my mother in the face as she said she would pray for her, it completely consumed me. I wanted to give her the same penalty that she gave my mother: death. But then I did as I was taught as a Christian and by my mom, and I had to forgive. After some time I found it in my heart to forgive her, because it is easier for me to forgive than carry this burden of hatred every day for the rest of my life.

"As my sentence for you, I would like you to have those pictures of my mother hanging inside your cell as she was found dead lying out in that field, so you can be reminded two times a day of what you did. Because I have to drive by there two times a day, on my way to work and my way home, and I have to be reminded two times a day. I have to think about her lying out there, so you should be reminded two times a day, too.

"It takes a lot of courage and intestinal fortitude to knock off an eighty-year-old lady and steal her car. If you wanted a car, why didn't you just knock her aside and take the car? There are lots of cars out there, hundreds of cars, thou-sands of cars. Genesee County is full of them. If you wanted a car, just take a car. And I can't believe that my mom just voluntarily got into the car, and voluntarily got out of the car, and just walked into the woods; where you shot her. That's what you told us, but I cannot believe that.

"While I can never forget this senseless act of complete and utter lack of respect for human life, it is easier for me to forgive you than carry the burden of hatred every day for the rest of my life.

"From Dorothy's homicide, we've learned a lot about the court system. And we gained a lot of new friends. Our family is a lot closer together. Everyone's been just wonderful to us—the police department, the prosecutor, churches, prayer groups. And I would just like to thank everybody for all they have done for us. All the concern they have shown for us."

⊷⇥⊙ ⊙⇤⊶

It was now my turn to speak.

"Kimberly Angenette Morgan, a jury of twelve decent men and women has found you guilty of kidnapping and murdering our mother, Dorothy Lorraine Lee Murphy. On a number of occasions you have confessed to committing these acts.

"You *chose* to kidnap, and you *chose* to murder our mother, grandmother, sister, aunt, and friend. Dorothy was the eldest of ten children and the matriarch of her larger extended family. She was the mother of four, grandmother to four, and loved by many people in this community.

"Dorothy had deep religious conviction and truly lived her faith. She lived a life of service to others. She lived eighty good years on this earth, and should have lived to see her grandchildren grow up, graduate from college, marry, and have great-grandchildren. She should be alive today.

"You, Kimberly, chose to take her away from us. You could have taken the car; she would have given it to you. You chose instead to drive her to that desolate spot, walk her into those woods, and shoot her, three times. And then you chose to dispose of her in the most disrespectful way imaginable.

"You then chose to steal lunch money from this tiny, defenseless, elderly woman's purse, after irreverently leaving her body in a dump to rot. Then you stole her car and intentionally destroyed it in an attempt to cover your crimes.

"Do you have any idea how much torment, pain, and suffering you caused this family and this community? Do you have any concept of the anguish we felt as we spent months uselessly searching for our beloved mother's body? This ordeal has traumatized us, and part of us shall never fully recover, all because of your selfish act.

"Do you ever think about the amount of time or the resources and the money that were spent to investigate and prosecute your crimes? That amount is enormous. And we are grateful that our community did these things in our behalf. We will recover.

"Throughout this trial the only emotion you displayed were the tears you shed for the lost love of Savannah Liddel. But there were no tears shed for our mother as you ate potato chips and calmly confessed to killing her.

"And as you were preparing to take her life, this devout old woman prayed for *you*, Kimberly Morgan, and not for herself or her own deliverance. Thy will be done. May you use the rest of your life to contemplate the horrible things you have done to all of us that loved her."

Kimberly Morgan's Last Words

Judge Neithercut sighed heavily. "Everyone in town sympathizes with you, you know that. You've seen the prayers and felt the outpouring, and specifically... I am really sorry that you had to look at those bad pictures during the trial. That's a terrible thing to have to see. I am sorry you had to go through that.

"Mr. Beauvais, will you speak for your client?"

"Your Honor, given the fact as to the sentence, the seriousness of this crime, it is the mandatory sentence. So everything that I could possibly say on behalf of my client I said in trial, and I have nothing further to say. I believe my client has something she wishes to say."

"Then it is your turn to speak, Miss Morgan," the judge said and he shifted his gaze back to his desk and correspondence.

Kimberly Morgan walked up to the podium in her oversize orange jumpsuit with her chains clanking as she went. Taking a deep breath, she began while looking directly at the four of us.

⋅⇒ ⇐⋅

"Before I read my statement to the family and everyone else, I just want to say that, um...I know you think I am a heartless person, but it's not that at all. I know you saw the videotape and it looked like I was just confessing to a murder while eating potato chips and drinking water. But what you didn't see was"— Kimberly exhaled deeply, audibly—"that I did break down and cry because of what happened, and I feel really bad. I'm very hurt about what has happened to your mother, and what has happened to a lot of people in this situation."

She then looked down and began to read directly from her notes. "I want to take this time and express my feel-ings, not because it will change anything or because I'm being sentenced, but because this is what my heart leads me to do.

"I'm sure this last year has been emotionally hard for a lot of people. I never thought, on July 2, that the events that took place would change the lives of so many people."

"My deepest apologies go out to the Murphy family. There's not a day that goes by that I don't feel your pain. I know that Miss. Murphy was very dear to you, and I truly apologize because you didn't have a chance to say good-bye.

"Miss Murphy did not deserve to be put in the middle of such a violent rela-tionship. I pray that the Lord will comfort you in your time of grief. I also pray that God puts it in your heart to forgive, for the wrong that's been done.

"To my parents, I'm sorry that you have to go through this pain, and to put you through such a hurtful predicament. I never wanted to hurt you. And yes, you raised me right. It's just that, some things that happen in life, even our pat-ents can't protect us from: or prepare us for. Also, thank you for your love, your prayers, and your support.

"To my attorney, who helped me, thank you for helping me and fighting for me. May God bless you throughout your career.

"To my friends and those that did not judge me, thank you for being you. I hope we can learn something from this. One, that life is too short and live every day to the fullest. Two, to be watchful of the people you call friends.

"What we need in the city of Flint and all over the world is to follow God's instructions, and that is to love your neighbors as well as your enemies, and to stop the violence, because if one person is killed, many are left to deal with the pain.

"I pray that throughout my incarceration, that I can help someone and help myself to lead a more positive life. I hope that what I said today will not offend anyone. Please know that this comes from the heart. I ask you to take the time to pray for peace and love, and comfort those that have been hurt behind this tragedy.

"Thank you. Sincerely, Kimberly A. Morgan.

⋅‣═◉ ◉═┤⋅

Ms. Morgan finished reading her statement, and it seemed sincere, moving, and heartfelt. But the fact is, she used the words *me, myself,* and *I* a total of forty-one times during her final statement, and she mentioned Dorothy Murphy, our mother and the victim, a total of two times. This proved that she was still thinking much more about herself than Mother and what she did to her—and to us.

This was the desperate act of a desperate person with a misguided idea of love that led us all to this place. But it was love and the goodness of fellow man that assisted us and brought us through this tragedy, revealed the truth, and provided justice and righteousness.

⋅‣═◉ ◉═┤⋅

Sentencing

Judge Neithercut began the sentencing phase now. "I don't need to say anything. I think the family's said everything that needs to be said. We just need to get on with this."

Mrs. Hanson, the prosecutor, stood and said, "Your Honor, the people move to have the murder convictions sentenced as one offense."

"I will acknowledge that this will be sentenced as one offense, first-degree premeditated murder," the judge verified.

"Yes, Judge," agreed Attorney Philip H. Beauvais III.

Peering over his Benjamin Franklin reading glasses, the judge spoke directly to Kimberly Morgan, looking her squarely in the eye.

"Madam, *you* are the one they built prisons for. *You* are the reason they made prisons. *You* are smart, you are impulsive, and you are giddy. You rob banks and you kill old ladies, and *you* are a danger to the rest of us. That's why they built prisons.

"You will be sentenced on counts one and two, as they are merged, and you are to be remanded to the custody of the Michigan Department of Corrections for the rest of your life. On counts four, five, and six, which are kidnapping, armed robbery, and assault with intent to commit murder, you will serve the rest of you life in the custody of the Michigan Department of Corrections.

"On count three, which is carjacking, you will serve a minimum time of five hundred and sixty-two months, a maximum of nine hundred months.

"On counts seven, eight, and nine, which are the arson and the two weapons charges, you will serve a minimum term of sixty months and a maximum of ninety months.

"On count ten, which is felony firearm, you'll serve two years in prison. Because this is a consecutive charge, you will get credit for the two hundred and seventy-four days you already served. You must finish that sentence, as it is preced-ing the commencement of sentences on counts one through nine.

"Because you are convicted by a jury, you have the right to an appeal and a free lawyer to assist you with that. Mr. Beauvais is going to give you a paper to fill out. You must sign and return it to the court no later than forty-two days from today. It could cause you to have a free lawyer to assist you with your appeal."

The judge sat back, placed his glasses upon the top of his head, and watched as Kimberly signed the paper. When finished, her lawyer walked them up to him.

"Your Honor," Mr. Beauvais said humbly, "for the record, Miss Morgan has signed the receipt of the notice of her appellate rights, I've given her a copy of that document, and I've assigned the original to the court."

"Go ahead, Deputies," Judge Neithercut said, and he motioned toward the deputy, and Kimberly Morgan was escorted out of the courtroom, with her arm and leg restraints clanking as she went.

Prosecutor Karen Hanson walked over to the front row where we were all assembled, and we all thanked her for a job well done.

After * words

THIS BOOK WAS first written ten years ago, shortly after all this happened. Then I put it away. In theory, that was because I wanted to "move on with my life." Now, a decade later, I have the time, energy, and wherewithal to finish it properly. This epilogue is included to inform you of what has happened in the decade since the disappearance and trial.

To quote Ms. Morgan at her sentencing, "It's just that some things that happen in life, even our parents can't protect us from." We could not protect Mother, save her life, or even say good-bye, because she was gone before we even knew she was missing. Mother was abducted and murdered; we were part of the resulting collateral damage. We were all affected in one way or another. An entire community was traumatized.

There are insights that I'd like to share with you, to give you some idea how the abduction and murder of a loved one can affect your life and the lives of those close to you. We found that some people quickly stepped forward to offer their support and assistance, while others were noticeably absent, retreating and not knowing what to do or say. Through this ordeal we have learned who was truly connected to us.

Our lives were permanently altered starting the day Mother vanished. The world has changed. Just as pure light is bent when passing through a prism; our view of the world has also been shifted. There are still many unanswered questions remaining, but we have learned to accept this. It is probably better that we don't know some things, because they would be far too disturbing. You have to learn how to turn off the "what-if mechanism," tune out the extra noise, and find peace within yourself, because you cannot be fully in the present if you haven't resolved your past.

⋅→⊨◉ ◉⊨←⋅

Time has moved on for all of us, if we like it or not. Our dear sister, Mary Ann, is now engaged to a good man named Jim, and we are all very happy for her. Her son, Ryan, has married his childhood sweet-heart, Darci, and they are happily building a life together in Traverse City. My sweet niece Erin graduated from college with a master's degree, got a job, bought a house, was married, and has produced a beautiful blue-eyed blonde grandchild for Mary.

Since her marriage, Aimee has produced three beautiful grandchildren for Tim and Patty, too. Patrick has grown up, graduated from college, and entered the workforce. Tim was "downsized" by General Motors and involuntarily retired. Since then he has taken up cross-country running and furniture making, and is doing very well at both.

Mike left his home in Mott Park and moved to the country, west of Flint, into an older farmhouse that he shares with his companion, Theresa, and her son, Tyler. He seems to be quite happy with his new life, and we're pleased he has found someone special. The popular Tiki Bar still continues to operate, only now in a new and improved location.

There was a change of residence for me too, as I sold my lovely cottage in Manistee, and I am now happily residing in sunny southern Florida, where I have taken up writing.

Weddings, births, deaths, and everything in between are happening as life continues moving on. Sadly, our mother was not able to share in her family's many accomplishments.

At first the holidays were particularly hard, because we certainly missed Mother, but they're becoming easier now. Family traditions are being carried on by the next generation, as Erin is now making Grandma's notorious green layered Jell-O salad for the holiday gatherings. It helps having a large and supportive family, with our warts and all.

The sense of needing to be hyper-vigilant has retreated to more normal levels now, but it is still there; I will never feel as safe as I once did. While living in Manistee I never locked my doors, but I would never leave them unlocked anymore.

The world is a more dangerous place than it was a decade ago, and so is Flint. We cope with the added dangers and stresses in our own ways. Mary took up yoga. Tim bought a gun, but he also started running. Mike got a pit bull and then moved out of the city, into the country. I had a heart attack.

Ms. Morgan was found guilty on all ten counts and given multiple life sentences without any chance of parole. When last notified, she was incarcerated in a women's prison in Plymouth, in southeast Michigan. Right after the trial we were notified of any appeals she would be having and of her movements within the penal system. This program has been terminated because of budget cuts, and there has not been any news about her or the case in quite some time.

Ms. Morgan did have an appeal shortly after her initial incarceration, and that was denied. For all we know she may be mounting another appeal at taxpayers' expense. There wasn't any further action taken against her ex-lover, Savannah Liddel, either because law enforcement officials said they did not have enough evidence to charge her with a crime. She was last seen leaving court, hand in hand with Alan Johnson, demonstrating that justice and love may both be blind.

We filed affidavits with the court to ensure that Ms. Morgan could not profit from the commission of this crime. We were told we could not sue her personally for damages, because she had no assets. But our attorney, Thomas Warda, suggested that we should initiate a lawsuit against Walgreens. "Someone should pay for this tragedy," he said. "It was their store where the abduction originated, ergo; they did not provide adequate security. So sue 'em good!"

We felt we were adequately compensated when all the forces of law and order were made available to us to help us find our missing mother and to prosecute the person who was found guilty of kidnapping and murdering her. Plus we felt we'd spent enough time in court to last a lifetime, so we let it go.

Flint is more violent than ever, and there are fewer police officers patrolling the streets, simply because the city can't afford them. For the past two decades the city has had a steadily shrinking population, so consequently the city's tax revenues have steadily declined as well. These budget short-falls have hit the police department particularly hard. Sixty-nine officers are left to patrol a city of one hundred thousand people. The fire department and the other city services did not escape the budget ax, either, with deep cuts happening across the board.

Over the past few years Flint has often been often been cited as one of the most violent cities in America, and it also has one of the highest unemployment rates in the country. When there are few jobs being created, and not many chances for young people to build a future, many just give up, turn to crime and drugs, or just get out of town.

·•►═◉ ◉═◄•·

Many people have commented on the grace that our family exhibited during this terrible ordeal. We have to give credit to our parents, because they raised us to be respectful children from a good working-class family. If our mother could with her last breath pray for her executioner, how could we harbor hatred toward her? The old lady set the bar high.

·•►═◉ ◉═◄•·

Mother's possessions have been dissolved, and now the memories of her are all that remain. I have been able to move past the events that were the cause of her awful death and can once again focus on what was her abundant life.

While the circumstances of Mother's death are difficult to deal with, because no one wants a loved one to suffer, the worst part for me was during her extended disappearance when we did not even know where she was.

·•►═◉ ◉═◄•·

A year after the trial, in late November 2005, my close friend Mike Putnam had a massive heart attack and died at his home. This came as an awful shock to all of us, but especially to me. He was only forty-seven, and apparently more fragile than any of us knew.

There was a memorial service and funeral held by his family, in Vassar, which many attended. Mike was well-liked, close to and loved by his family. His early and unexpected death was difficult for me. My family didn't really know how significant he was to me, and his family didn't know who I was, or what we meant to each other through the years. That is part of the price you pay for not being "out" to your family.

I was slowly beginning to regain some emotional footing after Mother's death and trial, and Mike's untimely death knocked me down and set me back severely. I mourned his death deeply; and I once again saw how quickly a loved one could leave without any notice.

⋅›▌⊜ ⊜▐‹⋅

During a routine dental exam it was discovered that I'd been grinding my teeth at night, and that was after break-ing three teeth, which required crowns. Consequently I was fitted with a mouth guard to wear at night to keep from doing any further damage. While lunching with Mary, I told her about the new problem I'd developed. She shared that she was also fitted with a mouth guard, because she was having the same problem. Stress can have many manifestations; you have to learn to deal with it.

⋅›▌⊜ ⊜▐‹⋅

After a very dark winter, and nearly a year had passed since the trial, the sun finally returned. Spring encouraged new life, new growth, and it felt like time for me to get up off the couch and rejoin the world.

On a lovely May morning, most unexpectedly, I had a heart attack, at age fifty-two. I didn't recognize the symptoms as being a heart attack, but I knew something was definitely wrong and I should probably get myself to the hospital.

I was immediately taken into the hospital's cardiac care ward, where I was given an EKG and blood was drawn for testing. Tests confirmed that I had a myocardial infarction, a heart attack. Balloon angioplasty opened the blockage, and then a medicated stent was surgically implanted inside the plugged vessel to keep it open.

Recuperation took several weeks. I was placed on a regimen of medications, and I will probably be on many of them for life. Many lifestyle changes were also introduced, such as a lower-salt and reduced-fat diet and regular exercise. Upon entering the hospital I became a nonsmoker, and that continues to this day. Eliminating stress from one's life is also very important, but *that* is a continual and ongoing challenge. Good luck with that one.

After the heart attack, I made the decision to cash in a few chips early and enjoy life a bit more, if that was possible. So I sold my cottage in Manistee and moved to sunny Florida to begin my new, semiretired life. There is not a guarantee of a future for any of us. There isn't a promise that any of us will make it to retirement, either; life is way too short. Who knows when your number is up? So start enjoying life while you are still living. Have the dessert.

➤═══ ═══◄

By banding together, we all survived Mother's murder, and I believe we are closer in many ways because of it. But it's a terrible way to learn closeness.

So my advice to everyone reading this book is this: make a practice of laughing more often. Hug the people you are close to, and tell them that you love them. Help a friend, or even a stranger, and remember we are all in this together. *We* are the community.

This is a piece of my life story; I will not let this tragedy define it. We have not put our mother upon a pedestal or made her out to be a saint. We can now speak about her and remember what fun she could be when we were young, and what a feisty, devout, and warm old woman she became. We all love and miss her terribly.

On Flint

FLINT IS DEFINED as being a very hard gray or brown stone that makes a spark when struck against steel. In prehist-oric times flint was considered a highly valued commodity, and primitive people would walk many miles to secure this precious rock, which was necessary for making spears, arrowheads, and, most importantly, fire.

Flint the city is often described as a rock-hard place. This gritty town was conceived by the shaping of metal and the spark of an ignition. The hardy people of Flint took steel and sparked the automobile industry.

For over one hundred years, "The Vehicle City" was a dirty factory town, and it was this scrappy environment that shaped me. Don't get me wrong, Flint is not all bad, it has many admirable qualities and has created products that have revolutionized the world. General Motors was conceived in Flint. And the 1937 Flint sit-down strike helped to create the U.A.W, {United Auto Workers}, which sparked the organized labor movement and helped create the American middle class.

Many characters were conceived there as well, some more colorful than others. Michael Moore was born there, as were the jazz vocalists Betty Carter and Dee Dee Bridgewater. Grand Funk Railroad departed from there in 1969. And *The Newlywed Game's* Bob Eubanks and the actress Sandra Bernhard were Flint products as well.

Most of our factories are closed now so they are no longer spewing soot and smog 24/7; the air is much cleaner. Without the factories' constant toxic discharges the water is much cleaner too, and the Flint River hasn't caught fire for over twenty years. People are actually canoeing down it for recreation.

Flint is slowly becoming a small Midwestern college town, as Mott Community College and the University of Michigan campuses continue to grow. Their expansion has rejuvenated downtown, given the city a better self-image and breathed new life into the entire community. And God bless the Mott Foundation for its continued largess in funding many community-minded projects.

People make up the fabric of the town, and many good people still live in Flint. This city was once my home, and it was Mother's adopted home as well; as she lived there over sixty years. These were her people, too. They stepped forward to help us search for her when she was lost, they fed us when we were hungry, and comforted us when we were weary. This community provided its resources to investigate Mother's case, and its judicial system brought the person responsible for her murder to trial.

I don't believe this outcome could have been possible anywhere else but in Flint. The community cared about what happened to one of its own, an old lady, and her family, too. Flint will always be my home-town – no matter where I live, my family is there, and I am loved there.

The good guys still outnumber the bad guys, and I shall be eternally grateful to all of "the good guys" from Flint. For we alone could not have done what our community did for us, and for Mother. God bless them all: the police, the courts, the jurors, and the people of Flint.

The end.

Amen.

About the Author

In 1954 Daniel Murphy was born in Flint, Michigan. In 1976 he graduated from the University of Michigan, with a bachelor of fine arts degree. For many years now he's been a visual artist, decorative painter, designer and restoration artist; who is now exploring another new and challenging medium, writing.

Dan now lives in sunny Cortez, Florida, a National Register of Historic Places community, and quaint fishing village, on the northern shore of the Gulf of Mexico's' Sarasota bay. He continues to write daily, and hopes this is the first book of many that he will produce at his adopted retirement home.

CPSIA information can be obtained at www.ICGtesting.com
Printed in the USA
LVOW11s1139280815

451935LV00003B/150/P